The Mediterranean Diet Cookbook for Beginners

600 Healthy and Delicious Mediterranean Diet Recipes with 28-Day Meal Plan to Live A Healthier Life

By Sarah Maurer

Table of Content

Introduction 1

Chapter 1: Mediterranean Lifestyle Breakdown 2

The ABCs of the Mediterranean Diet 3
The Mediterranean Food Pyramid 3
Foods to Enjoy 4
Forbidden Foods 6
Common Mistakes 6
You're Not Obeying the 10 Commandments 7
Eating Out on the Mediterranean Diet 8
28-Day Meal Plan Sample 9

Chapter 2 Breakfasts 13

Mediterranean Eggs (Shakshuka)........... 13
Ricotta Toast with Strawberries 13
Apple-Tahini Toast............................... 13
Egg Bake... 14
Tomato and Egg Scramble 14
Cinnamon Oatmeal with Dried Cranberries 14
Creamy Peach Smoothie...................... 15
Blackberry-Yogurt Green Smoothie......... 15
Blueberry Smoothie 15
Healthy Chia Pudding 15
Morning Overnight Oats with Raspberries 16
Cauliflower Breakfast Porridge............... 16
Baked Eggs in Avocado....................... 16
Creamy Vanilla Oatmeal 17
Fluffy Almond Flour Pancakes with
Strawberries 17
Pumpkin Pie Parfait............................. 17
Avocado Toast with Goat Cheese........... 18
Banana-Blueberry Breakfast Cookies...... 18
Warm Bulgur Breakfast Bowls with Fruits 18
5-Ingredient Quinoa Breakfast Bowls...... 19
Spinach and Egg Breakfast Wraps.......... 19
Easy Buckwheat Porridge..................... 19
Breakfast Yogurt Sundae 20
Spinach Cheese Pie............................. 20
Creamy Breakfast Bulgur with Berries 20
Cinnamon Pistachio Smoothie 21
Breakfast Pancakes with Berry Sauce 21
Feta and Olive Scrambled Eggs............. 21
Banana Corn Fritters........................... 22
Crustless Tiropita (Greek Cheese Pie)..... 22
Marinara Poached Eggs........................ 22
Parmesan Oatmeal with Greens 23
Avocado and Egg Toast........................ 23
Kale and Apple Smoothie..................... 23
Savory Breakfast Oatmeal 24
Cheesy Broccoli and Mushroom Egg
Casserole 24
Tomato and Egg Breakfast Pizza 24
Baked Ricotta with Honey Pears............. 25
Avocado Smoothie.............................. 25
Feta and Spinach Frittata...................... 25
Berry and Nut Parfait 26
Basil Scrambled Eggs 26
Mediterranean Omelet.......................... 26
Classic Shakshuka 27

Chapter 3 Sides, Salads, and Soups 27

Greek Chicken, Tomato, and Olive Salad .. 27
Artichoke and Arugula Salad 28
Baby Potato and Olive Salad 28
Garlic Wilted Greens 28
Barley, Parsley, and Pea Salad 29
Sumptuous Greek Vegetable Salad.......... 29
Cheesy Peach and Walnut Salad 29
Ritzy Summer Fruit Salad 30
Arugula and Fig Salad 30
Roasted Broccoli and Tomato Panzanella .. 30
Lemon and Spinach Orzo 31
Grilled Bell Pepper and Anchovy Antipasto 31
Butternut Squash and Cauliflower Curry
Soup... 31
Brussels Sprout and Apple Slaw 32
Hearty Veggie Slaw.............................. 32
Marinated Mushrooms and Olives........... 32
Cherry, Plum, Artichoke, and Cheese Board 33
Root Vegetable Roast 33
Mushroom and Soba Noodle Soup.......... 33
Cheesy Roasted Broccolini 34
Sardines with Lemony Tomato Sauce....... 34
Arugula, Watermelon, and Feta Salad...... 34
Cucumber Gazpacho 35

Greens, Fennel, and Pear Soup with Cashews 35
Sautéed White Beans with Rosemary 35
Easy Roasted Cauliflower 36
Rich Chicken and Small Pasta Broth 36
Orange-Honey Glazed Carrots 36
Lemon-Tahini Hummus 37
Simple Mushroom Barley Soup 37
Chicken and Pastina Soup 37
Zesty Spanish Potato Salad 38
Moroccan Lentil, Tomato, and Cauliflower Soup 38
Moroccan Spiced Couscous 38
Tricolor Summer Salad 39
Pumpkin Soup with Crispy Sage Leaves ... 39

Greek Salad with Dressing 39
Vegetable Fagioli Soup 40
Mixed Salad With Balsamic Honey Dressing 40
Mediterranean Tomato Hummus Soup 40
Citrus Salad with Kale and Fennel 41
Balsamic Brussels Sprouts and Delicata Squash 41
Green Beans with Tahini-Lemon Sauce 41
Roasted Root Vegetable Soup 42
Super Mushroom and Red Wine Soup 42
Paella Soup 43
Avgolemono (Lemon Chicken Soup) 43
Parmesan Roasted Red Potatoes 44
Sautéed Kale with Olives 44
Green Bean and Halloumi Salad 45

Chapter 4 Sandwiches, Pizzas, and Wraps 45

Sumptuous Vegetable and Cheese Lavash Pizza 45
Cheesy Fig Pizzas with Garlic Oil 46
Tuna and Olive Salad Sandwiches 46
Eggplant, Spinach, and Feta Sandwiches . 47
Easy Alfalfa Sprout and Nut Rolls 47
Greek Vegetable Salad Pita 47
Mini Pork and Cucumber Lettuce Wraps ... 48
Mashed Grape Tomato Pizzas 48
Salmon Salad Wraps 48
Classic Socca 49
Samosas in Potatoes 49
Za'atar Pizza 49
Brown Rice and Black Bean Burgers 50
Chickpea Lettuce Wraps 50
Mushroom and Caramelized Onion Musakhan 51
Grilled Caesar Salad Sandwiches 51
Spicy Black Bean and Poblano Dippers 52
Veg Mix and Blackeye Pea Burritos 52
Red Pepper Coques with Pine Nuts 53

Zucchini Hummus Wraps 53
Falafel Balls with Tahini Sauce 54
Mushroom-Pesto Baked Pizza 54
Easy Pizza Pockets 55
Open-Faced Margherita Sandwiches 55
Tuna and Hummus Wraps 55
Ritzy Garden Burgers 56
Dulse, Avocado, and Tomato Pitas 56
Glazed Mushroom and Vegetable Fajitas .. 57
Artichoke and Cucumber Hoagies 57
Mediterranean Greek Salad Wraps 58
Spicy Tofu Tacos with Cherry Tomato Salsa 58
Super Cheeses and Mushroom Tart 59
Roasted Tomato Panini 59
Roasted Vegetable Panini 60
White Pizzas with Arugula and Spinach 60
Green Veggie Sandwiches 61
Turkish Eggplant and Tomatoes Pide with Mint 61
Baked Parmesan Chicken Wraps 62

Chapter 5 Beans, Grains, and Pastas 63

Quinoa and Chickpea Vegetable Bowls 63
Lentil and Vegetable Curry Stew 63
Lush Moroccan Chickpea, Vegetable, and Fruit Stew 64
Wild Rice, Celery, and Cauliflower Pilaf 64
Slow Cooked Turkey and Brown Rice 65
Pearl Barley Risotto with Parmesan Cheese 65
Spicy Italian Bean Balls with Marinara 66
Italian Sautéed Cannellini Beans 66
Baked Rolled Oat with Pears and Pecans .. 67
Rich Cauliflower Alfredo 67
Black Bean Chili with Mangoes 68

Hearty Butternut Spinach, and Cheeses Lasagna 68
Israeli Style Eggplant and Chickpea Salad 69
Caprese Pasta with Roasted Asparagus 69
Spaghetti with Pine Nuts and Cheese 70
Papaya, Jicama, and Peas Rice Bowl 70
Black-Eyed Peas Salad with Walnuts 70
Turkish Canned Pinto Bean Salad 71
Minestrone Chickpeas and Macaroni Casserole 71
Ritzy Veggie Chili 72
Swoodles with Almond Butter Sauce 72

Roasted Ratatouille Pasta........................73
Mediterranean Lentils.............................73
Roasted Butternut Squash and Zucchini with Penne...74
Brown Rice Pilaf with Pistachios and Raisins 74
Garlic and Parsley Chickpeas...................75
Tomato Sauce and Basil Pesto Fettuccine . 75
Cherry, Apricot, and Pecan Brown Rice Bowl 76
Cranberry and Almond Quinoa.................76
Curry Apple Couscous with Leeks and Pecans...76
Rice and Blueberry Stuffed Sweet Potatoes 77
Mint Brown Rice 77
Mashed Beans with Cumin 77
Lebanese Flavor Broken Thin Noodles 78
Lemony Farro and Avocado Bowl 78
Easy Walnut and Ricotta Spaghetti..........79
Small Pasta and Beans Pot......................79
Fava and Garbanzo Bean Ful 80

Triple-Green Pasta with Cheese 80
Garlic Shrimp Fettuccine.........................80
Easy Simple Pesto Pasta 81
Creamy Garlic Parmesan Chicken Pasta ...81
Bulgur Pilaf with Garbanzo 81
Israeli Couscous with Asparagus.............82
Freekeh Pilaf with Dates and Pistachios ...82
Quinoa with Baby Potatoes and Broccoli...82
Black-Eyed Pea and Vegetable Stew 83
Chickpea Salad with Tomatoes and Basil .. 83
Bean and Veggie Pasta 83
Lentil and Mushroom Pasta 84
Mediterranean-Style Beans and Greens ...84
Broccoli and Carrot Pasta Salad 84
Tomato Basil Pasta.................................85
Simple Lentil Risotto 85
Bulgur Pilaf with Kale and Tomatoes........85
Cumin Quinoa Pilaf 86

Chapter 6 Vegetable Mains 86

Fried Eggplant Rolls 86
Roasted Veggies and Brown Rice Bowl....87
Beet and Watercress Salad 87
Eggplant and Zucchini Gratin 88
Veggie-Stuffed Portabello Mushrooms.....88
Cauliflower Hash with Carrots................89
Zucchini and Artichokes Bowl with Farro . 89
Garlicky Zucchini Cubes with Mint 89
Roasted Vegetables...............................90
5-Ingredient Zucchini Fritters 90
Moroccan Tagine with Vegetables...........91
Zoodles with Walnut Pesto 91
Potato Tortilla with Leeks and Mushrooms 92
Cheesy Sweet Potato Burgers................92
Wilted Dandelion Greens with Sweet Onion 93
Celery and Mustard Greens 93
Lentil and Tomato Collard Wraps............93
Vegetable and Tofu Scramble 94
Simple Zoodles 94
Vegan Lentil Bolognese 94
Vegetable and Red Lentil Stew 95
Cauliflower Rice Risotto with Mushrooms 95
Sautéed Green Beans with Tomatoes......95
Creamy Cauliflower Chickpea Curry........96
Grilled Vegetable Skewers 96
Chickpea Lettuce Wraps with Celery.......96
Stuffed Portobello Mushroom with Tomatoes 97
Stir-Fry Baby Bok Choy 97
Parmesan Stuffed Zucchini Boats...........97
Sweet Pepper Stew 98

Sautéed Spinach and Leeks 98
Baked Tomatoes and chickpeas 98
Stuffed Portobello Mushrooms with Spinach 99
Creamy Polenta with Mushrooms 99
Ratatouille 100
Brussels Sprouts Linguine 100
Garlicky Broccoli Rabe.........................101
Quick Steamed Broccoli.......................101
Sautéed Cabbage with Parsley 101
Braised Cauliflower with White Wine......102
Cauliflower Steaks with Arugula...........102
Baby Kale and Cabbage Salad 103
Grilled Romaine Lettuce.......................103
Mini Crustless Spinach Quiches............103
Veggie Rice Bowls with Pesto Sauce 104
Butternut Noodles with Mushrooms.......104
Zoodles with Beet Pesto 104
Roasted Vegetables and Chickpeas........105
Sweet Potato Chickpea Buddha Bowl.....105
Easy Zucchini Patties 106
Garlic-Butter Asparagus with Parmesan . 106
Simple Honey-Glazed Baby Carrots.......106
Zucchini Crisp 107
Creamy Sweet Potatoes and Collards.....107
Paprika Cauliflower Steaks with Walnut Sauce 108
Stir-Fried Eggplant 108
Grilled Lemon Chicken.........................109
Quick Chicken Salad Wraps.................109

Chapter 7 Poultry and Meats 109

Roasted Chicken Thighs With Basmati Rice110
Slow Cook Lamb Shanks with Cannellini
Beans Stew 110
Lamb Tagine with Couscous and Almonds .111
Grilled Chicken and Zucchini Kebabs 111
Panko Grilled Chicken Patties 112
Coconut Chicken Tenders......................112
Easy Grilled Pork Chops.......................112
Gyro Burgers with Tahini Sauce 113
Yogurt Chicken Breasts........................113
Potato Lamb and Olive Stew 114
Spiced Roast Chicken 114
Parsley-Dijon Chicken and Potatoes.......115
Chicken Cacciatore 115
Sautéed Ground Turkey with Brown Rice116
Beef Stew with Beans and Zucchini.......116

Baked Teriyaki Turkey Meatballs 117
Beef, Tomato, and Lentils Stew.............117
Ground Beef, Tomato, and Kidney Bean Chili118
Herbed-Mustard-Coated Pork Tenderloin 118
Macadamia Pork 119
Almond-Crusted Chicken Tenders with
Honey..119
Beef Kebabs with Onion and Pepper 120
Greek-Style Lamb Burgers 120
Chicken Bruschetta Burgers 120
Chicken Gyros with Tzatziki Sauce 121
Crispy Pesto Chicken...........................121
Greek Beef Kebabs 122
Chermoula Roasted Pork Tenderloin 122
Lamb Kofta (Spiced Meatballs) 123

Chapter 8 Fish and Seafood 123

Mediterranean Grilled Sea Bass 123
Air-Fried Flounder Fillets......................124
Glazed Broiled Salmon 124
Simple Fried Cod Fillets 124
10-Minute Cod with Parsley Pistou 125
Mediterranean Braised Cod with Vegetables 125
Baked Salmon with Basil and Tomato 125
Lemon-Parsley Swordfish......................126
Baked Salmon with Tarragon Mustard Sauce126
Peppercorn-Seared Tuna Steaks 126
Baked Lemon Salmon 127
Honey-Mustard Roasted Salmon 127
Salmon and Mushroom Hash with Pesto.127
Spiced Citrus Sole 128
Asian-Inspired Tuna Lettuce Wraps 128
Canned Sardine Donburi (Rice Bowl) 128
Orange Flavored Scallops.....................129
Instant Pot Poached Salmon.................129
Spicy Grilled Shrimp with Lemon Wedges....129
Crispy Tilapia with Mango Salsa 130
Lemon Rosemary Roasted Branzino.......130
Braised Branzino with Wine Sauce 131
Cioppino (Seafood Tomato Stew) 131
Lemon Grilled Shrimp 132
Baked Halibut Steaks with Vegetables ...132
Spicy Haddock Stew 133
Garlic Shrimp with Mushrooms 133
Lemony Shrimp with Orzo Salad 134
Avocado Shrimp Ceviche 134
Garlic Skillet Salmon...........................135

Salmon Baked in Foil...........................135
Balsamic-Honey Glazed Salmon............135
Seared Salmon with Lemon Cream Sauce ..136
Slow Cooker Salmon in Foil..................136
Baked Fish with Pistachio Crust 136
Mackerel and Green Bean Salad 137
Fennel Poached Cod with Tomatoes.......137
Sole Piccata with Capers......................137
Dill Baked Sea Bass 138
Tuna and Zucchini Patties 138
Mediterranean Cod Stew......................138
Haddock with Cucumber Sauce.............139
Crispy Herb Crusted Halibut 139
Roasted Trout Stuffed with Veggies 139
Garlic-Butter Parmesan Salmon and
Asparagus 140
Easy Breaded Shrimp..........................140
Pesto Shrimp over Zoodles...................140
Salt and Pepper Calamari and Scallops ..141
Easy Tomato Tuna Melts 141
Steamed Trout with Lemon Herb Crust ..141
Hazelnut Crusted Sea Bass 142
Lemony Trout with Caramelized Shallots 142
Garlic Shrimp with Arugula Pesto 142
Baked Cod with Vegetables 143
Baked Oysters with Vegetables.............143
Dill Chutney Salmon 144
Shrimp and Pea Paella.........................144
Grilled Lemon Pesto Salmon.................144

Chapter 9 Fruits and Desserts 145

Apple and Berries Ambrosia 145
Easy Blueberry and Oat Crisp..............145
Banana, Cranberry, and Oat Bars..........145
Lemony Tea and Chia Pudding 146
Berry and Rhubarb Cobbler.................146
Sweet Spiced Pumpkin Pudding 146
Coconut Blueberries with Brown Rice.....147
Citrus Cranberry and Quinoa Energy Bites..147
Chocolate, Almond, and Cherry Clusters 147
Chocolate and Avocado Mousse 148
Glazed Pears with Hazelnuts 148
Lemony Blackberry Granita 148
Mango and Coconut Frozen Pie 149
Mini Nuts and Fruits Crumble 149
Mint Banana Chocolate Sorbet.............149
Pecan and Carrot Cake 150
Raspberry Yogurt Basted Cantaloupe.....150
Simple Apple Compote 150
Simple Peanut Butter and Chocolate Balls . 151
Strawberries with Balsamic Vinegar.......151
Simple Spiced Sweet Pecans 151
Greek Yogurt Affogato with Pistachios....151
Grilled Peaches with Whipped Ricotta 152
Cherry Walnut Brownies 152
Grilled Stone Fruit with Honey.............152
Watermelon and Blueberry Salad.........153
Rice Pudding with Roasted Orange 153
Crispy Sesame Cookies 153
Crunchy Almond Cookies 154
Walnut and Date Balls 154
Frozen Mango Raspberry Delight..........154
Honey Baked Cinnamon Apples 155
Mascarpone Baked Pears 155
Easy Mixed Berry Crisp......................155
Orange Mug Cakes............................156
Fruit and Nut Chocolate Bark 156
Cozy Superfood Hot Chocolate 156

Chapter 10 Sauces, Dips, and Dressings 157

Peanut Sauce with Honey 157
Cilantro-Tomato Salsa 157
Simple Italian Dressing 157
Pineapple Salsa 157
Cheesy Pea Pesto 158
Parsley Vinaigrette.............................158
Hot Pepper Sauce 158
Garlic Lemon-Tahini Dressing 158
Lemon-Tahini Sauce...........................159
Easy Aioli 159
Vinaigrette 159
Lentil-Tahini Dip 159
Ginger Teriyaki Sauce.........................160
Asian-Inspired Vinaigrette 160
Creamy Grapefruit and Tarragon Dressing. 160
Basil Pesto..160
Peri-Peri Sauce..................................161
Not Old Bay Seasoning.......................161
Ranch-Style Cauliflower Dressing..........161
Homemade Blackened Seasoning..........162
Guacamole 162
Creamy Cucumber Dip 162
Lemon-Dill Cashew Dip.......................163
Tzatziki 163
Harissa Sauce 163
Orange-Garlic Dressing 164
Creamy Cider Yogurt Dressing 164
Basic French Vinaigrette 164
Appendix 1: Measurement Conversion Chart.. 165
Appendix 2: Recipes Index............ 166

Introduction

Let me start off by saying I am not a fan of diets. I personally don't know of any 'diet' that doesn't end badly—with you gaining the weight you lost and then some! So, before we move on, I have to clarify one thing: the Mediterranean diet is not a diet in the traditional sense...it is a lifestyle. Now, I know you're probably thinking, "Yeah, that's what all diets claim," and you won't be wholly wrong. But it is my hope that after reading this cookbook, you'll realize that eating the Mediterranean way is not about changing what you put into your body for only a few weeks or months, it is about changing your relationship with food entirely.

Okay, now that I got that out of the way, let me tell you about my love affair with Mediterranean cuisine. I started following this way of eating after my husband had a health scare, and we were forced to rethink our food choices. We used to eat the standard American diet—a 50/50 split of meat and starch washed down by a tall glass of soda, followed by my favorite, store-bought double-layer brownies. Sounds healthy, right? No wonder my husband had a heart attack!

I'm not going to bore you with all the details, but one thing is for sure, the Mediterranean diet with its colorful fruits and veggies, fatty fish, healthy grains, and a good helping of olive oil changed our lives. We've been following this diet for the last four years and have honestly never felt better.

In this cookbook, I want to share with you the health benefits of eating the Mediterranean way, but I also want to make it as easy as possible for you to replace the standard American diet with healthy, nutritious food. There's a reason why doctors all over the world recommend the Mediterranean diet to their patients; you will soon see why! And, after you're completely convinced that this way of eating is the most beneficial option out there, you'll find various delicious recipes to start your journey to a healthier you.

I've made all the recipes included in this cookbook, and they're always a major hit with friends and family. They find it difficult to believe that eating such delectable meals is in any way part of a wholesome eating plan that will heal you from the inside out and prolong your lifespan.

Your whole body will thank you if you make the change!

Chapter 1: Mediterranean Lifestyle Breakdown

In the 1950s, physiologist Ancel Keys and his colleagues discovered the advantages of following a simple, clean, and wholesome diet (Altomare et al., 2013). They found that the disadvantaged population of Italy had better health than well-off New Yorkers. This was attributed to the fact that fast-food chains were yet to arrive in the Mediterranean Basin.

Keys later went on to lead the Seven Countries Study, where he noticed that there is a link between what you eat, how you live, and cardiovascular disease (Keys et al., 1986). People who followed a Mediterranean diet have a lower risk of developing heart disease and were overall healthier, chiefly due to the high olive oil intake, as well as eating primarily fruits, vegetables, whole grains, beans, and nuts.

The research doesn't stop there. Study after study has shown that the Mediterranean diet is an effective way to prevent cardiovascular disease (Trichopoulou, 2001). And, if you're a woman, there are additional advantages such as warding off chronic diseases linked to old age, including kidney disease, lung disease, and cancer.

What makes the Mediterranean diet so potent is the focus on wholesome, natural foods. The average American diet, on the other hand, involves copious amounts of sugar, refined carbs, saturated fat, and sodium by the spoonful! This leads to obesity, which leads to a slew of other health issues. In fact, 42% of adults in America are obese, and a staggering one in five kids struggle with their weight (Centers for Disease Control and Prevention, 2015).

Those figures alone should convince you to change your eating habits!

In addition to a healthy heart, your brain will stay in tip-top shape well into your golden years when following the Mediterranean diet (American Geriatrics Society, 2017).

It should be apparent why switching from the standard American diet to the Mediterranean will bring nothing but good things your way!

The ABCs of the Mediterranean Diet

Antioxidants, broccoli, chickpeas; you can easily create a plate filled with healthy food starting with each letter of the alphabet! As long as you're eating a balance of high-antioxidant foods, healthy fats, and enough fiber, you're eating the Mediterranean way. Easy, isn't it?

However, as I mentioned in the introduction, the Mediterranean diet is not only about what you fuel your body with; it's about changing your lifestyle. Spending time with your family, exercising, getting enough sleep, and reducing stress all form part of living the Mediterranean way.

I have to mention that the Mediterranean diet does not require you to count calories, weigh your food, or give yourself a headache trying to work out your macronutrients. The only thing you have to do is eat within moderation. That may be difficult if you're trying to lose weight or if you struggle with binge eating, but don't feel dismayed. You will be feeding your body wholesome food, which will make you feel better physically and emotionally, and this will make you instinctively eat less.

But, let's quickly have a look at the foods you'll be enjoying when you follow this diet.

The Mediterranean Food Pyramid

We've all seen the standard food pyramid—carbohydrates and refined grains take up the whole first tier of it! If we pay attention to the research, that's not a good thing at all. Simple carbs—that's your white bread, pasta, cakes, pastries, doughnuts, sweets and candy, soda, everything we Americans love so much—is terrible for you. It plays havoc on your blood sugar and insulin levels, which leads to diabetes and affects your overall well-being negatively (Dyson, 2015).

This is why you'll see a more low-carb approach to the Mediterranean diet in this cookbook. It can only be good for you if you limit your carbohydrate intake to complex carbs like whole grains, oatmeal, etc.

So, let's break down the Mediterranean food pyramid.

- ✿ **Tier one:** Reduce stress, get more exercise, spend time with your family, go outside more often—all the lifestyle aspects that will increase the quality of your life.

- ✿ **Tier two:** Fruits, veggies, whole grains, beans and legumes, nuts, seeds, herbs and spices, olive oil, and other good fats. It is recommended that you eat these foods daily.

- ✿ **Tier three:** Fish, seafood, poultry, eggs, and dairy. You can eat these foods three to five times a week, but poultry, eggs, and dairy portions should be smaller than fish and seafood.

- ✿ **Tier four:** Red meat, rice, pasta, potatoes, refined flour products, and sweets. These types of food you should limit as much as possible. I'd say treat yourself to eating it once or twice a month and no more.

A FEW TIMES PER MONTH — Red Meat, Sweets, Flour Products, Potatoes

SEVERAL TIMES (3-5) PER WEEK — Fish And Seafood, Poultry, Eggs, Whole Grains, Probiotic-rich Dairy (Including Cheese)

DAILY — Vegetables, Fruits, Beans, Nuts, Olive Oil And Other Smart Fats, Herbs And Spices, Yogurt, Dark Chocolate, Red Wine, Coffee, Tea, Water

FOUNDATION — Outdoor Activity And Exercise, Market Shopping, Group Cooking, Relaxation, Leisurely Dining With Social Interaction, And Mindful Eating

Foods to Enjoy

Your plate will, most of the time, be packed to the brim with a colorful array of vegetables since the Mediterranean diet is primarily plant-based.

Let's look at the types of food that are staples in this diet.

Whole grains

Whole grains are superior to refined grains because they haven't been stripped of the fibrous layer that also contains all the vitamins and nutrients. Quinoa, barley, kasha, and oatmeal (I highly recommend steel cut oats for maximum benefit) are some of the healthy grains you'll be consuming with the Mediterranean diet.

Fruits and vegetables

Turn your plate into a rainbow! Colorful vegetables usually contain a lot of phytonutrients and antioxidants that will counter any free radicals. But if you're in the mood to go all-green, that's fine too. The bottom line is that all fruit and veggies are packed with vitamins and minerals and contain a lot of fiber—all of the things you need in your diet.

Nuts

A perfect way to fight hunger pangs in between meals. Nuts contain monounsaturated fat and Omega-3 fatty acids, but they're also a good source of protein. These delicious tiny treats also fight bad cholesterol and promote the overall health of your arteries (Mayo Clinic, n.d.).

Beans and legumes

Beans will make you feel fuller for longer because they are so fiber-rich. Regularly consuming beans will lower your cholesterol and prevent diabetes (Nierenberg, 2014).

Fish

I can't over-emphasize the value of consuming fish on a regular basis. Oily fish like salmon, sardines, trout, herring, flounder, shad, and pollock have a high Omega-3 fatty acid content, which is excellent news. Not getting enough Omega-3 in your diet causes a spike of inflammation in your body that can cause anything from acne to arthritis.

Just keep in mind that fish contain mercury, which is dangerous to pregnant women and children. However, the oilier the fish, the lower its mercury levels, so stick to the fish mentioned above and avoid tilefish, king mackerel, shark, and swordfish.

Olive oil

Olive oil is high in monounsaturated fat, which is great for your heart. On the Mediterranean diet, olive oil will be your go-to fat, and this means your chances of getting diabetes and heart disease will be decreased. Even more exciting is the fact that olive oil can actually help you lose weight since it will make you feel satiated for longer.

Red wine

Red wine contains two power substances called polyphenols and resveratrol that are linked to heart health. This doesn't mean you can drink a bottle a night—the Mediterranean diet is all about moderation. Limit yourself to one or two 5-ounce glasses a day.

Before the coffee and tea lovers get up in arms, I didn't forget about you! You're more than welcome to drink these beverages but also in moderation. Of course, if you drink green tea, forget about limiting your intake at all. That's one drink (after water) that you can't drink enough of—it's just so good for you.

Dark chocolate

Packed with flavanols—a potent antioxidant—dark chocolate is healthy. Again, self-control is important. What do they say? Too much of a good thing is a bad thing. So, keep the moderation principle in mind when you indulge in some dark chocolate. No more than an ounce at a time, a few times each week.

Forbidden Foods

Okay, the word forbidden may be a little too harsh. The only foods that aren't allowed on the Mediterranean diet are those that are harmful to your health. This includes sugary foods like candy, soda, energy drinks, cookies, and overly processed foods, etc.

That being said, there are some foods that you should limit.

✿ **Fructose:** Throughout our lives, we're told that natural sugars like those found in fruits and honey are good for us when, in actual fact, fructose may even be worse than table sugar. Our bodies don't use this type of sugar for energy—it has no need for it at all. So, fructose gets sent straight to the liver, which, as you can imagine, puts a lot of strain on the liver since it has to convert it all into triglycerides. In turn, the triglycerides get stored as fat, and this increases your risk of heart disease, diabetes, and other health issues linked to excessive fat storage.

✿ **Milk:** Full-cream milk is high in saturated fat. If you drink milk, make sure it is from grass fed cows, which raises the Omega-3 fatty acid count. Keep in mind, milk contains a lot of calories, and it is never a good idea to drink your calories when you're trying to lose or maintain your weight.

✿ **Red meat:** Also high in saturated fat, conventional red meat increases your chances of heart disease, hypertension, diabetes, and can cause chronic inflammation when consumed daily. Like milk, and other animal proteins, if you can find beef that is grass-fed, it is higher in Omega-3 fatty acids, so moderate intake can be helpful.

Common Mistakes

Mistakes are unavoidable when you first start the Mediterranean diet—you're changing your relationship with food entirely! I made so many blunders when I started, but at least something good can come from my slip-ups; I can share them with you so that you know what to look out for.

Portion Control

Although you don't have to control your vegetable consumption—since veggies are so fiber-rich, you'll only be able to eat a limited quantity anyway—you do have to keep an eye on everything else on your plate. Nuts and healthy fats are the main culprits because a small amount translates to a lot of calories. This is particularly important if you're following the Mediterranean diet to lose weight.

Carb Overkill

Yes, complex carbs are better for you than refined carbohydrates, but it still doesn't mean you should overindulge. As mentioned earlier, it is better for your health to limit your carb intake—even the right kind of carbs.

Forgetting to Eat Fish

You have to eat enough fish on the Mediterranean diet to reap the heart- and brain-boosting benefits. I know poultry falls on the same tier as fish, but if you have a choice, always choose seafood. You need to get enough of those Omega-3 fatty acids in your diet. If you really struggle to eat enough fish, or you're a vegan, consider fish and seaweed oil supplements.

Consuming the Wrong Dairy

Pasteurized cheese has been stripped of all nutrients and most probiotics. Choose feta, mozzarella, Camembert, or other non-pasteurized cheeses instead to get all the probiotic goodness your gut is craving.

Similarly, artificially flavored yogurt contains a lot of sugar and also doesn't have most probiotics. You can flavor and sweeten plain Greek yogurt with fruits and honey - paying attention to overall sugar and fructose consumption.

As you can see, not all dairy is equal. The more natural option is always better. Sources from grass-fed cows, as mentioned before, should be your go-to.

Limiting the Beans

Beans and legumes are superfoods—so don't leave them off your plate. I know they can take longer to prepare, but they're so excellent at regulating your blood sugar, it's worth the extra effort you have to go through to make them. If you have a pressure cooker, they can be ready within an hour. If necessary, you can also look for canned varieties, but they don't offer the same fiber count and can disrupt blood sugar levels.

Not Drinking Enough Water

Don't underplay the advantages of drinking enough water. It flushes out toxins from your body, is good for your kidneys and other organs, keeps your digestive system running, and helps keep you satiated; the list of benefits is endless. While we're on the topic of drinking, consuming too much wine is another mistake I made when I started the Mediterranean diet. Remember that you're allowed no more than two 5-ounce glasses of red wine a day.

Overheating Extra-Virgin Olive Oil

Extra-virgin olive oil is best ingested without cooking it. As soon as you heat it and it reaches 400 degrees Fahrenheit, the oil becomes pro-inflammatory. This is damaging to your health. It also tends to lose all its flavor when you overheat it, so it's a waste all-around to cook with extra-virgin olive oil. Reserve it for salad dressing, making your own mayo, or anything else that doesn't require heating. Extra virgin coconut oil is a great option for cooking - although it's a saturated fat, it does have some health benefits, and is also stable at higher temperatures.

You're Not Obeying the 10 Commandments

Yes, the Mediterranean diet comes with its own commandments! I use them as a quick reference if I'm not sure about something since it sums up precisely what the Mediterranean diet is all about.

The ten commandments of the Mediterranean diet and lifestyle are:

1. Your plate should contain copious amounts of fresh, non-processed foods.
2. Saturated fat, trans fat, sodium, refined sugar should be banned from your house.
3. Olive oil is your best friend. Don't cheat on it by using margarine or butter.
4. Control how much you eat, except when it comes to non-starchy vegetables.
5. Drink enough water.
6. Don't drink too much red wine.
7. Exercise daily.
8. Don't smoke.
9. Find ways to relax with your family.
10. Laugh a lot, smile, and enjoy life.

Eating Out on the Mediterranean Diet

We're social creatures, and that sometimes complicates our lives. It can be extra hard when you're trying to maintain a healthy lifestyle, surrounded by friends and family who don't really care about their health.

I don't want you to go into a panic when invited out to dinner. I know I used to break out in a light sweat when someone asked me to eat anywhere else other than my own house. But, after I trained myself to spot all the Mediterranean friendly foods, it was a joy to order at restaurants. Of course, being allowed a glass or two of wine with my meal was the cherry on top!

Here are some tips I always use when I dine out with friends or family.

Stick to the Basics

If you know your food pyramid by heart, there is no way that you will order the wrong food. Always choose plant-based dishes over steak with a side of starch; if you can select fish or a seafood dish, even better.

Turn Vegetarian

Vegetarian options on the menu are usually always Mediterranean diet-friendly. They're high in plant-based proteins, contain a lot of fiber and vitamins and nutrients. You'll be eating a well-rounded meal even if you don't have any animal protein on your plate.

Wine Is the Drink of Choice

You're allowed two 5-ounce glasses of wine. I always sip slowly and really enjoy the taste of whatever red I chose. If you're not in the mood for alcohol, you can't go wrong with drinking water. Always stay away from soda—even the diet kind.

Eat Only Half

Portion control isn't something restaurants are known for—unless you're enjoying some French cuisine. I always divide my plate in two if I am worried that I'm overeating. You can take the other half of the food home to eat later.

The Oil Issue

Most restaurants use sunflower and other vegetable oils instead of olive oil—it's cheaper. For this reason, I suggest you avoid any food that is oily. It's always best to select grilled, baked, or roasted. That way, you'll know no harmful oils were used for cooking your food, and you can load up on the olive oil in other ways!

28-Day Meal Plan Sample

Week 1

Meal Plan	Breakfast	Lunch	Dinner	Snack or Dessert	Reminder
Day-1	Blueberry Smoothie	Fried Eggplant Rolls	Spicy Italian Bean Balls with Marinara	Baby Potato and Olive Salad	
Day-2	Egg Bake	Lush Moroccan Chickpea, Vegetable, and Fruit Stew	Simple Fried Cod Fillets	Ritzy Summer Fruit Salad	
Day-3	Cauliflower Breakfast Porridge	Spicy Tofu Tacos with Cherry Tomato Salsa	Sautéed Green Beans with Tomatoes	Cherry, Plum, Artichoke, and Cheese Board	
Day-4	Morning Overnight Oats with Raspberries	Hearty Butternut Squash, Spinach, and Cheeses Lasagna	Baked Tomatoes and Chickpeas	Root Vegetable Roast	
Day-5	Breakfast Yogurt Sundae	Spicy Grilled Shrimp with Lemon Wedges	Mango and Coconut Frozen Pie	Brown Rice and Black Bean Burgers	
Weekend	Ricotta Toast with Strawberries	Stir-Fry Baby Bok Choy	Slow Cooked Turkey and Brown Rice	Glazed Pears with Hazelnuts	

Equipped with the recipes in this book, you can organize a group meal or a family dinner and wow them with the newly learned dishes, don't forget to make a toast with your favorite glass of wine and celebrate even tiny achievements you had in aspects of your life. Having a content mindset and enjoying the moment is also key to the Mediterranean diet.

Week 2

Meal Plan	Breakfast	Lunch	Dinner	Snack or Dessert	Reminder
Day-1	Creamy Peach Smoothie	Ritzy Garden Burgers	Greek Chicken, Tomato, and Olive Salad	Chocolate and Avocado Mousse	
Day-2	Spinach and Egg Breakfast Wraps	Air-Fried Flounder Fillets	Black Bean Chili with Mangoes	Healthy Chia Pudding	
Day-3	Pumpkin Pie Parfait	Sumptuous Vegetable and Cheese Lavash Pizza	Cheesy Peach and Walnut Salad	Pecan and Carrot Cake	
Day-4	Avocado Toast with Goat Cheese	Sardines with Lemony Tomato Sauce	Samosas in Potatoes	Marinated Mushrooms and Olives	
Day-5	Banana-Blueberry Breakfast Cookies	Lentil and Vegetable Curry Stew	Rice and Blueberry Stuffed Sweet Potatoes	Artichoke and Arugula Salad	
Weekend	Easy Buckwheat Porridge	Sweet Pepper Stew	Brown Rice Pilaf with Pistachios and Raisins	Blackberry-Yogurt Green Smoothie	

Equipped with the recipes in this book, you can organize a group meal or a family dinner and wow them with the newly learned dishes, don't forget to make a toast with your favorite glass of wine and celebrate even tiny achievements you had in aspects of your life. Having a content mindset and enjoying the moment is also key to the Mediterranean diet.

Week 3

Meal Plan	Breakfast	Lunch	Dinner	Snack or Dessert	Reminder
Day-1	Mediterranean Eggs (Shakshuka)	Red Pepper Coques with Pine Nuts	Barley, Parsley, and Pea Salad	Apple and Berries Ambrosia	
Day-2	5-Ingredient Quinoa Breakfast Bowls	Greek Vegetable Salad Pita	Baked Lemon Salmon	Raspberry Yogurt Basted Cantaloupe	
Day-3	Creamy Vanilla Oatmeal	Butternut Squash and Cauliflower Coconut Curry Soup	Cheesy Fig Pizzas with Garlic Oil	Lemony Tea and Chia Pudding	
Day-4	Blueberry Smoothie	Mediterranean Braised Cod with Vegetables	Cauliflower Hash with Carrots	Mint Banana Chocolate Sorbet	
Day-5	Cauliflower Breakfast Porridge	Falafel Balls with Tahini Sauce	Italian Sautéd Cannellini Beans	Simple Peanut Butter and Chocolate Balls	
Weekend	Tomato and Egg Scramble	Vegan Lentil Bolognese	Super Cheeses and Mushroom Tart	Simple Spiced Sweet Pecans	

Equipped with the recipes in this book, you can organize a group meal or a family dinner and wow them with the newly learned dishes, don't forget to make a toast with your favorite glass of wine and celebrate even tiny achievements you had in aspects of your life. Having a content mindset and enjoying the moment is also key to the Mediterranean diet.

Week 4

Meal Plan	Breakfast	Lunch	Dinner	Snack or Dessert	Reminder
Day-1	Cheesy Broccoli and Mushroom Egg Casserole	Quinoa and Chickpea Vegetable Bowls with Mango Sauce	Rich Chicken and Small Pasta Broth	Banana, Cranberry, and Oat Bars	
Day-2	Creamy Peach Smoothie	Ritzy Veggie Chili	Cherry, Apricot, and Pecan Brown Rice Bowl	Cucumber Gazpacho	
Day-3	Baked Eggs in Avocado	Lemon-Parsley Swordfish	Mushroom and Soba Noodle Soup	Berry and Rhubarb Cobbler	
Day-4	Breakfast Yogurt Sundae	Glazed Mushroom and Vegetable Fajitas	Grilled Bell Pepper and Anchovy Antipasto	Simple Apple Compote	
Day-5	Crustless Tiropita (Greek Cheese Pie)	Glazed Broiled Salmon	Coconut Blueberries with Brown Rice	Sweet Spiced Pumpkin Pudding	
Weekend	Greens, Fennel, and Pear Soup with Cashews	Baked Rolled Oat with Pears and Pecans	Roasted Tomato Panini	Mini Nuts and Fruits Crumble	

Equipped with the recipes in this book, you can organize a group meal or a family dinner and wow them with the newly learned dishes, don't forget to make a toast with your favorite glass of wine and celebrate even tiny achievements you had in aspects of your life. Having a content mindset and enjoying the moment is also key to the Mediterranean diet.

Chapter 2 Breakfasts

Mediterranean Eggs (Shakshuka)

Prep time: 5 minutes | Cook time: 20 minutes | Serves 4

2 tablespoons extra-virgin olive oil
1 cup chopped shallots
1 teaspoon garlic powder
1 cup finely diced potato
1 cup chopped red bell peppers
1 (14.5-ounce/ 411-g) can diced tomatoes, drained
¼ teaspoon ground cardamom
¼ teaspoon paprika
¼ teaspoon turmeric
4 large eggs
¼ cup chopped fresh cilantro

1. Preheat the oven to 350ºF (180ºC).
2. Heat the olive oil in an ovenproof skillet over medium-high heat until it shimmers.
3. Add the shallots and sauté for about 3 minutes, stirring occasionally, until fragrant.
4. Fold in the garlic powder, potato, and bell peppers and stir to combine.
5. Cover and cook for 10 minutes, stirring frequently.
6. Add the tomatoes, cardamon, paprika, and turmeric and mix well.
7. When the mixture begins to bubble, remove from the heat and crack the eggs into the skillet.
8. Transfer the skillet to the preheated oven and bake for 5 to 10 minutes, or until the egg whites are set and the yolks are cooked to your liking.
9. Remove from the oven and garnish with the cilantro before serving.

Tip: If you prefer a spicy shakshuka, you can stir in ¼ teaspoon red pepper flakes to the tomatoes.

Per Serving
calories: 223 | fat: 11.8g | protein: 9.1g
carbs: 19.5g | fiber: 3.0g | sodium: 277mg

Ricotta Toast with Strawberries

Prep time: 10 minutes | Cook time: 0 minutes | Serves 2

½ cup crumbled ricotta cheese
1 tablespoon honey, plus additional as needed
Pinch of sea salt, plus additional as needed
4 slices of whole-grain bread, toasted
1 cup sliced fresh strawberries
4 large fresh basil leaves, sliced into thin shreds

1. Mix together the cheese, honey, and salt in a small bowl until well incorporated.
2. Taste and add additional salt and honey if needed.
3. Spoon 2 tablespoons of the cheese mixture onto each slice of bread and spread it all over.
4. Sprinkle the sliced strawberry and basil leaves on top before serving.

Tip: If you don't like the honey and cheese, you can omit them. And the strawberries can be replaced with sliced cucumber.

Per Serving
calories: 274 | fat: 7.9g | protein: 15.1g
carbs: 39.8g | fiber: 5.0g | sodium: 322mg

Apple-Tahini Toast

Prep time: 5 minutes | Cook time: 0 minutes | Serves 1

2 slices whole-wheat bread, toasted
2 tablespoons tahini
1 small apple of your
choice, cored and thinly sliced
1 teaspoon honey

1. Spread the tahini on the toasted bread.
2. Place the apple slices on the bread and drizzle with the honey. Serve immediately.

Per Serving
calories: 458 | fat: 17.8g | protein: 11.0g
carbs: 63.5g | fiber: 10.5g | sodium: 285mg

Egg Bake

Prep time: 10 minutes | Cook time: 30 minutes | Serves 2

1 tablespoon olive oil
1 slice whole-grain bread
4 large eggs
3 tablespoons unsweetened almond milk
½ teaspoon onion powder
¼ teaspoon garlic powder
¾ cup chopped cherry tomatoes
¼ teaspoon salt
Pinch freshly ground black pepper

1. Preheat the oven to 375ºF (190ºC).
2. Coat two ramekins with the olive oil and transfer to a baking sheet. Line the bottom of each ramekin with ½ of bread slice.
3. In a medium bowl, whisk together the eggs, almond milk, onion powder, garlic powder, tomatoes, salt, and pepper until well combined.
4. Pour the mixture evenly into two ramekins. Bake in the preheated oven for 30 minutes, or until the eggs are completely set.
5. Cool for 5 minutes before serving.

Tips: You can add any of your favorite chopped vegetables to the egg mixture, such as mushrooms, spinach or broccoli. To add more flavors to this meal, serve topped with a sprinkle of shredded cheese.

Per Serving
calories: 240 | fat: 17.4g | protein: 9.0g
carbs: 12.2g | fiber: 2.8g | sodium: 396mg

Tomato and Egg Scramble

Prep time: 10 minutes | Cook time: 20 minutes | Serves 4

2 tablespoons extra-virgin olive oil
¼ cup finely minced red onion
1½ cups chopped fresh tomatoes
2 garlic cloves, minced
½ teaspoon dried thyme
½ teaspoon dried oregano
8 large eggs
½ teaspoon salt
¼ teaspoon freshly ground black pepper
¾ cup crumbled feta cheese
¼ cup chopped fresh mint leaves

1. Heat the olive oil in a large skillet over medium heat.
2. Sauté the red onion and tomatoes in the hot skillet for 10 to 12 minutes, or until the tomatoes are softened.
3. Stir in the garlic, thyme, and oregano and sauté for 2 to 4 minutes, or until the garlic is fragrant.
4. Meanwhile, beat the eggs with the salt and pepper in a medium bowl until frothy.
5. Pour the beaten eggs into the skillet and reduce the heat to low. Scramble
6. for 3 to 4 minutes, stirring constantly, or until the eggs are set.
7. Remove from the heat and scatter with the feta cheese and mint. Serve warm.

Tips: For an extra dose of micronutrients, try adding sautéed kale or spinach to this tomato and egg scramble. And fresh herbs (1 to 2 teaspoons) will work just as well as dried in this dish.

Per Serving
calories: 260 | fat: 21.9g | protein: 10.2g
carbs: 5.8g | fiber: 1.0g | sodium: 571mg

Cinnamon Oatmeal with Dried Cranberries

Prep time: 5 minutes | Cook time: 8 minutes | Serves 2

1 cup almond milk
1 cup water
Pinch sea salt
1 cup old-fashioned oats
½ cup dried cranberries
1 teaspoon ground cinnamon

1. In a medium saucepan over high heat, bring the almond milk, water, and salt to a boil.
2. Stir in the oats, cranberries, and cinnamon. Reduce the heat to medium and cook for 5 minutes, stirring occasionally.
3. Remove the oatmeal from the heat. Cover and let it stand for 3 minutes. Stir before serving.

Per Serving
calories: 107 | fat: 2.1g | protein: 3.2g
carbs: 18.2g | fiber: 4.1g | sodium: 122mg

Creamy Peach Smoothie

Prep time: 15 minutes | Cook time: 0 minutes | Serves 2

2 cups packed frozen peaches, partially thawed
½ ripe avocado
½ cup plain or vanilla Greek yogurt
2 tablespoons flax meal
1 tablespoon honey
1 teaspoon orange extract
1 teaspoon vanilla extract

1. Place all the ingredients in a blender and blend until completely mixed and smooth.
2. Divide the mixture into two bowls and serve immediately.

Tip: You can serve the smoothie with any toppings of your choice, such as sunflower seeds, chia seeds, cocoa nibs, chopped nuts, or shredded unsweetened coconut.

Per Serving
calories: 212 | fat: 13.1g | protein: 6.0g
carbs: 22.5g | fiber: 7.2g | sodium: 40mg

Blackberry-Yogurt Green Smoothie

Prep time: 5 minutes | Cook time: 0 minutes | Serves 2

1 cup plain Greek yogurt
1 cup baby spinach
½ cup frozen blackberries
½ cup unsweetened almond milk
½ teaspoon peeled and grated fresh ginger
¼ cup chopped pecans

1. Process the yogurt, baby spinach, blackberries, almond milk, and ginger in a food processor until smoothly blended.
2. Divide the mixture into two bowls and serve topped with the chopped pecans.

Tips: If you prefer a stronger flavor, you can use the fresh turmeric. For extra healthy fats, protein and carbohydrates, you can increase the amount of chopped pecans.

Per Serving
calories: 201 | fat: 14.5g | protein: 7.1g
carbs: 14.9g | fiber: 4.3g | sodium: 103mg

Blueberry Smoothie

Prep time: 5 minutes | Cook time: 0 minutes | Serves 1

1 cup unsweetened almond milk, plus additional as needed
¼ cup frozen blueberries
2 tablespoons unsweetened almond butter
1 tablespoon extra-virgin olive oil
1 tablespoon ground flaxseed or chia seeds
1 to 2 teaspoons maple syrup
½ teaspoon vanilla extract
¼ teaspoon ground cinnamon

1. Blend all the ingredients in a blender until smooth and creamy.
2. You can add additional almond milk to reach your preferred consistency if needed. Serve immediately.

Tip: The blueberries can be replaced with the raspberries or strawberries and the fresh berries will work just as well as frozen in this recipe.

Per Serving
calories: 459 | fat: 40.1g | protein: 8.9g
carbs: 20.0g | fiber: 10.1g | sodium: 147mg

Healthy Chia Pudding

Prep time: 5 minutes | Cook time: 0 minutes | Serves 4

4 cups unsweetened almond milk
¾ cup chia seeds
1 teaspoon ground cinnamon
Pinch sea salt

1. In a medium bowl, whisk together the almond milk, chia seeds, cinnamon, and sea salt until well incorporated.
2. Cover and transfer to the refrigerator to thicken for about 1 hour, or until a pudding-like texture is achieved.
3. Serve chilled.

Tip: You can serve it with your favorite toppings, like blueberries or raspberries. This chia pudding is the perfect healthy breakfast or snack to meal prep.

Per Serving
calories: 236 | fat: 9.8g | protein: 13.1g
carbs: 24.8g | fiber: 11.0g | sodium: 133mg

Morning Overnight Oats with Raspberries

Prep time: 5 minutes | Cook time: 0 minutes | Serves 2

²/₃ cup unsweetened almond milk
¼ cup raspberries
¹/₃ cup rolled oats
1 teaspoon honey
¼ teaspoon turmeric
⅛ teaspoon ground cinnamon
Pinch ground cloves

1. Place the almond milk, raspberries, rolled oats, honey, turmeric, cinnamon, and cloves in a mason jar. Cover and shake to combine.
2. Transfer to the refrigerator for at least 8 hours, preferably 24 hours.
3. Serve chilled.

Tip: For added crunch and flavor, you can serve it with any of your favorite toppings, such as chopped nuts, shredded coconut or fruits.

Per Serving
calories: 81 | fat: 1.9g | protein: 2.1g
carbs: 13.8g | fiber: 3.0g | sodium: 97mg

Cauliflower Breakfast Porridge

Prep time: 5 minutes | Cook time: 5 minutes | Serves 2

2 cups riced cauliflower
¾ cup unsweetened almond milk
4 tablespoons extra-virgin olive oil, divided
2 teaspoons grated fresh orange peel (from ½ orange)
½ teaspoon almond extract or vanilla extract
½ teaspoon ground cinnamon
⅛ teaspoon salt
4 tablespoons chopped walnuts, divided
1 to 2 teaspoons maple syrup (optional)

1. Place the riced cauliflower, almond milk, 2 tablespoons of olive oil, orange peel, almond extract, cinnamon, and salt in a medium saucepan.
2. Stir to incorporate and bring the mixture to a boil over medium-high heat, stirring often.
3. Remove from the heat and add 2 tablespoons of chopped walnuts and maple syrup (if desired).
4. Stir again and divide the porridge into bowls. To serve, sprinkle each bowl evenly with remaining 2 tablespoons of walnuts and olive oil.

Tip: For a slightly sweeter taste, you can substitute the chopped pecans or shelled pistachios for the walnuts.

Per Serving
calories: 381 | fat: 37.8g | protein: 5.2g
carbs: 10.9g | fiber: 4.0g | sodium: 228mg

Baked Eggs in Avocado

Prep time: 5 minutes | Cook time: 10 to 15 minutes | Serves 2

1 ripe large avocado
2 large eggs
Salt and freshly ground black pepper, to taste
4 tablespoons jarred pesto, for serving
2 tablespoons chopped tomato, for serving
2 tablespoons crumbled feta cheese, for serving (optional)

1. Preheat the oven to 425ºF (220ºC).
2. Slice the avocado in half, remove the pit and scoop out a generous tablespoon of flesh from each half to create a hole big enough to fit an egg.
3. Transfer the avocado halves (cut-side up) to a baking sheet.
4. Crack 1 egg into each avocado half and sprinkle with salt and pepper.
5. Bake in the preheated oven for 10 to 15 minutes, or until the eggs are cooked to your preferred doneness.
6. Remove the avocado halves from the oven. Scatter each avocado half evenly with the jarred pesto, chopped tomato, and crumbled feta cheese (if desired). Serve immediately.

Tip: To add more flavors to this breakfast, you can serve it with your favorite toppings like fresh vegetables or a dollop of plain Greek yogurt.

Per Serving
calories: 301 | fat: 25.9g | protein: 8.1g
carbs: 9.8g | fiber: 5.0g | sodium: 435mg

Creamy Vanilla Oatmeal

Prep time: 5 minutes | Cook time: 40 minutes | Serves 4

4 cups water
Pinch sea salt
1 cup steel-cut oats
¾ cup unsweetened

almond milk
2 teaspoons pure
vanilla extract

1. Add the water and salt to a large saucepan over high heat and bring to a boil.
2. Once boiling, reduce the heat to low and add the oats. Mix well and cook for 30 minutes, stirring occasionally.
3. Fold in the almond milk and vanilla and whisk to combine. Continue cooking for about 10 minutes, or until the oats are thick and creamy.
4. Ladle the oatmeal into bowls and serve warm.

Tip: For added crunch and flavor, sprinkle the fresh berries, chopped peaches, sliced almonds, sunflower seeds, or flaxseeds on top before serving.

Per Serving
calories: 117 | fat: 2.2g | protein: 4.3g
carbs: 20.0g | fiber: 3.8g | sodium: 38mg

Fluffy Almond Flour Pancakes with Strawberries

Prep time: 5 minutes | Cook time: 15 minutes | Serves 4

1 cup plus 2
tablespoons
unsweetened almond
milk
1 cup almond flour
2 large eggs, whisked
⅓ cup honey

1 teaspoon baking
soda
¼ teaspoon salt
2 tablespoons extra-
virgin olive oil
1 cup sliced
strawberries

1. Combine the almond milk, almond flour, whisked eggs, honey, baking soda, and salt in a large bowl and whisk to incorporate.
2. Heat the olive oil in a large skillet over medium-high heat.

3. Make the pancakes: Pour ⅓ cup of batter into the hot skillet and swirl the pan so the batter covers the bottom evenly. Cook for 2 to 3 minutes until the pancake turns golden brown around the edges. Gently flip the pancake with a spatula and cook for 2 to 3 minutes until cooked through. Repeat with the remaining batter.
4. Serve the pancakes with the sliced strawberries on top.

Tip: To add more flavors to this meal, you can serve the pancakes with a drizzle of maple syrup or some fresh fruits like sliced banana or blueberries.

Per Serving
calories: 298 | fat: 11.7g | protein: 11.8g
carbs: 34.8g | fiber: 3.9g | sodium: 195mg

Pumpkin Pie Parfait

Prep time: 5 minutes | Cook time: 0 minutes | Serves 4

1 (15-ounce / 425-
g) can pure pumpkin
purée
4 teaspoons honey
1 teaspoon pumpkin
pie spice

¼ teaspoon ground
cinnamon
2 cups plain Greek
yogurt
1 cup honey granola

1. Combine the pumpkin purée, honey, pumpkin pie spice, and cinnamon in a large bowl and stir to mix well.
2. Cover the bowl with plastic wrap and chill in the refrigerator for at least 2 hours.
3. Make the parfaits: Layer each parfait glass with ¼ cup pumpkin mixture in the bottom. Top with ¼ cup of yogurt and scatter each top with ¼ cup of honey granola. Repeat the layers until the glasses are full.
4. Serve immediately.

Tip: If you want to make it a gluten-free dish, be sure to use a gluten-free honey granola.

Per Serving
calories: 263 | fat: 8.9g | protein: 15.3g
carbs: 34.6g | fiber: 6.0g | sodium: 91mg

Avocado Toast with Goat Cheese

Prep time: 5 minutes | Cook time: 2 to 3 minutes | Serves 2

2 slices whole-wheat thin-sliced bread
½ avocado
2 tablespoons
crumbled goat cheese
Salt, to taste

1. Toast the bread slices in a toaster for 2 to 3 minutes on each side until browned.
2. Scoop out the flesh from the avocado into a medium bowl and mash it with a fork to desired consistency. Spread the mash onto each piece of toast.
3. Scatter the crumbled goat cheese on top and season as needed with salt.
4. Serve immediately.

Tip: To make this a complete meal, you can serve the avocado toast with any of your favorite toppings, such as crushed nuts, shredded Parmesan cheese, a handful of microgreens, or tomato slices.

Per Serving
calories: 136 | fat: 5.9g | protein: 5.0g
carbs: 17.5g | fiber: 5.1g | sodium: 194mg

Banana-Blueberry Breakfast Cookies

Prep time: 10 minutes | Cook time: 13 minutes | Serves 4

2 medium bananas, sliced
4 tablespoons almond butter
4 large eggs, lightly beaten
½ cup unsweetened
applesauce
1 teaspoon vanilla extract
⅔ cup coconut flour
¼ teaspoon salt
1 cup fresh or frozen blueberries

1. Preheat the oven to 375ºF (190ºC). Line a baking sheet with parchment paper.
2. Stir together the bananas and almond butter in a medium bowl until well incorporated.
3. Fold in the beaten eggs, applesauce, and vanilla and blend well.
4. Add the coconut flour and salt and mix well. Add the blueberries and stir to just incorporate.

5. Drop about 2 tablespoons of dough onto the parchment paper-lined baking sheet for each cookie. Using your clean hand, flatten each into a rounded biscuit shape, until it is 1 inch thick.
6. Bake in the preheated oven for about 13 minutes, or until the top is golden brown and a toothpick inserted in the center comes out clean.
7. Let the cookies cool for 5 to 10 minutes before serving.

Tip: To make this a complete meal, you can serve it with 1 or 2 hard-boiled eggs.

Per Serving (3 cookies)
calories: 264 | fat: 13.9g | protein: 7.3g
carbs: 27.6g | fiber: 5.2g | sodium: 219mg

Warm Bulgur Breakfast Bowls with Fruits

Prep time: 5 minutes | Cook time: 15 minutes | Serves 6

2 cups unsweetened almond milk
1½ cups uncooked bulgur
1 cup water
½ teaspoon ground cinnamon
2 cups frozen (or
fresh, pitted) dark sweet cherries
8 dried (or fresh) figs, chopped
½ cup chopped almonds
¼ cup loosely packed fresh mint, chopped

1. Combine the milk, bulgur, water, and cinnamon in a medium saucepan, stirring, and bring just to a boil.
2. Cover, reduce the heat to medium-low, and allow to simmer for 10 minutes, or until the liquid is absorbed.
3. Turn off the heat, but keep the pan on the stove, and stir in the frozen cherries (no need to thaw), figs, and almonds. Cover and let the hot bulgur thaw the cherries and partially hydrate the figs, about 1 minute.
4. Fold in the mint and stir to combine, then serve.

Per Serving
calories: 207 | fat: 6.0g | protein: 8.0g
carbs: 32.0g | fiber: 4.0g | sodium: 82mg

5-Ingredient Quinoa Breakfast Bowls

Prep time: 5 minutes | Cook time: 17 minutes | Serves 1

¼ cup quinoa, rinsed
¾ cup water, plus additional as needed
1 carrot, grated
½ small broccoli
head, finely chopped
¼ teaspoon salt
1 tablespoon chopped fresh dill

1. Add the quinoa and water to a small pot over high heat and bring to a boil.
2. Once boiling, reduce the heat to low. Cover and cook for 5 minutes, stirring occasionally.
3. Stir in the carrot, broccoli, and salt and continue cooking for 1o to 12 minutes, or until the quinoa is cooked though and the vegetables are fork-tender. If the mixture gets too thick, you can add additional water as needed.
4. Add the dill and serve warm.

Tips: You can try this recipe with different gluten-free grains, such as millet, rolled oats, buckwheat, or sorghum for variety. And you can grind the gluten-free grains in a food processor until they are ground into a powder-like consistency.

Per Serving
calories: 219 | fat: 2.9g | protein: 10.0g
carbs: 40.8g | fiber: 7.1g | sodium: 666mg

Spinach and Egg Breakfast Wraps

Prep time: 10 minutes | Cook time: 7 minutes | Serves 2

1 tablespoon olive oil
¼ cup minced onion
3 to 4 tablespoons minced sun-dried tomatoes in olive oil and herbs
3 large eggs, whisked
1½ cups packed baby spinach
1 ounce (28 g) crumbled feta cheese
Salt, to taste
2 (8-inch) whole-wheat tortillas

1. Heat the olive oil in a large skillet over medium-high heat.
2. Sauté the onion and tomatoes for about 3 minutes, stirring occasionally, until softened.
3. Reduce the heat to medium. Add the whisked eggs and stir-fry for 1 to 2 minutes.
4. Stir in the baby spinach and scatter with the crumbled feta cheese. Season as needed with salt.
5. Remove the egg mixture from the heat to a plate. Set aside.
6. Working in batches, place 2 tortillas on a microwave-safe dish and microwave for about 20 seconds to make them warm.
7. Spoon half of the egg mixture into each tortilla. Fold them in half and roll up, then serve.

Tip: For a spicy dish, you can use a few teaspoons of harissa sauce to substitute for the sun-dried tomatoes.

Per Serving
calories: 434 | fat: 28.1g | protein: 17.2g
carbs: 30.8g | fiber: 6.0g | sodium: 551mg

Easy Buckwheat Porridge

Prep time: 5 minutes | Cook time: 40 minutes | Serves 4

3 cups water
2 cups raw buckwheat groats
Pinch sea salt
1 cup unsweetened almond milk

1. In a medium saucepan, add the water, buckwheat groats, and sea salt and bring to a boil over medium-high heat.
2. Once it starts to boil, reduce the heat to low. Cook for about 20 minutes, stirring occasionally, or until most of the water is absorbed.
3. Fold in the almond milk and whisk well. Continue cooking for about 15 minutes, or until the buckwheat groats are very softened.
4. Ladle the porridge into bowls and serve warm.

Tip: To add more flavors to this meal, you can serve it with sliced banana, fresh berries, chopped nuts, or a dollop of plain Greek yogurt.

Per Serving
calories: 121 | fat: 1.0g | protein: 6.3g
carbs: 21.5g | fiber: 3.0g | sodium: 47mg

Breakfast Yogurt Sundae

Prep time: 5 minutes | Cook time: 0 minutes | Serves 1

¾ cup plain Greek yogurt
¼ cup fresh mixed berries (blueberries, strawberries, blackberries)
2 tablespoons walnut pieces
1 tablespoon ground flaxseed
2 fresh mint leaves, shredded

1. Pour the yogurt into a tall parfait glass and sprinkle with the mixed berries, walnut pieces, and flaxseed.
2. Garnish with the shredded mint leaves and serve immediately.

Tips: The frozen mixed berries will work just as well as the fresh in this sundae. And you can substitute the cashew or almond pieces for the walnut.

Per Serving
calories: 236 | fat: 10.8g | protein: 21.1g
carbs: 15.9g | fiber: 4.1g | sodium: 63mg

Spinach Cheese Pie

Prep time: 5 minutes | Cook time: 25 minutes | Serves 8

2 tablespoons extra-virgin olive oil
1 onion, chopped
1 pound (454 g) frozen spinach, thawed
¼ teaspoon ground nutmeg
¼ teaspoon garlic salt
¼ teaspoon freshly
ground black pepper
4 large eggs, divided
1 cup grated Parmesan cheese, divided
2 puff pastry doughs, at room temperature
4 hard-boiled eggs, halved
Nonstick cooking spray

1. Preheat the oven to 350ºF (180ºC). Spritz a baking sheet with nonstick cooking spray and set aside.
2. Heat a large skillet over medium-high heat. Add the olive oil and onion and sauté for about 5 minutes, stirring occasionally, or until translucent.
3. Squeeze the excess water from the spinach, then add to the skillet and cook, uncovered, so that any excess water from the spinach can evaporate.
4. Season with the nutmeg, garlic salt, and black pepper. Remove from heat and set aside to cool.
5. Beat 3 eggs in a small bowl. Add the beaten eggs and ½ cup of Parmesan cheese to the spinach mixture, stirring well.
6. Roll out the pastry dough on the prepared baking sheet. Layer the spinach mixture on top of the dough, leaving 2 inches around each edge.
7. Once the spinach is spread onto the pastry dough, evenly place the hard-boiled egg halves throughout the pie, then cover with the second pastry dough. Pinch the edges closed.
8. Beat the remaining 1 egg in the bowl. Brush the egg wash over the pastry dough.
9. Bake in the preheated oven for 15 to 20 minutes until golden brown.
10. Sprinkle with the remaining ½ cup of Parmesan cheese. Cool for 5 minutes before cutting and serving.

Per Serving
calories: 417 | fat: 28.0g | protein: 17.0g
carbs: 25.0g | fiber: 3.0g | sodium: 490mg

Creamy Breakfast Bulgur with Berries

Prep time: 2 minutes | Cook time: 10 minutes | Serves 2

½ cup medium-grain bulgur wheat
1 cup water
Pinch sea salt
¼ cup unsweetened almond milk
1 teaspoon pure vanilla extract
¼ teaspoon ground cinnamon
1 cup fresh berries of your choice

1. Put the bulgur in a medium saucepan with the water and sea salt, and bring to a boil.
2. Cover, remove from heat, and let stand for 10 minutes until water is absorbed.
3. Stir in the milk, vanilla, and cinnamon until fully incorporated. Divide between 2 bowls and top with the fresh berries to serve.

Per Serving
calories: 173 | fat: 1.6g | protein: 5.7g
carbs: 34.0g | fiber: 6.0g | sodium: 197mg

Cinnamon Pistachio Smoothie

Prep time: 5 minutes | Cook time: 0 minutes | Serves 1

½ cup unsweetened almond milk, plus more as needed
½ cup plain Greek yogurt
Zest and juice of ½ orange
1 tablespoon extra-virgin olive oil

1 tablespoon shelled pistachios, coarsely chopped
¼ to ½ teaspoon ground allspice
¼ teaspoon vanilla extract
¼ teaspoon ground cinnamon

1. In a blender, combine ½ cup almond milk, yogurt, orange zest and juice, olive oil, pistachios, allspice, vanilla, and cinnamon. Blend until smooth and creamy, adding more almond milk to achieve your desired consistency.
2. Serve chilled.

Per Serving
calories: 264 | fat: 22.0g | protein: 6.0g
carbs: 12.0g | fiber: 2.0g | sodium: 127mg

Breakfast Pancakes with Berry Sauce

Prep time: 5 minutes | Cook time: 10 minutes | Serves 4

Pancakes:
1 cup almond flour
1 teaspoon baking powder
¼ teaspoon salt
6 tablespoon extra-virgin olive oil,

divided
2 large eggs, beaten
Zest and juice of 1 lemon
½ teaspoon vanilla extract

Berry Sauce:
1 cup frozen mixed berries
1 tablespoon water,

plus more as needed
½ teaspoon vanilla extract

Make the Pancakes
1. In a large bowl, combine the almond flour, baking powder, and salt and stir to break up any clumps.
2. Add 4 tablespoons olive oil, beaten eggs, lemon zest and juice, and vanilla extract and stir until well mixed.

3. Heat 1 tablespoon of olive oil in a large skillet. Spoon about 2 tablespoons of batter for each pancake. Cook until bubbles begin to form, 4 to 5 minutes. Flip and cook for another 2 to 3 minutes. Repeat with the remaining 1 tablespoon of olive oil and batter.

Make the Berry Sauce
1. Combine the frozen berries, water, and vanilla extract in a small saucepan and heat over medium-high heat for 3 to 4 minutes until bubbly, adding more water as needed. Using the back of a spoon or fork, mash the berries and whisk until smooth.
2. Serve the pancakes with the berry sauce.

Per Serving
calories: 275 | fat: 26.0g | protein: 4.0g
carbs: 8.0g | fiber: 2.0g | sodium: 271mg

Feta and Olive Scrambled Eggs

Prep time: 5 minutes | Cook time: 5 minutes | Serves 2

4 large eggs
1 tablespoon unsweetened almond milk
Sea salt and freshly ground pepper, to taste
1 tablespoon olive oil

¼ cup crumbled feta cheese
10 Kalamata olives, pitted and sliced
Small bunch fresh mint, chopped, for garnish

1. Beat the eggs in a bowl until just combined. Add the milk and a pinch of sea salt and whisk well.
2. Heat a medium nonstick skillet over medium-high heat and add the olive oil.
3. Pour in the egg mixture and stir constantly, or until they just begin to curd and firm up, about 2 minutes. Add the feta cheese and olive slices, and stir until evenly combined. Season to taste with salt and pepper.
4. Divide the mixture between 2 plates and serve garnished with the fresh chopped mint.

Per Serving
calories: 244 | fat: 21.9g | protein: 8.4g
carbs:3.5g | fiber: 0.6g | sodium: 339mg

Banana Corn Fritters

Prep time: 5 minutes | Cook time: 10 minutes | Serves 2

½ cup yellow cornmeal
¼ cup flour
2 small ripe bananas, peeled and mashed
2 tablespoons unsweetened almond milk
1 large egg, beaten

½ teaspoon baking powder
¼ to ½ teaspoon ground chipotle chili
¼ teaspoon ground cinnamon
¼ teaspoon sea salt
1 tablespoon olive oil

1. Stir together all ingredients except for the olive oil in a large bowl until smooth.
2. Heat a nonstick skillet over medium-high heat. Add the olive oil and drop about 2 tablespoons of batter for each fritter. Cook for 2 to 3 minutes until the bottoms are golden brown, then flip. Continue cooking for 1 to 2 minutes more, until cooked through. Repeat with the remaining batter.
3. Serve warm.

Per Serving
calories: 396 | fat: 10.6g | protein: 7.3g
carbs: 68.0g | fiber: 4.8g | sodium: 307mg

Crustless Tiropita (Greek Cheese Pie)

Prep time: 10 minutes | Cook time: 35 to 40 minutes | Serves 6

4 tablespoons extra-virgin olive oil, divided
½ cup whole-milk ricotta cheese
1¼ cups crumbled feta cheese
1 tablespoon chopped fresh dill

2 tablespoons chopped fresh mint
½ teaspoon lemon zest
¼ teaspoon freshly ground black pepper
2 large eggs
½ teaspoon baking powder

1. Preheat the oven to 350ºF (180ºC). Coat the bottom and sides of a baking dish with 2 tablespoons of olive oil. Set aside.
2. Mix together the ricotta and feta cheese in a medium bowl and stir with a fork until well combined. Add the dill, mint, lemon zest, and black pepper and mix well.
3. In a separate bowl, whisk together the eggs and baking powder. Pour the whisked eggs into the bowl of cheese mixture. Blend well.
4. Slowly pour the mixture into the coated baking dish and drizzle with the remaining 2 tablespoons of olive oil.
5. Bake in the preheated oven for about 35 to 40 minutes, or until the pie is browned around the edges and cooked through.
6. Cool for 5 minutes before slicing into wedges.

Tip: To add more flavors to this breakfast, you can serve it with a cup of coffee. It also pairs perfectly with a traditional Greek salad as a light lunch.

Per Serving
calories: 181 | fat: 16.6g | protein: 7.0g
carbs: 1.8g | fiber: 0g | sodium: 321mg

Marinara Poached Eggs

Prep time: 5 minutes | Cook time: 15 minutes | Serves 6

1 tablespoon extra-virgin olive oil
1 cup chopped onion
2 garlic cloves, minced
2 (14.5-ounce / 411-

g) cans no-salt-added Italian diced tomatoes, undrained
6 large eggs
½ cup chopped fresh flat-leaf parsley

1. Heat the olive oil in a large skillet over medium-high heat.
2. Add the onion and sauté for 5 minutes, stirring occasionally. Add the garlic and cook for 1 minute more.
3. Pour the tomatoes with their juices over the onion mixture and cook for 2 to 3 minutes until bubbling.
4. Reduce the heat to medium and use a large spoon to make six indentations in the tomato mixture. Crack the eggs, one at a time, into each indentation.
5. Cover and simmer for 6 to 7 minutes, or until the eggs are cooked to your preference.
6. Serve with the parsley sprinkled on top.

Per Serving
calories: 89 | fat: 6.0g | protein: 4.0g
carbs: 4.0g | fiber: 1.0g | sodium: 77mg

Parmesan Oatmeal with Greens

Prep time: 10 minutes | Cook time: 18 minutes | Serves 2

1 tablespoon olive oil
¼ cup minced onion
2 cups greens (arugula, baby spinach, chopped kale, or Swiss chard)
¾ cup gluten-free old-fashioned oats
1½ cups water, or low-sodium chicken stock
2 tablespoons Parmesan cheese
Salt, to taste
Pinch freshly ground black pepper

1. Heat the olive oil in a saucepan over medium-high heat. Add the minced onion and sauté for 2 minutes, or until softened.
2. Add the greens and stir until they begin to wilt. Transfer this mixture to a bowl and set aside.
3. Add the oats to the pan and let them toast for about 2 minutes. Add the water and bring the oats to a boil.
4. Reduce the heat to low, cover, and let the oats cook for 10 minutes, or until the liquid is absorbed and the oats are tender.
5. Stir the Parmesan cheese into the oats, and add the onion and greens back to the pan. Add additional water if needed, so the oats are creamy and not dry.
6. Stir well and season with salt and black pepper to taste. Serve warm.

Per Serving
calories: 257 | fat: 14.0g | protein: 12.2g
carbs: 30.2g | fiber: 6.1g | sodium: 262mg

Avocado and Egg Toast

Prep time: 5 minutes | Cook time: 8 minutes | Serves 2

2 tablespoons ground flaxseed
½ teaspoon baking powder
2 large eggs, beaten
1 teaspoon salt, plus additional for serving
½ teaspoon freshly ground black pepper,
plus additional for serving
½ teaspoon garlic powder, sesame seed, caraway seed, or other dried herbs (optional)
3 tablespoons extra-virgin olive oil, divided
1 medium ripe avocado, peeled, pitted, and sliced
2 tablespoons chopped ripe tomato

1. In a small bowl, combine the flaxseed and baking powder, breaking up any lumps in the baking powder.
2. Add the beaten eggs, salt, pepper, and garlic powder (if desired) and whisk well. Let sit for 2 minutes.
3. In a small nonstick skillet, heat 1 tablespoon of olive oil over medium heat. Pour the egg mixture into the skillet and let cook undisturbed until the egg begins to set on bottom, 2 to 3 minutes.
4. Using a rubber spatula, scrape down the sides to allow uncooked egg to reach the bottom. Cook for an additional 2 to 3 minutes.
5. Once almost set, flip like a pancake and allow the top to fully cook, another 1 to 2 minutes.
6. Remove from the skillet and allow to cool slightly, then slice into 2 pieces.
7. Top each piece with avocado slices, additional salt and pepper, chopped tomato, and drizzle with the remaining 2 tablespoons of olive oil. Serve immediately.

Per Serving
calories: 297 | fat: 26.1g | protein: 8.9g
carbs: 12.0g | fiber: 7.1g | sodium: 1132mg

Kale and Apple Smoothie

Prep time: 5 minutes | Cook time: 0 minutes | Serves 2

2 cups shredded kale
1 cup unsweetened almond milk
¼ cup 2 percent plain Greek yogurt
½ Granny Smith apple, unpeeled, cored and chopped
½ avocado, diced
3 ice cubes

1. Put all ingredients in a blender and blend until smooth and thick.
2. Pour into two glasses and serve immediately.

Per Serving
calories: 177 | fat: 6.8g | protein: 8.2g
carbs: 22.0g | fiber: 4.1g | sodium: 112mg

Savory Breakfast Oatmeal

Prep time: 5 minutes | Cook time: 15 minutes | Serves 2

½ cup steel-cut oats
1 cup water
1 medium cucumber, chopped
1 large tomato, chopped
1 tablespoon olive oil
Pinch freshly grated

Parmesan cheese
Sea salt and freshly ground pepper, to taste
Flat-leaf parsley or mint, chopped, for garnish

1. Combine the oats and water in a medium saucepan and bring to a boil over high heat, stirring continuously, or until the water is absorbed, about 15 minutes.
2. Divide the oatmeal between 2 bowls and scatter the tomato and cucumber on top. Drizzle with the olive oil and sprinkle with the Parmesan cheese.
3. Season with salt and pepper to taste. Serve garnished with the parsley.

Per Serving
calories: 197| fat: 8.9g | protein: 6.3g
carbs: 23.1g | fiber: 6.4g | sodium: 27mg

Cheesy Broccoli and Mushroom Egg Casserole

Prep time: 10 minutes | Cook time: 40 minutes | Serves 4

2 tablespoons extra-virgin olive oil
½ sweet onion, chopped
1 teaspoon minced garlic
1 cup sliced button mushrooms
1 cup chopped broccoli

8 large eggs
¼ cup unsweetened almond milk
1 tablespoon chopped fresh basil
1 cup shredded Cheddar cheese
Sea salt and freshly ground black pepper, to taste

1. Preheat the oven to 375ºF (190ºC).
2. Heat the olive oil in a large ovenproof skillet over medium-high heat.
3. Add the onion, garlic, and mushrooms to the skillet and sauté for about 5 minutes, stirring occasionally.
4. Stir in the broccoli and sauté for 5

minutes until the vegetables start to soften.
5. Meanwhile, beat the eggs with the almond milk and basil in a small bowl until well mixed.
6. Remove the skillet from the heat and pour the egg mixture over the top. Scatter the Cheddar cheese all over.
7. Bake uncovered in the preheated oven for about 30 minutes, or until the top of the casserole is golden brown and a fork inserted in the center comes out clean.
8. Remove from the oven and sprinkle with the sea salt and pepper. Serve hot.

Tip: To add more flavors to this meal, you can try adding a can (14.5-ounce / 411-g) of diced tomatoes to this casserole.

Per Serving
calories: 326 | fat: 27.2g | protein: 14.1g
carbs: 6.7g | fiber: 0.7g | sodium: 246mg

Tomato and Egg Breakfast Pizza

Prep time: 5 minutes | Cook time: 15 minutes | Serves 2

2 (6- to 8-inch-long) slices of whole-wheat naan bread
2 tablespoons

prepared pesto
1 medium tomato, sliced
2 large eggs

1. Heat a large nonstick skillet over medium-high heat. Place the naan bread in the skillet and let warm for about 2 minutes on each side, or until softened.
2. Spread 1 tablespoon of the pesto on one side of each slice and top with tomato slices.
3. Remove from the skillet and place each one on its own plate.
4. Crack the eggs into the skillet, keeping them separated, and cook until the whites are no longer translucent and the yolk is cooked to desired doneness.
5. Using a spatula, spoon one egg onto each bread slice. Serve warm.

Per Serving
calories: 429 | fat: 16.8g | protein: 18.1g
carbs: 12.0g | fiber: 4.8g | sodium: 682mg

Baked Ricotta with Honey Pears

Prep time: 5 minutes | Cook time: 22 to 25 minutes | Serves 4

1 (1-pound / 454-g) container whole-milk ricotta cheese
2 large eggs
¼ cup whole-wheat pastry flour
1 tablespoon sugar
1 teaspoon vanilla extract
¼ teaspoon ground nutmeg
1 pear, cored and diced
2 tablespoons water
1 tablespoon honey
Nonstick cooking spray

1. Preheat the oven to 400ºF (205ºC). Spray four ramekins with nonstick cooking spray.
2. Beat together the ricotta, eggs, flour, sugar, vanilla, and nutmeg in a large bowl until combined. Spoon the mixture into the ramekins.
3. Bake in the preheated oven for 22 to 25 minutes, or until the ricotta is just set.
4. Meanwhile, in a small saucepan over medium heat, simmer the pear in the water for 10 minutes, or until slightly softened. Remove from the heat, and stir in the honey.
5. Remove the ramekins from the oven and cool slightly on a wire rack. Top the ricotta ramekins with the pear and serve.

Per Serving
calories: 329 | fat: 19.0g | protein: 17.0g
carbs: 23.0g | fiber: 3.0g | sodium: 109mg

Avocado Smoothie

Prep time: 2 minutes | Cook time: 0 minutes | Serves 2

1 large avocado
1½ cups unsweetened coconut
milk
2 tablespoons honey

1. Place all ingredients in a blender and blend until smooth and creamy. Serve immediately.

Per Serving
calories: 686 | fat: 57.6g | protein: 6.2g
carbs: 35.8g | fiber: 10.7g | sodium: 35mg

Feta and Spinach Frittata

Prep time: 10 minutes | Cook time: 15 minutes | Serves 2

4 large eggs, beaten
2 tablespoons fresh chopped herbs, such as rosemary, thyme, oregano, basil or 1 teaspoon dried herbs
¼ teaspoon salt
Freshly ground black pepper, to taste
4 tablespoons extra-virgin olive oil, divided
1 cup fresh spinach, arugula, kale, or other leafy greens
4 ounces (113 g) quartered artichoke hearts, rinsed, drained, and thoroughly dried
8 cherry tomatoes, halved
½ cup crumbled soft goat cheese

1. Preheat the broiler to Low.
2. In a small bowl, combine the beaten eggs, herbs, salt, and pepper and whisk well with a fork. Set aside.
3. In an ovenproof skillet, heat 2 tablespoons of olive oil over medium heat. Add the spinach, artichoke hearts, and cherry tomatoes and sauté until just wilted, 1 to 2 minutes.
4. Pour in the egg mixture and let it cook undisturbed over medium heat for 3 to 4 minutes, until the eggs begin to set on the bottom.
5. Sprinkle the goat cheese across the top of the egg mixture and transfer the skillet to the oven.
6. Broil for 4 to 5 minutes, or until the frittata is firm in the center and golden brown on top.
7. Remove from the oven and run a rubber spatula around the edge to loosen the sides. Slice the frittata in half and serve drizzled with the remaining 2 tablespoons of olive oil.

Per Serving
calories: 529 | fat: 46.5g | protein: 21.4g
carbs: 7.1g | fiber: 3.1g | sodium: 762mg

Berry and Nut Parfait

Prep time: 10 minutes | Cook time: 0 minutes | Serves 2

2 cups plain Greek yogurt
2 tablespoons honey
1 cup fresh raspberries
1 cup fresh blueberries
½ cup walnut pieces

1. In a medium bowl, whisk the yogurt and honey. Spoon into 2 serving bowls.
2. Top each with ½ cup blueberries, ½ cup raspberries, and ¼ cup walnut pieces. Serve immediately.

Per Serving
calories: 507 | fat: 23.0g | protein: 24.1g
carbs: 57.0g | fiber: 8.2g | sodium: 172mg

Basil Scrambled Eggs

Prep time: 5 minutes | Cook time: 8 minutes | Serves 2

4 large eggs
2 tablespoons grated Gruyère cheese
2 tablespoons finely chopped fresh basil
1 tablespoon plain Greek yogurt
1 tablespoon olive oil
2 cloves garlic, minced
Sea salt and freshly ground pepper, to taste

1. In a large bowl, beat together the eggs, cheese, basil, and yogurt with a whisk until just combined.
2. Heat the oil in a large, heavy nonstick skillet over medium-low heat. Add the garlic and cook until golden, about 1 minute.
3. Pour the egg mixture into the skillet over the garlic. Work the eggs continuously and cook until fluffy and soft.
4. Season with sea salt and freshly ground pepper to taste. Divide between 2 plates and serve immediately.

Per Serving
calories: 243 | fat: 19.7g | protein: 15.6g
carbs: 3.4g | fiber: 0.1g | sodium: 568mg

Mediterranean Omelet

Prep time: 8 minutes | Cook time: 15 minutes | Serves 2

2 teaspoons extra-virgin olive oil, divided
1 garlic clove, minced
½ yellow bell pepper, thinly sliced
½ red bell pepper, thinly sliced
¼ cup thinly sliced red onion
2 tablespoons chopped fresh parsley, plus extra for garnish
2 tablespoons chopped fresh basil
½ teaspoon salt
½ teaspoon freshly ground black pepper
4 large eggs, beaten

1. In a large, heavy skillet, heat 1 teaspoon of the olive oil over medium heat. Add the garlic, peppers, and onion to the skillet and sauté, stirring frequently, for 5 minutes.
2. Add the parsley, basil, salt, and pepper, increase the heat to medium-high, and sauté for 2 minutes. Slide the vegetable mixture onto a plate and return the skillet to the heat.
3. Heat the remaining 1 teaspoon of olive oil in the skillet and pour in the beaten eggs, tilting the pan to coat evenly. Cook the eggs just until the edges are bubbly and all but the center is dry, 3 to 5 minutes.
4. Spoon the vegetable mixture onto one-half of the omelet and use a spatula to fold the empty side over the top. Slide the omelet onto a platter or cutting board.
5. To serve, cut the omelet in half and garnish with extra fresh parsley.

Per Serving
calories: 206 | fat: 14.2g | protein: 13.7g
carbs: 7.2g | fiber: 1.2g | sodium: 729mg

Classic Shakshuka

Prep time: 15 minutes | Cook time: 30 minutes | Serves 2

1 tablespoon olive oil
½ red pepper, diced
½ medium onion, diced
2 small garlic cloves, minced
½ teaspoon smoked paprika
½ teaspoon cumin
Pinch red pepper flakes
1 (14.5-ounce / 411- g) can fire-roasted tomatoes
¼ teaspoon salt
Pinch freshly ground black pepper
1 ounce (28 g) crumbled feta cheese (about ¼ cup)
3 large eggs
3 tablespoons minced fresh parsley

1. Heat the olive oil in a skillet over medium-high heat and add the pepper, onion, and garlic. Sauté until the vegetables start to turn golden.
2. Add the paprika, cumin, and red pepper flakes and stir to toast the spices for about 30 seconds. Add the tomatoes with their juices.
3. Reduce the heat and let the sauce simmer for 10 minutes, or until it starts to thicken. Add the salt and pepper. Taste the sauce and adjust seasonings as necessary.
4. Scatter the feta cheese on top. Make 3 wells in the sauce and crack one egg into each well.
5. Cover and let the eggs cook for about 7 minutes. Remove the lid and continue cooking for 5 minutes more, or until the yolks are cooked to desired doneness.
6. Garnish with fresh parsley and serve.

Per Serving
calories: 289 | fat: 18.2g | protein: 15.1g
carbs: 18.5g | fiber: 4.9g | sodium: 432mg

Chapter 3 Sides, Salads, and Soups

Greek Chicken, Tomato, and Olive Salad

Prep time: 10 minutes | Cook time: 0 minutes | Serves 2

Salad:
2 grilled boneless, skinless chicken breasts, sliced (about 1 cup)
10 cherry tomatoes, halved
8 pitted Kalamata olives, halved
½ cup thinly sliced red onion

Dressing:
¼ cup balsamic vinegar
1 teaspoon freshly squeezed lemon juice
¼ teaspoon sea salt
¼ teaspoon freshly ground black pepper
2 teaspoons extra-virgin olive oil

For Serving:
2 cups roughly chopped romaine lettuce
½ cup crumbled feta cheese

1. Combine the ingredients for the salad in a large bowl. Toss to combine well.
2. Combine the ingredients for the dressing in a small bowl. Stir to mix well.
3. Pour the dressing the bowl of salad, then toss to coat well. Wrap the bowl in plastic and refrigerate for at least 2 hours.
4. Remove the bowl from the refrigerator. Spread the lettuce on a large plate, then top with marinated salad. Scatter the salad with feta cheese and serve immediately.

Tip: How to grill the chicken breast: Preheat the grill to medium high heat, then grease the grill grates with olive oil. Place the chicken breast on the grill grate and grill for 15 minutes or until the internal temperature of the chicken reaches at least 165ºF (74ºC). Flip the chicken breast halfway through. Allow to cool before using.

Per Serving
calories: 328 | fat: 16.9g | protein: 27.6g
carbs: 15.9g | fiber: 3.1g| sodium: 1102mg

Artichoke and Arugula Salad

Prep time: 10 minutes | Cook time: 0 minutes | Serves 6

Salad:

6 canned oil-packed artichoke hearts, sliced
6 cups baby arugula leaves
6 fresh olives, pitted and chopped
1 cup cherry tomatoes, sliced in half

Dressing:

1 teaspoon Dijon mustard
2 tablespoons balsamic vinegar
1 clove garlic, minced
2 tablespoons extra-virgin olive oil

For Garnish:

4 fresh basil leaves, thinly sliced

1. Combine the ingredients for the salad in a large salad bowl, then toss to combine well.
2. Combine the ingredients for the dressing in a small bowl, then stir to mix well.
3. Dressing the salad, then serve with basil leaves on top.

Tip: If you don't like canned food, and good at dealing with or want to deal with the fresh artichokes, you can use the same amount of fresh artichoke to replace the canned artichoke hearts.

Per Serving
calories: 134 | fat: 12.1g | protein: 1.6g
carbs: 6.2g | fiber: 3.0g| sodium: 65mg

Baby Potato and Olive Salad

Prep time: 10 minutes | Cook time: 20 minutes | Serves 6

2 pounds (907 g) baby potatoes, cut into 1-inch cubes
1 tablespoon low-sodium olive brine
3 tablespoons freshly squeezed lemon juice (from about 1 medium lemon)
¼ teaspoon kosher salt
3 tablespoons extra-virgin olive oil
½ cup sliced olives
2 tablespoons torn fresh mint
1 cup sliced celery (about 2 stalks)
2 tablespoons chopped fresh oregano

1. Put the tomatoes in a saucepan, then pour in enough water to submerge the tomatoes about 1 inch.
2. Bring to a boil over high heat, then reduce the heat to medium-low. Simmer for 14 minutes or until the potatoes are soft.
3. Meanwhile, combine the olive brine, lemon juice, salt, and olive oil in a small bow. Stir to mix well.
4. Transfer the cooked tomatoes in a colander, then rinse with running cold water. Pat dry with paper towels.
5. Transfer the tomatoes in a large salad bowl, then drizzle with olive brine mixture. Spread with remaining ingredients and toss to combine well.
6. Serve immediately.

Tip: You can toss the hot tomatoes with half of the olive brine mixture after patting dry and let it to infuse before combining with remaining ingredients.

Per Serving
calories: 220 | fat: 6.1g | protein: 4.3g
carbs: 39.2g | fiber: 5.0g | sodium: 231mg

Garlic Wilted Greens

Prep time: 10 minutes | Cook time: 5 minutes | Serves 2

1 tablespoon olive oil
2 garlic cloves, minced
3 cups sliced greens (spinach, chard, beet greens, dandelion
greens, or a combination)
Pinch salt
Pinch red pepper flakes (or more to taste)

1. Heat the olive oil in a skillet over medium-high heat.
2. Add garlic and sauté for 30 seconds, or just until fragrant.
3. Add the greens, salt, and pepper flakes and stir to combine. Let the greens wilt, but do not overcook.
4. Remove from the skillet and serve on a plate.

Per Serving
calories: 93 | fat: 6.8g | protein: 1.2g
carbs: 7.3g | fiber: 3.1g | sodium: 112mg

Barley, Parsley, and Pea Salad

Prep time: 10 minutes | Cook time: 10 minutes | Serves 4

2 cups water
1 cup quick-cooking barley
1 small bunch flat-leaf parsley, chopped (about 1 to 1½ cups)
2 cups sugar snap pea pods
Juice of 1 lemon
½ small red onion, diced
2 tablespoons extra-virgin olive oil
Sea salt and freshly ground pepper, to taste

1. Pour the water in a saucepan. Bring to a boil. Add the barley to the saucepan, then put the lid on.
2. Reduce the heat to low. Simmer the barley for 10 minutes or until the liquid is absorbed, then let sit for 5 minutes.
3. Open the lid, then transfer the barley in a colander and rinse under cold running water.
4. Pour the barley in a large salad bowl and add the remaining ingredients. Toss to combine well.
5. Serve immediately.

Tip: If you have enough time, you can use pearl barley to replace the quick-cooking barley, and it may cost 15 more minutes to simmer the barley.

Per Serving
calories: 152 | fat: 7.4g | protein: 3.7g
carbs: 19.3g | fiber: 4.7g| sodium: 20mg

Sumptuous Greek Vegetable Salad

Prep time: 20 minutes | Cook time: 0 minutes | Serves 6

Salad:
1 (15-ounce / 425-g) can chickpeas, drained and rinsed
1 (14-ounce / 397-g) can artichoke hearts, drained and halved
1 head Bibb lettuce, chopped (about 2½ cups)
1 cucumber, peeled deseeded, and
chopped (about 1½ cups)
1½ cups grape tomatoes, halved
¼ cup chopped basil leaves
½ cup sliced black olives
½ cup cubed feta cheese

Dressing:
1 tablespoon freshly squeezed lemon juice (from about ½ small lemon)
¼ teaspoon freshly ground black pepper
1 tablespoon chopped
fresh oregano
2 tablespoons extra-virgin olive oil
1 tablespoon red wine vinegar
1 teaspoon honey

1. Combine the ingredients for the salad in a large salad bowl, then toss to combine well.
2. Combine the ingredients for the dressing in a small bowl, then stir to mix well.
3. Dressing the salad and serve immediately.

Tip: You can use ½ head romaine lettuce or other fresh leaves to replace the Bibb lettuce.

Per Serving
calories: 165 | fat: 8.1g | protein: 7.2g
carbs: 17.9g | fiber: 7.0g | sodium: 337mg

Cheesy Peach and Walnut Salad

Prep time: 10 minutes | Cook time: 0 minutes | Serves 1

1 ripe peach, pitted and sliced
¼ cup chopped walnuts, toasted
¼ cup shredded Parmesan cheese
1 teaspoon raw honey
Zest of 1 lemon
1 tablespoon chopped fresh mint

1. Combine the peach, walnut, and cheese in a medium bowl, then drizzle with honey. Spread the lemon zest and mint on top. Toss to combine everything well.
2. Serve immediately.

Tip: You can serve this salad as breakfast, and serve it with plain almond yogurt and toss with cubed whole wheat bread, if desired.

Per Serving
calories: 373 | fat: 26.4g | protein: 12.9g
carbs: 27.0g | fiber: 4.7g | sodium: 453mg

Ritzy Summer Fruit Salad

Prep time: 10 minutes | Cook time: 0 minutes | Serves 8

Salad:

1 cup fresh blueberries

2 cups cubed cantaloupe

2 cups red seedless grapes

1 cup sliced fresh strawberries

2 cups cubed honeydew melon

Zest of 1 large lime

½ cup unsweetened toasted coconut flakes

Dressing:

¼ cup raw honey

Juice of 1 large lime

¼ teaspoon sea salt

½ cup extra-virgin olive oil

1. Combine the ingredients for the salad in a large salad bowl, then toss to combine well.
2. Combine the ingredients for the dressing in a small bowl, then stir to mix well.
3. Dressing the salad and serve immediately.

Tip: You can enjoy this fruit salad between breakfast and lunchtime. Because during this time, the nutritional value of the fruits are highest and they can also give you a bright day.

Per Serving

calories: 242 | fat: 15.5g | protein: 1.3g carbs: 28.0g | fiber: 2.4g | sodium: 90mg

Arugula and Fig Salad

Prep time: 15 minutes | Cook time: 0 minutes | Serves 2

3 cups arugula

4 fresh, ripe figs (or 4 to 6 dried figs), stemmed and sliced

2 tablespoons olive oil

¼ cup lightly toasted pecan halves

2 tablespoons crumbled blue cheese

1 to 2 tablespoons balsamic glaze

1. Toss the arugula and figs with the olive oil in a large bowl until evenly coated.
2. Add the pecans and blue cheese to the bowl. Toss the salad lightly.
3. Drizzle with the balsamic glaze and serve immediately.

Per Serving

calories: 517 | fat: 36.2g | protein: 18.9g carbs: 30.2g | fiber: 6.1g | sodium: 481mg

Roasted Broccoli and Tomato Panzanella

Prep time: 10 minutes | Cook time: 20 minutes | Serves 4

1 pound (454 g) broccoli (about 3 medium stalks), trimmed, cut into 1-inch florets and ½-inch stem slices

2 tablespoons extra-virgin olive oil, divided

1½ cups cherry tomatoes

1½ teaspoons honey, divided

3 cups cubed whole-grain crusty bread

1 tablespoon balsamic vinegar

¼ teaspoon kosher salt

½ teaspoon freshly ground black pepper

¼ cup grated Parmesan cheese, for serving (optional)

¼ cup chopped fresh oregano leaves, for serving (optional)

1. Preheat the oven to 450ºF (235ºC).
2. Toss the broccoli with 1 tablespoon of olive oil in a large bowl to coat well.
3. Arrange the broccoli on a baking sheet, then add the tomatoes to the same bowl and toss with the remaining olive oil. Add 1 teaspoon of honey and toss again to coat well. Transfer the tomatoes on the baking sheet beside the broccoli.
4. Place the baking sheet in the preheated oven and roast for 15 minutes, then add the bread cubes and flip the vegetables. Roast for an additional 3 minutes or until the broccoli is lightly charred and the bread cubes are golden brown.
5. Meanwhile, combine the remaining ingredients, except for the Parmesan and oregano, in a small bowl. Stir to mix well.
6. Transfer the roasted vegetables and bread cubes to the large salad bowl, then dress them and spread with Parmesan and oregano leaves. Toss and serve immediately.

Tip: You can use sun-dried tomatoes, ripped yellow tomatoes, or just grape tomatoes to replace the cherry tomatoes. Remember to reserve the juice and drizzle the salad with the juice for more freshness.

Per Serving

calories: 162 | fat: 6.8g | protein: 8.2g carbs: 18.9g | fiber: 6.0g | sodium: 397mg

Lemon and Spinach Orzo

Prep time: 5 minutes | Cook time: 10 minutes | Makes 2 cups

1 cup dry orzo
1 (6-ounce / 170-g) bag baby spinach
1 cup halved grape tomatoes
2 tablespoons extra-virgin olive oil
¼ teaspoon salt
Freshly ground black pepper
¾ cup crumbled feta cheese
1 lemon, juiced and zested

1. Bring a medium pot of water to a boil. Stir in the orzo and cook uncovered for 8 minutes. Drain the water, then return the orzo to medium heat.
2. Add the spinach and tomatoes and cook until the spinach is wilted.
3. Sprinkle with the olive oil, salt, and pepper and mix well. Top with the feta cheese, lemon juice and zest, then toss one or two more times and serve.

Per Serving (1 cup)
calories: 610 | fat: 27.0g | protein: 21.0g
carbs: 74.0g | fiber: 6.0g | sodium: 990mg

Grilled Bell Pepper and Anchovy Antipasto

Prep time: 15 minutes | Cook time: 8 minutes | Serves 4

2 tablespoons extra-virgin olive oil, divided
4 medium red bell peppers, quartered, stem and seeds removed
6 ounces (170 g) anchovies in oil, chopped
2 tablespoons capers, rinsed and drained
1 cup Kalamata olives, pitted
1 small shallot, chopped
Sea salt and freshly ground pepper, to taste

1. Heat the grill to medium-high heat. Grease the grill grates with 1 tablespoon of olive oil.
2. Arrange the red bell peppers on the preheated grill grates, then grill for 8 minutes or until charred.
3. Turn off the grill and allow the pepper to cool for 10 minutes.

4. Transfer the charred pepper in a colander. Rinse and peel the peppers under running cold water, then pat dry with paper towels.
5. Cut the peppers into chunks and combine with remaining ingredients in a large bowl. Toss to mix well.
6. Serve immediately.

Tip: As an antipasto, you can serve this dish with whole-wheat bread, or you can use it as the filling for whole wheat pita pockets.

Per Serving
calories: 227 | fat: 14.9g | protein: 13.9g
carbs: 9.9g | fiber: 3.8g| sodium: 1913mg

Butternut Squash and Cauliflower Curry Soup

Prep time: 15 minutes | Cook time: 4 hours | Serves 4 to 6

1 pound (454 g) butternut squash, peeled and cut into 1-inch cubes
1 small head cauliflower, cut into 1-inch pieces
1 onion, sliced
2 cups unsweetened coconut milk
1 tablespoon curry powder
½ cup no-added-sugar apple juice
4 cups low-sodium vegetable soup
2 tablespoons coconut oil
1 teaspoon sea salt
¼ teaspoon freshly ground white pepper
¼ cup chopped fresh cilantro, divided

1. Combine all the ingredients, except for the cilantro, in the slow cooker. Stir to mix well.
2. Cook on high heat for 4 hours or until the vegetables are tender.
3. Pour the soup in a food processor, then pulse until creamy and smooth.
4. Pour the puréed soup in a large serving bowl and garnish with cilantro before serving.

Tip: To make this a complete meal, you can serve this soup with salmon filet or grilled scallops.

Per Serving
calories: 415 | fat: 30.8g | protein: 10.1g
carbs: 29.9g | fiber: 7.0g | sodium: 1386mg

Brussels Sprout and Apple Slaw

Prep time: 15 minutes | Cook time: 0 minutes | Serves 4

Salad:

1 pound (454 g) Brussels sprouts, stem ends removed and sliced thinly

1 apple, cored and sliced thinly
½ red onion, sliced thinly

Dressing:

1 teaspoon Dijon mustard
2 teaspoons apple cider vinegar
1 tablespoon raw

honey
1 cup plain coconut yogurt
1 teaspoon sea salt

For Garnish:

½ cup pomegranate seeds
½ cup chopped toasted hazelnuts

1. Combine the ingredients for the salad in a large salad bowl, then toss to combine well.
2. Combine the ingredients for the dressing in a small bowl, then stir to mix well.
3. Dressing the salad. Let sit for 30 minutes, then serve with pomegranate seeds and toasted hazelnuts on top.

Tip: If you don't like pomegranate seeds, you can replace it with sunflower seeds, pumpkin seeds, or chia seeds.

Per Serving
calories: 248 | fat: 11.2g | protein: 12.7g carbs: 29.9g | fiber: 8.0g | sodium: 645mg

Hearty Veggie Slaw

Prep time: 20 minutes | Cook time: 0 minutes | Serves 4 to 6

Salad:

2 large broccoli stems, peeled and shredded
½ celery root bulb, peeled and shredded
¼ cup chopped fresh Italian parsley

1 large beet, peeled and shredded
2 carrots, peeled and shredded
1 small red onion, sliced thin
2 zucchinis, shredded

Dressing:

1 teaspoon Dijon   mustard

½ cup apple cider vinegar
1 tablespoon raw honey
1 teaspoon sea salt

¼ teaspoon freshly ground black pepper
2 tablespoons extra-virgin olive oil

Topping:
½ cup crumbled feta cheese

1. Combine the ingredients for the salad in a large salad bowl, then toss to combine well.
2. Combine the ingredients for the dressing in a small bowl, then stir to mix well.
3. Dressing the salad, then serve with feta cheese on top.

Tip: You can use this slaw as a side dish to serve with chicken and potato stew or grilled salmon.

Per Serving
calories: 387 | fat: 30.2g | protein: 8.1g carbs: 25.9g | fiber: 6.0g | sodium: 980mg

Marinated Mushrooms and Olives

Prep time: 1 hour 10 minutes | Cook time: 0 minutes | Serves 8

1 pound (454 g) white button mushrooms, rinsed and drained
1 pound (454 g) fresh olives
½ tablespoon crushed fennel seeds
1 tablespoon white

wine vinegar
2 tablespoons fresh thyme leaves
Pinch chili flakes
Sea salt and freshly ground pepper, to taste
2 tablespoons extra-virgin olive oil

1. Combine all the ingredients in a large bowl. Toss to mix well.
2. Wrap the bowl in plastic and refrigerate for at least 1 hour to marinate.
3. Remove the bowl from the refrigerate and let sit under room temperature for 10 minutes, then serve.

Tip: As a side dish, you can serve it with seared salmon filet or you can pour this dish into a bowl of cooked pasta and stir to serve.

Per Serving
calories: 111 | fat: 9.7g | protein: 2.4g carbs: 5.9g | fiber: 2.7g | sodium: 449mg

Cherry, Plum, Artichoke, and Cheese Board

Prep time: 15 minutes | Cook time: 0 minutes | Serves 4

2 cups rinsed cherries
2 cups rinsed and sliced plums
2 cups rinsed carrots, cut into sticks
1 cup canned low-

sodium artichoke hearts, rinsed and drained
1 cup cubed feta cheese

1. Arrange all the ingredients in separated portions on a clean board or a large tray, then serve with spoons, knife, and forks.

Tip: If you don't like canned food, you can replace the canned artichoke hearts with ½ cup of fresh olives.

Per Serving
calories: 417 | fat: 13.8g | protein: 20.1g
carbs: 56.2g | fiber: 3.0g | sodium: 715mg

Root Vegetable Roast

Prep time: 15 minutes | Cook time: 25 minutes | Serves 4 to 6

1 bunch beets, peeled and cut into 1-inch cubes
2 small sweet potatoes, peeled and cut into 1-inch cubes
3 parsnips, peeled and cut into 1-inch rounds
4 carrots, peeled and cut into 1-inch

rounds
1 tablespoon raw honey
1 teaspoon sea salt
½ teaspoon freshly ground black pepper
1 tablespoon extra-virgin olive oil
2 tablespoons coconut oil, melted

1. Preheat the oven to 400ºF (205ºC). Line a baking sheet with parchment paper.
2. Combine all the ingredients in a large bowl. Toss to coat the vegetables well.
3. Pour the mixture in the baking sheet, then place the sheet in the preheated oven.
4. Roast for 25 minutes or until the vegetables are lightly browned and soft. Flip the vegetables halfway through the cooking time.

5. Remove the vegetables from the oven and allow to cool before serving.

Tip: If one baking sheet is not large enough to hold all the mixture, then you can use two or more baking sheets to work in batches to avoid overcrowding.

Per Serving
calories: 461 | fat: 18.1g | protein: 5.9g
carbs: 74.2g | fiber: 14.0g | sodium: 759mg

Mushroom and Soba Noodle Soup

Prep time: 15 minutes | Cook time: 10 minutes | Serves 4

2 tablespoons coconut oil
8 ounces (227 g) shiitake mushrooms, stemmed and sliced thin
1 tablespoon minced fresh ginger
4 scallions, sliced thin
1 garlic clove, minced

1 teaspoon sea salt
4 cups low-sodium vegetable broth
3 cups water
4 ounces (113 g) soba noodles
1 bunch spinach, blanched, rinsed and cut into strips
1 tablespoon freshly squeezed lemon juice

1. Heat the coconut oil in a stockpot over medium heat until melted.
2. Add the mushrooms, ginger, scallions, garlic, and salt. Sauté for 5 minutes or until fragrant and the mushrooms are tender.
3. Pour in the vegetable broth and water. Bring to a boil, then add the soba noodles and cook for 5 minutes or until al dente.
4. Turn off the heat and add the spinach and lemon juice. Stir to mix well.
5. Pour the soup in a large bowl and serve immediately.

Tip: If you can't find the soda noodles, just use common long pastas to replace it.

Per Serving
calories: 254 | fat: 9.2g | protein: 13.1g
carbs: 33.9g | fiber: 4.0g | sodium: 1773mg

Cheesy Roasted Broccolini

Prep time: 5 minutes | Cook time: 10 minutes | Serves 2

1 bunch broccolini (about 5 ounces / 142 g)
1 tablespoon olive oil
½ teaspoon garlic powder
¼ teaspoon salt
2 tablespoons grated Romano cheese

1. Preheat the oven to 400ºF (205ºC). Line a sheet pan with parchment paper.
2. Slice the tough ends off the broccolini and put in a medium bowl. Add the olive oil, garlic powder, and salt and toss to coat well. Arrange the broccolini on the prepared sheet pan.
3. Roast in the preheated oven for 7 minutes, flipping halfway through the cooking time.
4. Remove the pan from the oven and sprinkle the cheese over the broccolini. Using tongs, carefully flip the broccolini over to coat all sides.
5. Return to the oven and cook for an additional 2 to 3 minutes, or until the cheese melts and starts to turn golden. Serve warm.

Per Serving
calories: 114 | fat: 9.0g | protein: 4.0g
carbs: 5.0g | fiber: 2.0g | sodium: 400mg

Sardines with Lemony Tomato Sauce

Prep time: 10 minutes | Cook time: 40 minutes | Serves 4

2 tablespoons olive oil, divided
4 Roma tomatoes, peeled and chopped, reserve the juice
1 small onion, sliced thinly
Zest of 1 orange
Sea salt and freshly
ground pepper, to taste
1 pound (454 g) fresh sardines, rinsed, spine removed, butterflied
½ cup white wine
2 tablespoons whole-wheat breadcrumbs

1. Preheat the oven to 425ºF (220ºC). Grease a baking dish with 1 tablespoon of olive oil.
2. Heath the remaining olive oil in a nonstick skillet over medium-low heat until shimmering.
3. Add the tomatoes with juice, onion, orange zest, salt, and ground pepper to the skillet and simmer for 20 minutes or until it thickens.
4. Pour half of the mixture on the bottom of the baking dish, then top with the butterflied sardines. Pour the remaining mixture and white wine over the sardines.
5. Spread the breadcrumbs on top, then place the baking dish in the preheated oven. Bake for 20 minutes or until the fish is opaque.
6. Remove the baking sheet from the oven and serve the sardines warm.

Tip: You can replace the whole wheat breadcrumbs with Parmesan cheese shreds to gift the sardines a cheese flavor.

Per Serving
calories: 363 | fat: 20.2g | protein: 29.7g
carbs: 9.7g | fiber: 2.0g| sodium: 381mg

Arugula, Watermelon, and Feta Salad

Prep time: 10 minutes | Cook time: 0 minutes | Serves 2

3 cups packed arugula
2½ cups watermelon, cut into bite-size cubes
2 ounces (57 g) feta cheese, crumbled
2 tablespoons balsamic glaze

1. Divide the arugula between two plates.
2. Divide the watermelon cubes between the beds of arugula.
3. Scatter half of the feta cheese over each salad.
4. Drizzle about 1 tablespoon of the glaze (or more if desired) over each salad. Serve immediately.

Per Serving
calories: 157 | fat: 6.9g | protein: 6.1g
carbs: 22.0g | fiber: 1.1g | sodium: 328mg

Cucumber Gazpacho

Prep time: 10 minutes | Cook time: 0 minutes | Serves 4

2 cucumbers, peeled, deseeded, and cut into chunks
½ cup mint, finely chopped
2 cups plain Greek yogurt
2 garlic cloves, minced

2 cups low-sodium vegetable soup
1 tablespoon no-salt-added tomato paste
3 teaspoons fresh dill
Sea salt and freshly ground pepper, to taste

1. Put the cucumber, mint, yogurt, and garlic in a food processor, then pulse until creamy and smooth.
2. Transfer the puréed mixture in a large serving bowl, then add the vegetable soup, tomato paste, dill, salt, and ground black pepper. Stir to mix well.
3. Keep the soup in the refrigerator for at least 2 hours, then serve chilled.

Tip: You can use the almond yogurt or coconut yogurt to replace the plain Greek yogurt, just to make sure they are unsweetened.

Per Serving
calories: 133 | fat: 1.5g | protein: 14.2g
carbs: 16.5g | fiber: 2.9g | sodium: 331mg

Greens, Fennel, and Pear Soup with Cashews

Prep time: 15 minutes | Cook time: 15 minutes | Serves 4 to 6

2 tablespoons olive oil
1 fennel bulb, cut into ¼-inch-thick slices
2 leeks, white part only, sliced
2 pears, peeled, cored, and cut into

½-inch cubes
1 teaspoon sea salt
¼ teaspoon freshly ground black pepper
½ cup cashews
2 cups packed blanched spinach
3 cups low-sodium vegetable soup

1. Heat the olive oil in a stockpot over high heat until shimmering.
2. Add the fennel and leeks, then sauté for 5 minutes or until tender.
3. Add the pears and sprinkle with salt and pepper, then sauté for another 3 minutes or until the pears are soft.
4. Add the cashews, spinach, and vegetable soup. Bring to a boil. Reduce the heat to low. Cover and simmer for 5 minutes.
5. Pour the soup in a food processor, then pulse until creamy and smooth.
6. Pour the soup back to the pot and heat over low heat until heated through.
7. Transfer the soup to a large serving bowl and serve immediately.

Tips: If you like, you can use arugula to replace the spinach. And if you don't like cashews, you can replace it with other kinds of nuts, such as walnuts.

Per Serving
calories: 266 | fat: 15.1g | protein: 5.2g
carbs: 32.9g | fiber: 7.0g | sodium: 628mg

Sautéed White Beans with Rosemary

Prep time: 10 minutes | Cook time: 12 minutes | Serves 2

1 tablespoon olive oil
2 garlic cloves, minced
1 (15-ounce / 425-g) can white cannellini beans, drained and rinsed
1 teaspoon minced

fresh rosemary plus 1 whole fresh rosemary sprig
¼ teaspoon dried sage
½ cup low-sodium chicken stock
Salt, to taste

1. Heat the olive oil in a saucepan over medium-high heat.
2. Add the garlic and sauté for 30 seconds until fragrant.
3. Add the beans, minced and whole rosemary, sage, and chicken stock and bring the mixture to a boil.
4. Reduce the heat to medium and allow to simmer for 10 minutes, or until most of the liquid is evaporated. If desired, mash some of the beans with a fork to thicken them.
5. Season with salt to taste. Remove the rosemary sprig before serving.

Per Serving
calories: 155 | fat: 7.0g | protein: 6.0g
carbs: 17.0g | fiber: 8.0g | sodium: 153mg

Easy Roasted Cauliflower

Prep time: 10 minutes | Cook time: 20 minutes | Serves 2

½ large head cauliflower, stemmed and broken into florets (about 3 cups)
1 tablespoon olive oil
2 tablespoons freshly

squeezed lemon juice
2 tablespoons tahini
1 teaspoon harissa paste
Pinch salt

1. Preheat the oven to 400ºF (205ºC). Line a sheet pan with parchment paper.
2. Toss the cauliflower florets with the olive oil in a large bowl and transfer to the sheet pan.
3. Roast in the preheated oven for 15 minutes, flipping the cauliflower once or twice, or until it starts to become golden.
4. Meanwhile, in a separate bowl, combine the lemon juice, tahini, harissa, and salt and stir to mix well.
5. Remove the pan from the oven and toss the cauliflower with the lemon tahini sauce. Return to the oven and roast for another 5 minutes. Serve hot.

Per Serving
calories: 205 | fat: 15.0g | protein: 4.0g
carbs: 15.0g | fiber: 7.0g | sodium: 161mg

Rich Chicken and Small Pasta Broth

Prep time: 10 minutes | Cook time: 4 hours | Serves 6

6 boneless, skinless chicken thighs
4 stalks celery, cut into ½-inch pieces
4 carrots, cut into 1-inch pieces
1 medium yellow onion, halved
2 garlic cloves, minced

2 bay leaves
Sea salt and freshly ground black pepper, to taste
6 cups low-sodium chicken stock
½ cup stelline pasta
¼ cup chopped fresh flat-leaf parsley

1. Combine the chicken thighs, celery, carrots, onion, and garlic in the slow cooker. Spread with bay leaves and sprinkle with salt and pepper. Toss to mix well.

2. Pour in the chicken stock. Put the lid on and cook on high for 4 hours or until the internal temperature of chicken reaches at least 165ºF (74ºC).
3. In the last 20 minutes of the cooking, remove the chicken from the slow cooker and transfer to a bowl to cool until ready to reserve.
4. Discard the bay leaves and add the pasta to the slow cooker. Put the lid on and cook for 15 minutes or until al dente.
5. Meanwhile, slice the chicken, then put the chicken and parsley in the slow cooker and cook for 5 minutes or until well combined.
6. Pour the soup in a large bowl and serve immediately.

Tip: If you don't have stelline pasta, you can use any other small pastas, such as alphabet pasta.

Per Serving
calories: 285 | fat: 10.8g | protein: 27.4g
carbs: 18.8g | fiber: 2.6g | sodium: 815mg

Orange-Honey Glazed Carrots

Prep time: 10 minutes | Cook time: 15 to 20 minutes | Serves 2

½ pound (227 g) rainbow carrots, peeled
2 tablespoons fresh

orange juice
1 tablespoon honey
½ teaspoon coriander
Pinch salt

1. Preheat the oven to 400ºF (205ºC).
2. Cut the carrots lengthwise into slices of even thickness and place in a large bowl.
3. Stir together the orange juice, honey, coriander, and salt in a small bowl. Pour the orange juice mixture over the carrots and toss until well coated.
4. Spread the carrots in a baking dish in a single layer. Roast for 15 to 20 minutes until fork-tender.
5. Let cool for 5 minutes before serving.

Per Serving
calories: 85 | fat: 0g | protein: 1.0g
carbs: 21.0g | fiber: 3.0g | sodium: 156mg

Lemon-Tahini Hummus

Prep time: 15 minutes | Cook time: 0 minutes | Serves 6

1 (15-ounce / 425-g) can chickpeas, drained and rinsed
4 tablespoons extra-virgin olive oil, divided
4 to 5 tablespoons tahini (sesame seed paste)
2 lemons, juiced
1 lemon, zested, divided
1 tablespoon minced garlic
Pinch salt

1. In a food processor, combine the chickpeas, 2 tablespoons of olive oil, tahini, lemon juice, half of the lemon zest, and garlic and pulse for up to 1 minute, scraping down the sides of the food processor bowl as necessary.
2. Taste and add salt as needed. Feel free to add 1 teaspoon of water at a time to thin the hummus to a better consistency.
3. Transfer the hummus to a serving bowl. Serve drizzled with the remaining 2 tablespoons of olive oil and remaining half of the lemon zest.

Per Serving
calories: 216 | fat: 15.0g | protein: 5.0g carbs: 17.0g | fiber: 5.0g | sodium: 12mg

Simple Mushroom Barley Soup

Prep time: 5 minutes | Cook time: 20 to 23 minutes | Serves 6

2 tablespoons extra-virgin olive oil
1 cup chopped carrots
1 cup chopped onion
5½ cups chopped mushrooms
6 cups no-salt-added vegetable broth
1 cup uncooked pearled barley
¼ cup red wine
2 tablespoons tomato paste
4 sprigs fresh thyme or ½ teaspoon dried thyme
1 dried bay leaf
6 tablespoons grated Parmesan cheese

1. In a large stockpot over medium heat, heat the oil. Add the onion and carrots and cook for 5 minutes, stirring frequently. Turn up the heat to medium-high and add the mushrooms. Cook for 3 minutes, stirring frequently.
2. Add the broth, barley, wine, tomato paste, thyme, and bay leaf. Stir, cover, and bring the soup to a boil. Once it's boiling, stir a few times, reduce the heat to medium-low, cover, and cook for another 12 to 15 minutes, until the barley is cooked through.
3. Remove the bay leaf and serve the soup in bowls with 1 tablespoon of cheese sprinkled on top of each.

Per Serving
calories: 195 | fat: 4.0g | protein: 7.0g carbs: 34.0g | fiber: 6.0g | sodium: 173mg

Chicken and Pastina Soup

Prep time: 5 minutes | Cook time: 20 minutes | Serves 6

1 tablespoon extra-virgin olive oil
2 garlic cloves, minced
3 cups packed chopped kale, center ribs removed
1 cup minced carrots
8 cups no-salt-added chicken or vegetable broth
¼ teaspoon kosher or sea salt
¼ teaspoon freshly ground black pepper
¾ cup uncooked acini de pepe or pastina pasta
2 cups shredded cooked chicken (about 12 ounces / 340 g)
3 tablespoons grated Parmesan cheese

1. In a large stockpot over medium heat, heat the oil. Add the garlic and cook for 30 seconds, stirring frequently. Add the kale and carrots and cook for 5 minutes, stirring occasionally.
2. Add the broth, salt, and pepper, and turn the heat to high. Bring the broth to a boil, and add the pasta. Reduce the heat to medium and cook for 10 minutes, or until the pasta is cooked through, stirring every few minutes so the pasta doesn't stick to the bottom. Add the chicken, and cook for another 2 minutes to warm through.
3. Ladle the soup into six bowls. Top each with ½ tablespoon of cheese and serve.

Per Serving
calories: 275 | fat: 19.0g | protein: 16.0g carbs: 11.0g | fiber: 2.0g | sodium: 298mg

Zesty Spanish Potato Salad

Prep time: 10 minutes | Cook time: 5 to 7 minutes | Serves 6 to 8

4 russet potatoes, peeled and chopped
3 large hard-boiled eggs, chopped
1 cup frozen mixed vegetables, thawed
½ cup plain, unsweetened, full-fat Greek yogurt
5 tablespoons pitted

Spanish olives
½ teaspoon freshly ground black pepper
½ teaspoon dried mustard seed
½ tablespoon freshly squeezed lemon juice
½ teaspoon dried dill
Salt, to taste

1. Place the potatoes in a large pot of water and boil for 5 to 7 minutes, until just fork-tender, checking periodically for doneness. You don't have to overcook them.
2. Meanwhile, in a large bowl, mix the eggs, vegetables, yogurt, olives, pepper, mustard, lemon juice, and dill. Season with salt to taste. Once the potatoes are cooled somewhat, add them to the large bowl, then toss well and serve.

Per Serving
calories: 192 | fat: 5.0g | protein: 9.0g
carbs: 30.0g | fiber: 2.0g | sodium: 59mg

Moroccan Lentil, Tomato, and Cauliflower Soup

Prep time: 15 minutes | Cook time: 4 hours | Serves 6

1 cup chopped carrots
1 cup chopped onions
3 cloves garlic, minced
½ teaspoon ground coriander
1 teaspoon ground cumin
1 teaspoon ground turmeric
¼ teaspoon ground cinnamon
¼ teaspoon freshly ground black pepper
1 cup dry lentils
28 ounces (794 g)

tomatoes, diced, reserve the juice
1½ cups chopped cauliflower
4 cups low-sodium vegetable soup
1 tablespoon no-salt-added tomato paste
1 teaspoon extra-virgin olive oil
1 cup chopped fresh spinach
¼ cup chopped fresh cilantro
1 tablespoon red wine vinegar (optional)

1. Put the carrots and onions in the slow cooker, then sprinkle with minced garlic, coriander, cumin, turmeric, cinnamon, and black pepper. Stir to combine well.
2. Add the lentils, tomatoes, and cauliflower, then pour in the vegetable soup and tomato paste. Drizzle with olive oil. Stir to combine well.
3. Put the slow cooker lid on and cook on high for 4 hours or until the vegetables are tender.
4. In the last 30 minutes during the cooking time, open the lid and stir the soup, then fold in the spinach.
5. Pour the cooked soup in a large serving bowl, then spread with cilantro and drizzle with vinegar. Serve immediately.

Tip: For a healthier choice, you can use the freshly puréed tomato to replace the tomato paste.

Per Serving
calories: 131 | fat: 2.1g | protein: 5.6g
carbs: 25.0g | fiber: 5.5g | sodium: 364mg

Moroccan Spiced Couscous

Prep time: 10 minutes | Cook time: 8 minutes | Serves 2

1 tablespoon olive oil
¾ cup couscous
¼ teaspoon cinnamon
¼ teaspoon garlic powder
¼ teaspoon salt, plus

more as needed
1 cup water
2 tablespoons minced dried apricots
2 tablespoons raisins
2 teaspoons minced fresh parsley

1. Heat the olive oil in a saucepan over medium-high heat until it shimmers.
2. Add the couscous, cinnamon, garlic powder, and salt. Stir for 1 minute to toast the couscous and spices.
3. Add the water, apricots, and raisins and bring the mixture to a boil.
4. Cover and turn off the heat. Allow the couscous to sit for 4 to 5 minutes and then fluff it with a fork. Sprinkle with the fresh parsley. Season with more salt as needed and serve.

Per Serving
calories: 338 | fat: 8.0g | protein: 9.0g
carbs: 59.0g | fiber: 4.0g | sodium: 299mg

Tricolor Summer Salad

Prep time: 10 minutes | Cook time: 0 minutes | Serves 3 to 4

¼ cup while balsamic vinegar
2 tablespoons Dijon mustard
1 tablespoon sugar
½ teaspoon garlic salt
½ teaspoon freshly ground black pepper
¼ cup extra-virgin

olive oil
1½ cups chopped orange, yellow, and red tomatoes
½ cucumber, peeled and diced
1 small red onion, thinly sliced
¼ cup crumbled feta (optional)

1. In a small bowl, whisk the vinegar, mustard, sugar, pepper, and garlic salt. Then slowly whisk in the olive oil.
2. In a large bowl, add the tomatoes, cucumber, and red onion. Add the dressing. Toss once or twice, and serve with the feta crumbles (if desired) sprinkled on top.

Per Serving
calories: 246 | fat: 18.0g | protein: 1.0g carbs: 19.0g | fiber: 2.0g | sodium: 483mg

Pumpkin Soup with Crispy Sage Leaves

Prep time: 15 minutes | Cook time: 10 minutes | Serves 4

1 tablespoon olive oil
2 garlic cloves, cut into ⅛-inch-thick slices
1 onion, chopped
2 cups freshly puréed pumpkin
4 cups low-sodium vegetable soup

2 teaspoons chipotle powder
1 teaspoon sea salt
½ teaspoon freshly ground black pepper
½ cup vegetable oil
12 sage leaves, stemmed

1. Heat the olive oil in a stockpot over high heat until shimmering.
2. Add the garlic and onion, then sauté for 5 minutes or until the onion is translucent.
3. Pour in the puréed pumpkin and vegetable soup in the pot, then sprinkle with chipotle powder, salt, and ground black pepper. Stir to mix well.

4. Bring to a boil. Reduce the heat to low and simmer for 5 minutes.
5. Meanwhile, heat the vegetable oil in a nonstick skillet over high heat.
6. Add the sage leaf to the skillet and sauté for a minute or until crispy. Transfer the sage on paper towels to soak the excess oil.
7. Gently pour the soup in three serving bowls, then divide the crispy sage leaves in bowls for garnish. Serve immediately.

Tip: You can make your own chipotle powder by combining freshly ground chipotle chiles with garlic powder and herbs you like.

Per Serving
calories: 380 | fat: 20.1g | protein: 8.9g carbs: 45.2g | fiber: 18.0g | sodium: 1364mg

Greek Salad with Dressing

Prep time: 10 minutes | Cook time: 0 minutes | Serves 4 to 6

1 head iceberg lettuce
2 cups cherry tomatoes
1 large cucumber
1 medium onion
¼ cup lemon juice
½ cup extra-virgin

olive oil
1 teaspoon salt
1 clove garlic, minced
1 cup Kalamata olives, pitted
1 (6-ounce / 170-g) package feta cheese, crumbled

1. Cut the lettuce into 1-inch pieces and put them in a large salad bowl.
2. Cut the tomatoes in half and add them to the salad bowl.
3. Slice the cucumber into bite-sized pieces and add them to the salad bowl.
4. Thinly slice the onion and add it to the salad bowl.
5. In a separate bowl, whisk together the olive oil, lemon juice, salt, and garlic. Pour the dressing over the salad and gently toss to evenly coat.
6. Top the salad with the Kalamata olives and feta cheese and serve.

Per Serving
calories: 539 | fat: 50.0g | protein: 9.0g carbs: 18.0g | fiber: 4.0g | sodium: 1758mg

Vegetable Fagioli Soup

Prep time: 30 minutes | Cook time: 60 minutes | Serves 2

1 tablespoon olive oil
2 medium carrots, diced
2 medium celery stalks, diced
½ medium onion, diced
1 large garlic clove, minced
3 tablespoons tomato paste
4 cups low-sodium vegetable broth
1 cup packed kale, stemmed and chopped
1 (15-ounce / 425-g) can red kidney beans, drained and rinsed
1 (15-ounce / 425-g) can cannellini beans, drained and rinsed
½ cup chopped fresh basil
Salt and freshly ground black pepper, to taste

1. Heat the olive oil in a stockpot over medium-high heat. Add the carrots, celery, onion, and garlic and sauté for 10 minutes, or until the vegetables start to turn golden.
2. Stir in the tomato paste and cook for about 30 seconds.
3. Add the vegetable broth and bring the soup to a boil. Cover, and reduce the heat to low. Cook the soup for 45 minutes, or until the carrots are tender.
4. Using an immersion blender, purée the soup so that it's partly smooth, but with some chunks of vegetables.
5. Add the kale, beans, and basil. Season with salt and pepper to taste, then serve.

Per Serving
calories: 217 | fat: 4.2g | protein: 10.0g
carbs: 36.2g | fiber: 10.2g | sodium: 482mg

Mixed Salad With Balsamic Honey Dressing

Prep time: 15 minutes | Cook time: 0 minutes | Serves 2

Dressing:
¼ cup balsamic vinegar
¼ cup olive oil
1 tablespoon honey
1 teaspoon Dijon mustard
¼ teaspoon garlic powder
¼ teaspoon salt, or more to taste
Pinch freshly ground black pepper

Salad:
4 cups chopped red leaf lettuce
½ cup cherry or grape tomatoes, halved
½ English cucumber, sliced in quarters lengthwise and then cut into bite-size pieces
Any combination fresh, torn herbs (parsley, oregano, basil, or chives)
1 tablespoon roasted sunflower seeds

1. Make the Dressing
2. Combine the vinegar, olive oil, honey, mustard, garlic powder, salt, and pepper in a jar with a lid. Shake well.
3. Make the Salad
4. In a large bowl, combine the lettuce, tomatoes, cucumber, and herbs. Toss well.
5. Pour all or as much dressing as desired over the tossed salad and toss again to coat the salad with dressing.
6. Top with the sunflower seeds before serving.

Per Serving
calories: 337 | fat: 26.1g | protein: 4.2g
carbs: 22.2g | fiber: 3.1g | sodium: 172mg

Mediterranean Tomato Hummus Soup

Prep time: 10 minutes | Cook time: 10 minutes | Serves 2

1 (14.5-ounce / 411-g) can crushed tomatoes with basil
2 cups low-sodium chicken stock
1 cup roasted red pepper hummus
Salt, to taste
¼ cup thinly sliced fresh basil leaves, for garnish (optional)

1. Combine the canned tomatoes, hummus, and chicken stock in a blender and blend until smooth. Pour the mixture into a saucepan and bring it to a boil. Season with salt to taste.
2. Serve garnished with the fresh basil, if desired.

Per Serving
calories: 147 | fat: 6.2g | protein: 5.2g
carbs: 20.1g | fiber: 4.1g | sodium: 682mg

Citrus Salad with Kale and Fennel

Prep time: 15 minutes | Cook time: 0 minutes | Serves 2

Dressing:

3 tablespoons olive oil
2 tablespoons fresh orange juice
1 tablespoon blood orange vinegar, other

orange vinegar, or cider vinegar
1 tablespoon honey
Salt and freshly ground black pepper, to taste

Salad:

2 cups packed baby kale
1 medium navel or blood orange, segmented
½ small fennel bulb, stems and leaves

removed, sliced into matchsticks
3 tablespoons toasted pecans, chopped
2 ounces (57 g) goat cheese, crumbled

Make the Dressing

1. Mix the olive oil, orange juice, vinegar, and honey in a small bowl and whisk to combine. Season with salt and pepper to taste. Set aside.

Make the Salad

1. Divide the baby kale, orange segments, fennel, pecans, and goat cheese evenly between two plates.
2. Drizzle half of the dressing over each salad, and serve.

Per Serving

calories: 503 | fat: 39.1g | protein: 13.2g
carbs: 31.2g | fiber: 6.1g | sodium: 156mg

Balsamic Brussels Sprouts and Delicata Squash

Prep time: 10 minutes | Cook time: 30 minutes | Serves 2

½ pound (227 g) Brussels sprouts, ends trimmed and outer leaves removed
1 medium delicata squash, halved lengthwise, seeded, and cut into 1-inch pieces
1 cup fresh cranberries

2 teaspoons olive oil
Salt and freshly ground black pepper, to taste
½ cup balsamic vinegar
2 tablespoons roasted pumpkin seeds
2 tablespoons fresh pomegranate arils (seeds)

1. Preheat oven to 400ºF (205ºC). Line a sheet pan with parchment paper.
2. Combine the Brussels sprouts, squash, and cranberries in a large bowl. Drizzle with olive oil, and season lightly with salt and pepper. Toss well to coat and arrange in a single layer on the sheet pan.
3. Roast in the preheated oven for 30 minutes, turning vegetables halfway through, or until Brussels sprouts turn brown and crisp in spots.
4. Meanwhile, make the balsamic glaze by simmering the vinegar for 10 to 12 minutes, or until mixture has reduced to about ¼ cup and turns a syrupy consistency.
5. Remove the vegetables from the oven, drizzle with balsamic syrup, and sprinkle with pumpkin seeds and pomegranate arils before serving.

Per Serving

calories: 203 | fat: 6.8g | protein: 6.2g
carbs: 22.0g | fiber: 8.2g | sodium: 32mg

Green Beans with Tahini-Lemon Sauce

Prep time: 5 minutes | Cook time: 10 minutes | Serves 2

1 pound (454 g) green beans, washed and trimmed
2 tablespoons tahini
1 garlic clove, minced
Grated zest and juice of 1 lemon

Salt and black pepper, to taste
1 teaspoon toasted black or white sesame seeds (optional)

1. Steam the beans in a medium saucepan fitted with a steamer basket (or by adding ¼ cup water to a covered saucepan) over medium-high heat. Drain, reserving the cooking water.
2. Mix the tahini, garlic, lemon zest and juice, and salt and pepper to taste. Use the reserved cooking water to thin the sauce as desired.
3. Toss the green beans with the sauce and garnish with the sesame seeds, if desired. Serve immediately.

Per Serving

calories: 188 | fat: 8.4g | protein: 7.2g
carbs: 22.2g | fiber: 7.9g | sodium: 200mg

Roasted Root Vegetable Soup

Prep time: 10 minutes | Cook time: 35 minutes | Serves 6

2 parsnips, peeled and sliced
2 carrots, peeled and sliced
2 sweet potatoes, peeled and sliced
1 teaspoon chopped fresh rosemary
1 teaspoon chopped fresh thyme
1 teaspoon sea salt
½ teaspoon freshly ground black pepper
2 tablespoons extra-virgin olive oil
4 cups low-sodium vegetable soup
½ cup grated Parmesan cheese, for garnish (optional)

1. Preheat the oven to 400ºF (205ºC). Line a baking sheet with aluminum foil.
2. Combine the parsnips, carrots, and sweet potatoes in a large bowl, then sprinkle with rosemary, thyme, salt, and pepper, and drizzle with olive oil. Toss to coat the vegetables well.
3. Arrange the vegetables on the baking sheet, then roast in the preheated oven for 30 minutes or until lightly browned and soft. Flip the vegetables halfway through the roasting.
4. Pour the roasted vegetables with vegetable broth in a food processor, then pulse until creamy and smooth.
5. Pour the puréed vegetables in a saucepan, then warm over low heat until heated through.
6. Spoon the soup in a large serving bowl, then scatter with Parmesan cheese. Serve immediately.

Tip: If you don't have vegetable soup, just use the same amount of water to replace it.

Per Serving
calories: 192 | fat: 5.7g | protein: 4.8g
carbs: 31.5g | fiber: 5.7g | sodium: 797mg

Super Mushroom and Red Wine Soup

Prep time: 40 minutes | Cook time: 35 minutes | Serves 6

2 ounces (57 g) dried morels
2 ounces (57 g) dried porcini
1 tablespoon extra-virgin olive oil
8 ounces (227 g) button mushrooms, chopped
8 ounces (227 g) portobello mushrooms, chopped
3 shallots, finely chopped
2 cloves garlic, minced
1 teaspoon finely chopped fresh thyme
Sea salt and freshly ground pepper, to taste
$1/_3$ cup dry red wine
4 cups low-sodium chicken broth
½ cup heavy cream
1 small bunch flat-leaf parsley, chopped

1. Put the dried mushrooms in a large bowl and pour in enough water to submerge the mushrooms. Soak for 30 minutes and drain.
2. Heat the olive oil in a stockpot over medium-high heat until shimmering.
3. Add the mushrooms and shallots to the pot and sauté for 10 minutes or until the mushrooms are tender.
4. Add the garlic and sauté for an additional 1 minute or until fragrant. Sprinkle with thyme, salt, and pepper.
5. Pour in the dry red wine and chicken broth. Bring to a boil over high heat.
6. Reduce the heat to low. Simmer for 20 minutes.
7. After simmering, pour half of the soup in a food processor, then pulse until creamy and smooth.
8. Pour the puréed soup back to the pot, then mix in the cream and heat over low heat until heated through.
9. Pour the soup in a large serving bowl and spread with chopped parsley before serving.

Tip: If you don't have dry red wine, you can use white wine to replace it, such as sherry.

Per Serving
calories: 139 | fat: 7.4g | protein: 7.1g
carbs: 14.4g | fiber: 2.8g | sodium: 94mg

Paella Soup

Prep time: 6 minutes | Cook time: 24 minutes | Serves 6

2 tablespoons extra-virgin olive oil
1 cup chopped onion
1½ cups coarsely chopped green bell pepper
1½ cups coarsely chopped red bell pepper
2 garlic cloves, chopped
1 teaspoon ground turmeric
1 teaspoon dried thyme
2 teaspoons smoked paprika

2½ cups uncooked instant brown rice
2 cups low-sodium or no-salt-added chicken broth
2½ cups water
1 cup frozen green peas, thawed
1 (28-ounce / 794-g) can low-sodium or no-salt-added crushed tomatoes
1 pound (454 g) fresh raw medium shrimp, shells and tails removed

1. In a large stockpot over medium-high heat, heat the oil. Add the onion, bell peppers, and garlic. Cook for 8 minutes, stirring occasionally. Add the turmeric, thyme, and smoked paprika, and cook for 2 minutes more, stirring often. Stir in the rice, broth, and water. Bring to a boil over high heat. Cover, reduce the heat to medium-low, and cook for 10 minutes.
2. Stir the peas, tomatoes, and shrimp into the soup. Cook for 4 minutes, until the shrimp is cooked, turning from gray to pink and white. The soup will be very thick, almost like stew, when ready to serve.
3. Ladle the soup into bowls and serve hot.

Per Serving
calories: 431 | fat: 5.7g | protein: 26.0g
carbs: 69.1g | fiber: 7.4g | sodium: 203mg

Avgolemono (Lemon Chicken Soup)

Prep time: 15 minutes | Cook time: 60 minutes | Serves 2

½ large onion
2 medium carrots
1 celery stalk
1 garlic clove
5 cups low-sodium chicken stock
¼ cup brown rice
1½ cups (about 5 ounces / 142 g) shredded rotisserie

chicken
3 tablespoons freshly squeezed lemon juice
1 egg yolk
2 tablespoons chopped fresh dill
2 tablespoons chopped fresh parsley
Salt, to taste

1. Put the onion, carrots, celery, and garlic in a food processor and pulse until the vegetables are minced.
2. Add the vegetables and chicken stock to a stockpot and bring it to a boil over high heat.
3. Reduce the heat to medium-low and add the rice, shredded chicken and lemon juice. Cover, and let the soup simmer for 40 minutes, or until the rice is cooked.
4. In a small bowl, whisk the egg yolk lightly. Slowly, while whisking with one hand, pour about ½ of a ladle of the broth into the egg yolk to warm, or temper, the yolk. Slowly add another ladle of broth and continue to whisk.
5. Remove the soup from the heat and pour the whisked egg yolk–broth mixture into the pot. Stir well to combine.
6. Add the fresh dill and parsley. Season with salt to taste and serve.

Per Serving
calories: 172 | fat: 4.2g | protein: 18.2g
carbs: 16.1g | fiber: 2.1g | sodium: 232mg

Parmesan Roasted Red Potatoes

Prep time: 10 minutes | Cook time: 55 minutes | Serves 2

12 ounces (340 g) red potatoes (3 to 4 small potatoes), scrubbed and diced into 1-inch pieces
1 tablespoon olive oil
½ teaspoon garlic powder
¼ teaspoon salt
1 tablespoon grated Parmesan cheese
1 teaspoon minced fresh rosemary (from 1 sprig)

1. Preheat the oven to 425ºF (220ºC). Line a baking sheet with parchment paper.
2. In a mixing bowl, combine the potatoes, olive oil, garlic powder, and salt. Toss well to coat.
3. Lay the potatoes on the parchment paper and roast for 10 minutes. Flip the potatoes over and roast for another 10 minutes.
4. Check the potatoes to make sure they are golden brown on the top and bottom. Toss them again, turn the heat down to 350ºF (180ºC), and roast for 30 minutes more.
5. When the potatoes are golden brown, scatter the Parmesan cheese over them and toss again. Return to the oven for 3 minutes to melt the cheese.
6. Remove from the oven and sprinkle with the fresh rosemary before serving.

Per Serving
calories: 200 | fat: 8.2g | protein: 5.1g
carbs: 30.0g | fiber: 3.2g | sodium: 332mg

Sautéed Kale with Olives

Prep time: 10 minutes | Cook time: 10 minutes | Serves 2

1 bunch kale, leaves chopped and stems minced
½ cup celery leaves, roughly chopped, or additional parsley
½ bunch flat-leaf parsley, stems and leaves roughly chopped
4 garlic cloves, chopped
2 teaspoons olive oil
¼ cup pitted Kalamata olives, chopped
Grated zest and juice of 1 lemon
Salt and pepper, to taste

1. Place the kale, celery leaves, parsley, and garlic in a steamer basket set over a medium saucepan. Steam over medium-high heat, covered, for 15 minutes. Remove from the heat and squeeze out any excess moisture.
2. Place a large skillet over medium heat. Add the oil, then add the kale mixture to the skillet. Cook, stirring often, for 5 minutes.
3. Remove from the heat and add the olives and lemon zest and juice. Season with salt and pepper and serve.

Per Serving
calories: 86 | fat: 6.4g | protein: 1.8g
carbs: 7.5g | fiber: 2.1g | sodium: 276mg

Green Bean and Halloumi Salad

Prep time: 20 minutes | Cook time: 5 minutes | Serves 2

Dressing:

¼ cup unsweetened coconut milk
1 tablespoon olive oil
2 teaspoons freshly squeezed lemon juice
¼ teaspoon garlic powder
¼ teaspoon onion powder
Pinch salt
Pinch freshly ground black pepper

Salad:

½ pound (227 g) fresh green beans, trimmed
2 ounces (57 g) Halloumi cheese, sliced into 2 (½-inch-thick) slices
½ cup halved cherry or grape tomatoes
¼ cup thinly sliced sweet onion

Make the Dressing

1. Combine the coconut milk, olive oil, lemon juice, onion powder, garlic powder, salt, and pepper in a small bowl and whisk well. Set aside.

Make the Salad

1. Fill a medium-size pot with about 1 inch of water and add the green beans. Cover and steam them for about 3 to 4 minutes, or just until beans are tender. Do not overcook. Drain beans, rinse them immediately with cold water, and set them aside to cool.
2. Heat a nonstick skillet over medium-high heat and place the slices of Halloumi in the hot pan. After about 2 minutes, check to see if the cheese is golden on the bottom. If it is, flip the slices and cook for another minute or until the second side is golden.
3. Remove cheese from the pan and cut each piece into cubes (about 1-inch square).
4. Place the green beans, halloumi slices, tomatoes, and onion in a large bowl and toss to combine.
5. Drizzle the dressing over the salad and toss well to combine. Serve immediately.

Per Serving

calories: 274 | fat: 18.1g | protein: 8.0g
carbs: 16.8g | fiber: 5.1g | sodium: 499mg

Chapter 4
Sandwiches, Pizzas, and Wraps

Sumptuous Vegetable and Cheese Lavash Pizza

Prep time: 15 minutes | Cook time: 11 minutes | Serves 4

2 (12 by 9-inch) lavash breads
2 tablespoons extra-virgin olive oil
10 ounces (284 g) frozen spinach, thawed and squeezed dry
1 cup shredded fontina cheese
1 tomato, cored and cut into ½-inch pieces
½ cup pitted large green olives, chopped
¼ teaspoon red pepper flakes
3 garlic cloves, minced
¼ teaspoon sea salt
¼ teaspoon ground black pepper
½ cup grated Parmesan cheese

1. Preheat oven to 475ºF (246ºC).
2. Brush the lavash breads with olive oil, then place them on two baking sheet. Heat in the preheated oven for 4 minutes or until lightly browned. Flip the breads halfway through the cooking time.
3. Meanwhile, combine the spinach, fontina cheese, tomato pieces, olives, red pepper flakes, garlic, salt, and black pepper in a large bowl. Stir to mix well.
4. Remove the lavash bread from the oven and sit them on two large plates, spread them with the spinach mixture, then scatter with the Parmesan cheese on top.
5. Bake in the oven for 7 minutes or until the cheese melts and well browned.
6. Slice and serve warm.

Tip: You can replace the tomato, spinach, and olives with broccoli, fennel and artichoke for a different lavash pizza.

Per Serving

calories: 431 | fat: 21.5g | protein: 20.0g
carbs: 38.4g | fiber: 2.5g | sodium: 854mg

Cheesy Fig Pizzas with Garlic Oil

Prep time: 1 day 40 minutes | Cook time: 10 minutes | Makes 2 pizzas

Dough:

1 cup almond flour
1½ cups whole-wheat flour
¾ teaspoon instant or rapid-rise yeast
2 teaspoons raw honey
1¼ cups ice water
2 tablespoons extra-virgin olive oil
1¾ teaspoons sea salt

Garlic Oil:

4 tablespoons extra-virgin olive oil, divided
½ teaspoon dried thyme
2 garlic cloves, minced
⅛ teaspoon sea salt
½ teaspoon freshly ground pepper

Topping:

1 cup fresh basil leaves
1 cup crumbled feta cheese
8 ounces (227 g)
fresh figs, stemmed and quartered lengthwise
2 tablespoons raw honey

Make the Dough:

1. Combine the flours, yeast, and honey in a food processor, pulse to combine well. Gently add water while pulsing. Let the dough sit for 10 minutes.
2. Mix the olive oil and salt in the dough and knead the dough until smooth. Wrap in plastic and refrigerate for at least 1 day.

Make the Garlic Oil:

1. Heat 2 tablespoons of olive oil in a nonstick skillet over medium-low heat until shimmering.
2. Add the thyme, garlic, salt, and pepper and sauté for 30 seconds or until fragrant. Set them aside until ready to use.

Make the pizzas:

1. Preheat the oven to 500ºF (260ºC). Grease two baking sheets with 2 tablespoons of olive oil.
2. Divide the dough in half and shape into two balls. Press the balls into 13-inch rounds. Sprinkle the rounds with a tough of flour if they are sticky.
3. Top the rounds with the garlic oil and basil leaves, then arrange the rounds on the baking sheets. Scatter with feta cheese and figs.
4. Put the sheets in the preheated oven and bake for 9 minutes or until lightly browned. Rotate the pizza halfway through.
5. Remove the pizzas from the oven, then discard the bay leaves. Drizzle with honey. Let sit for 5 minutes and serve immediately.

Tip: You can replace the garlic oil with homemade pesto and top the pizzas with freshly chopped tomatoes, fried potatoes, and sautéed broccoli.

Per Serving (1 pizza)
calories: 1350 | fat: 46.5g | protein: 27.5g
carbs: 221.9g | fiber: 23.7g | sodium: 2898mg

Tuna and Olive Salad Sandwiches

Prep time: 10 minutes | Cook time: 0 minutes | Serves 4

3 tablespoons freshly squeezed lemon juice
2 tablespoons extra-virgin olive oil
1 garlic clove, minced
½ teaspoon freshly ground black pepper
2 (5-ounce / 142-g) cans tuna, drained
1 (2.25-ounce / 64-g) can sliced olives, any green or black variety
½ cup chopped fresh fennel, including fronds
8 slices whole-grain crusty bread

1. In a medium bowl, whisk together the lemon juice, oil, garlic, and pepper. Add the tuna, olives and fennel to the bowl. Using a fork, separate the tuna into chunks and stir to incorporate all the ingredients.
2. Divide the tuna salad equally among 4 slices of bread. Top each with the remaining bread slices.
3. Let the sandwiches sit for at least 5 minutes so the zesty filling can soak into the bread before serving.

Per Serving
calories: 952 | fat: 17.0g | protein: 165.0g
carbs: 37.0g | fiber: 7.0g | sodium: 2572mg

Eggplant, Spinach, and Feta Sandwiches

Prep time: 10 minutes | Cook time: 6 to 8 minutes | Serves 2

1 medium eggplant, sliced into ½-inch-thick slices
2 tablespoons olive oil
Sea salt and freshly ground pepper, to taste
5 to 6 tablespoons hummus
4 slices whole-wheat bread, toasted
1 cup baby spinach leaves
2 ounces (57 g) feta cheese, softened

1. Preheat the grill to medium-high heat.
2. Salt both sides of the sliced eggplant, and let sit for 20 minutes to draw out the bitter juices.
3. Rinse the eggplant and pat dry with a paper towel.
4. Brush the eggplant slices with olive oil and season with sea salt and freshly ground pepper to taste.
5. Grill the eggplant until lightly charred on both sides but still slightly firm in the middle, about 3 to 4 minutes per side.
6. Spread the hummus on the bread slices and top with the spinach leaves, feta cheese, and grilled eggplant. Top with the other slice of bread and serve immediately.

Per Serving
calories: 493 | fat: 25.3g | protein: 17.1g
carbs: 50.9g | fiber: 14.7g | sodium: 789mg

Easy Alfalfa Sprout and Nut Rolls

Prep time: 40 minutes | Cook time: 0 minutes | Makes 16 bite-size pieces

1 cup alfalfa sprouts
2 tablespoons Brazil nuts
½ cup chopped fresh cilantro
2 tablespoons flaked coconut
1 garlic clove, minced
2 tablespoons ground flaxseeds
Zest and juice of 1 lemon
Pinch cayenne pepper
Sea salt and freshly ground black pepper, to taste
1 tablespoon melted coconut oil
2 tablespoons water
2 whole-grain wraps

1. Combine all ingredients, except for the wraps, in a food processor, then pulse to combine well until smooth.
2. Unfold the wraps on a clean work surface, then spread the mixture over the wraps. Roll the wraps up and refrigerate for 30 minutes until set.
3. Remove the rolls from the refrigerator and slice into 16 bite-sized pieces, if desired, and serve.

Tip: You can replace the Brazil nuts with the same amount of almonds, if needed, and put the almonds in a preheated oven to roast over 325ºF (163ºC) for 10 minutes for more flavor.

Per Serving (1 piece)
calories: 67 | fat: 7.1g | protein: 2.2g
carbs: 2.9g | fiber: 1.0g | sodium: 61mg

Greek Vegetable Salad Pita

Prep time: 10 minutes | Cook time: 0 minutes | Serves 4

½ cup baby spinach leaves
½ small red onion, thinly sliced
½ small cucumber, deseeded and chopped
1 tomato, chopped
1 cup chopped romaine lettuce
1 tablespoon extra-virgin olive oil
½ tablespoon red wine vinegar
1 teaspoon Dijon mustard
1 tablespoon crumbled feta cheese
Sea salt and freshly ground pepper, to taste
1 whole-wheat pita

1. Combine all the ingredients, except for the pita, in a large bowl. Toss to mix well.
2. Stuff the pita with the salad, then serve immediately.

Tip: If you want to gift your salad pita bread with more flavor, you can sauté the red onion in a nonstick skillet over medium-high heat for 10 minutes or until the onion is caramelized. Stuff the pita with the hot caramelized onion.

Per Serving
calories: 137 | fat: 8.1g | protein: 3.1g
carbs: 14.3g | fiber: 2.4g | sodium: 166mg

Mini Pork and Cucumber Lettuce Wraps

Prep time: 20 minutes | Cook time: 0 minutes | Makes 12 wraps

8 ounces (227 g) cooked ground pork
1 cucumber, diced
1 tomato, diced
1 red onion, sliced
1 ounce (28 g) low-fat feta cheese, crumbled
Juice of 1 lemon
1 tablespoon extra-virgin olive oil
Sea salt and freshly ground pepper, to taste
12 small, intact iceberg lettuce leaves

1. Combine the ground pork, cucumber, tomato, and onion in a large bowl, then scatter with feta cheese. Drizzle with lemon juice and olive oil, and sprinkle with salt and pepper. Toss to mix well.
2. Unfold the small lettuce leaves on a large plate or several small plates, then divide and top with the pork mixture.
3. Wrap and serve immediately.

Tip: How to cook the ground pork: Heat 1 tablespoon of olive oil in a nonstick skillet over medium-high heat until shimmering. Add the ground pork and sauté for 5 minutes or until well browned. Remove from the skillet and use immediately.

Per Serving (1 warp)
calories: 78 | fat: 5.6g | protein: 5.5g
carbs: 1.4g | fiber: 0.3g | sodium: 50mg

Mashed Grape Tomato Pizzas

Prep time: 10 minutes | Cook time: 20 minutes | Serves 6

3 cups grape tomatoes, halved
1 teaspoon chopped fresh thyme leaves
2 garlic cloves, minced
¼ teaspoon kosher salt
¼ teaspoon freshly ground black pepper
1 tablespoon extra-virgin olive oil
¾ cup shredded Parmesan cheese
6 whole-wheat pita breads

1. Preheat the oven to 425ºF (220ºC).
2. Combine the tomatoes, thyme, garlic, salt, ground black pepper, and olive oil in a baking pan.

3. Roast in the preheated oven for 20 minutes. Remove the pan from the oven, mash the tomatoes with a spatula and stir to mix well halfway through the cooking time.
4. Meanwhile, divide and spread the cheese over each pita bread, then place the bread in a separate baking pan and roast in the oven for 5 minutes or until golden brown and the cheese melts.
5. Transfer the pita bread onto a large plate, then top with the roasted mashed tomatoes. Serve immediately.

Tip: If you want a more juicy pizza, you can replace the grape tomatoes to normal large tomatoes and chopped the tomatoes into chunks to make them easier for cooking.

Per Serving
calories: 140 | fat: 5.1g | protein: 6.2g
carbs: 16.9g | fiber: 2.0g | sodium: 466mg

Salmon Salad Wraps

Prep time: 10 minutes | Cook time: 0 minutes | Serves 6

1 pound (454 g) salmon fillets, cooked and flaked
½ cup diced carrots
½ cup diced celery
3 tablespoons diced red onion
3 tablespoons chopped fresh dill
2 tablespoons capers
1½ tablespoons
extra-virgin olive oil
1 tablespoon aged balsamic vinegar
¼ teaspoon kosher or sea salt
½ teaspoon freshly ground black pepper
4 whole-wheat flatbread wraps or soft whole-wheat tortillas

1. In a large bowl, stir together all the ingredients, except for the wraps.
2. On a clean work surface, lay the wraps. Divide the salmon mixture evenly among the wraps. Fold up the bottom of the wraps, then roll up the wrap.
3. Serve immediately.

Per Serving
calories: 194 | fat: 8.0g | protein: 18.0g
carbs: 13.0g | fiber: 3.0g | sodium: 536mg

Classic Socca

Prep time: 10 minutes | Cook time: 10 minutes | Serves 4

1½ cups chickpea flour
½ teaspoon ground turmeric
½ teaspoon sea salt
½ teaspoon ground

black pepper
2 tablespoons plus 2 teaspoons extra-virgin olive oil
1½ cups water

1. Combine the chickpea flour, turmeric, salt, and black pepper in a bowl. Stir to mix well, then gently mix in 2 tablespoons of olive oil and water. Stir to mix until smooth.
2. Heat 2 teaspoons of olive oil in an 8-inch nonstick skillet over medium-high heat until shimmering.
3. Add half cup of the mixture into the skillet and swirl the skillet so the mixture coat the bottom evenly.
4. Cook for 5 minutes or until lightly browned and crispy. Flip the socca halfway through the cooking time. Repeat with the remaining mixture.
5. Slice and serve warm.

Tip: When you cook the second batch of the socca, you can transfer the first batch of cooked socca in a baking pan and keep it warm in the oven under 200ºF (93ºC).

Per Serving
calories: 207 | fat: 10.2g | protein: 7.9g
carbs: 20.7g | fiber: 3.9g | sodium: 315mg

Samosas in Potatoes

Prep time: 20 minutes | Cook time: 30 minutes | Makes 8

4 small potatoes
1 teaspoon coconut oil
1 small onion, finely chopped
1 small piece ginger, minced
2 garlic cloves, minced
2 to 3 teaspoons

curry powder
Sea salt and freshly ground black pepper, to taste
¼ cup frozen peas, thawed
2 carrots, grated
¼ cup chopped fresh cilantro

1. Preheat the oven to 350ºF (180ºC).
2. Poke small holes into potatoes with a fork, then wrap with aluminum foil.
3. Bake in the preheated oven for 30 minutes until tender.
4. Meanwhile, heat the coconut oil in a nonstick skillet over medium-high heat until melted.
5. Add the onion and sauté for 5 minutes or until translucent.
6. Add the ginger and garlic to the skillet and sauté for 3 minutes or until fragrant.
7. Add the curry power, salt, and ground black pepper, then stir to coat the onion. Remove them from the heat.
8. When the cooking of potatoes is complete, remove the potatoes from the foil and slice in half.
9. Hollow to potato halves with a spoon, then combine the potato fresh with sautéed onion, peas, carrots, and cilantro in a large bowl. Stir to mix well.
10. Spoon the mixture back to the tomato skins and serve immediately.

Tip: You can replace the cilantro with the same amount of parsley, if necessary.

Per Serving (1 samosa)
calories: 131 | fat: 13.9g | protein: 3.2g
carbs: 8.8g | fiber: 3.0g | sodium: 111mg

Za'atar Pizza

Prep time: 10 minutes | Cook time: 1o to 12 minutes | Serves 4 to 6

1 sheet puff pastry
¼ cup extra-virgin olive oil

1/3 cup za'atar seasoning

1. Preheat the oven to 350ºF (180ºC). Line a baking sheet with parchment paper.
2. Place the puff pastry on the prepared baking sheet. Cut the pastry into desired slices.
3. Brush the pastry with the olive oil. Sprinkle with the za'atar seasoning.
4. Put the pastry in the oven and bake for 10 to 12 minutes, or until edges are lightly browned and puffed up.
5. Serve warm.

Per Serving
calories: 374 | fat: 30.0g | protein: 3.0g
carbs: 20.0g | fiber: 1.0g | sodium: 166mg

Brown Rice and Black Bean Burgers

Prep time: 20 minutes | Cook time: 40 minutes | Makes 8 burgers

1 cup cooked brown rice
1 (15-ounce / 425-g) can black beans, drained and rinsed
1 tablespoon olive oil
2 tablespoons taco or seasoning
½ yellow onion, finely diced
1 beet, peeled and grated
1 carrot, peeled and grated
2 tablespoons no-salt-added tomato paste
2 tablespoons apple cider vinegar
3 garlic cloves, minced
¼ teaspoon sea salt
Ground black pepper, to taste
8 whole-wheat hamburger buns

Toppings:

16 lettuce leaves, rinsed well
8 tomato slices, rinsed well
Whole-grain mustard, to taste

1. Line a baking sheet with parchment paper.
2. Put the brown rice and black beans in a food processor and pulse until mix well. Pour the mixture in a large bowl and set aside.
3. Heat the olive oil in a nonstick skillet over medium heat until shimmering.
4. Add the taco seasoning and stir for 1 minute or until fragrant.
5. Add the onion, beet, and carrot and sauté for 5 minutes or until the onion is translucent and beet and carrot are tender.
6. Pour in the tomato paste and vinegar, then add the garlic and cook for 3 minutes or until the sauce is thickened. Sprinkle with salt and ground black pepper.
7. Transfer the vegetable mixture to the bowl of rice mixture, then stir to mix well until smooth.
8. Divide and shape the mixture into 8 patties, then arrange the patties on the baking sheet and refrigerate for at least 1 hour.
9. Preheat the oven to 400ºF (205ºC).
10. Remove the baking sheet from the refrigerator and allow to sit under room temperature for 10 minutes.
11. Bake in the preheated oven for 40 minutes or until golden brown on both sides. Flip the patties halfway through the cooking time.
12. Remove the patties from the oven and allow to cool for 10 minutes.
13. Assemble the buns with patties, lettuce, and tomato slices. Top the filling with mustard and serve immediately.

Tip: How to cook the brown rice: Pour the brown rice in a pot, then pour in enough water to submerge the rice. Bring to a boil over medium-high heat. Reduce the heat to low and simmer for 45 minutes or until most liquid is absorbed and the rice is tender. Remove the rice from the pot and fluff with a fork. Allow to cool for 15 minutes before using.

Per Serving (1 burger)
calories: 544 | fat: 20.0g | protein: 15.8g
carbs: 76.0g | fiber: 10.6g | sodium: 446mg

Chickpea Lettuce Wraps

Prep time: 15 minutes | Cook time: 0 minutes | Serves 2

1 (15-ounce / 425-g) can chickpeas, drained and rinsed well
1 celery stalk, diced
½ shallot, minced
1 green apple, cored and diced
3 tablespoons tahini (sesame paste)
2 teaspoons freshly squeezed lemon juice
1 teaspoon raw honey
1 teaspoon Dijon mustard
Dash salt
Filtered water, to thin
4 romaine lettuce leaves

1. In a medium bowl, stir together the chickpeas, celery, shallot, apple, tahini, lemon juice, honey, mustard, and salt. If needed, add some water to thin the mixture.
2. Place the romaine lettuce leaves on a plate. Fill each with the chickpea filling, using it all. Wrap the leaves around the filling. Serve immediately.

Per Serving
calories: 397 | fat: 15.1g | protein: 15.1g
carbs: 53.1g | fiber: 15.3g | sodium: 409mg

Mushroom and Caramelized Onion Musakhan

Prep time: 20 minutes | Cook time: 1 hour 5 minutes | Serves 4

2 tablespoons sumac, plus more for sprinkling
1 teaspoon ground allspice
½ teaspoon ground cardamom
½ teaspoon ground cumin
3 tablespoons extra-virgin olive oil, divided
2 pounds (907 g) portobello mushroom caps, gills removed, caps halved and sliced ½ inch thick
3 medium white onions, coarsely chopped
¼ cup water
Kosher salt, to taste
1 whole-wheat Turkish flatbread
¼ cup pine nuts
1 lemon, wedged

1. Preheat the oven to 350ºF (180ºC).
2. Combine 2 tablespoons of sumac, allspice, cardamom, and cumin in a small bowl. Stir to mix well.
3. Heat 2 tablespoons of olive oil in an oven-proof skillet over medium-high heat until shimmering.
4. Add the mushroom to the skillet and sprinkle with half of sumac mixture. Sauté for 8 minutes or until the mushrooms are tender. You may need to work in batches to avoid overcrowding. Transfer the mushrooms to a plate and set side.
5. Heat 1 tablespoon of olive oil in the skillet over medium-high heat until shimmering.
6. Add the onion and sauté for 20 minutes or until caramelized. Sprinkle with remaining sumac mixture, then cook for 1 more minute.
7. Pour in the water and sprinkle with salt. Bring to a simmer.
8. Turn off the heat and put the mushroom back to the skillet.
9. Place the skillet in the preheated oven and bake for 30 minutes.
10. Remove the skillet from the oven and let the mushroom sit for 10 minutes until cooled down.
11. Heat the Turkish flatbread in a baking dish in the oven for 5 minutes or until warmed through.
12. Arrange the bread on a large plate and top with mushrooms, onions, and roasted pine nuts. Squeeze the lemon wedges over and sprinkle with more sumac. Serve immediately.

Tip: How to roast the pine nuts: Heat 1 tablespoon of olive oil in a separate skillet over medium heat until shimmering. Add the pine nuts and toast for 3 minutes or until lightly browned. Sprinkle with salt and set aside until ready to serve.

Per Serving
calories: 336 | fat: 18.7g | protein: 11.5g
carbs: 34.3g | fiber: 6.9g | sodium: 369mg

Grilled Caesar Salad Sandwiches

Prep time: 5 minutes | Cook time: 5 minutes | Serves 2

¾ cup olive oil, divided
2 romaine lettuce hearts, left intact
3 to 4 anchovy fillets
Juice of 1 lemon
2 to 3 cloves garlic, peeled
1 teaspoon Dijon mustard
¼ teaspoon Worcestershire sauce
Sea salt and freshly ground pepper, to taste
2 slices whole-wheat bread, toasted
Freshly grated Parmesan cheese, for serving

1. Preheat the grill to medium-high heat and oil the grates.
2. On a cutting board, drizzle the lettuce with 1 to 2 tablespoons of olive oil and place on the grates.
3. Grill for 5 minutes, turning until lettuce is slightly charred on all sides. Let lettuce cool enough to handle.
4. In a food processor, combine the remaining olive oil with the anchovies, lemon juice, garlic, mustard, and Worcestershire sauce.
5. Pulse the ingredients until you have a smooth emulsion. Season with sea salt and freshly ground pepper to taste. Chop the lettuce in half and place on the bread.
6. Drizzle with the dressing and serve with a sprinkle of Parmesan cheese.

Per Serving
calories: 949 | fat: 85.6g | protein: 12.9g
carbs: 34.1g | fiber: 13.9g | sodium: 786mg

Spicy Black Bean and Poblano Dippers

Prep time: 20 minutes | Cook time: 21 minutes | Serves 8

2 tablespoons avocado oil, plus more for brushing the dippers
1 (15 ounces / 425 g) can black beans, drained and rinsed
1 poblano, deseeded and quartered
1 jalapeño, halved and deseeded
½ cup fresh cilantro, leaves and tender stems
1 yellow onion, quartered
2 garlic cloves
1 teaspoon chili powder
1 teaspoon ground cumin
1 teaspoon sea salt
24 organic corn tortillas

1. Preheat the oven to 400ºF (205ºC). Line a baking sheet with parchment paper and grease with avocado oil.
2. Combine the remaining ingredients, except for the tortillas, in a food processor, then pulse until chopped finely and the mixture holds together. Make sure not to purée the mixture.
3. Warm the tortillas on the baking sheet in the preheated oven for 1 minute or until softened.
4. Add a tablespoon of the mixture in the middle of each tortilla. Fold one side of the tortillas over the mixture and tuck to roll them up tightly to make the dippers.
5. Arrange the dippers on the baking sheet and brush them with avocado oil. Bake in the oven for 20 minutes or until well browned. Flip the dippers halfway through the cooking time.
6. Serve immediately.

Tip: For more flavor, you can serve the dippers with homemade pesto, tomato paste, or other sauce you like.

Per Serving
calories: 388 | fat: 6.5g | protein: 16.2g
carbs: 69.6g | fiber: 13.5g | sodium: 340mg

Veg Mix and Blackeye Pea Burritos

Prep time: 15 minutes | Cook time: 40 minutes | Makes 6 burritos

1 teaspoon olive oil
1 red onion, diced
2 garlic cloves, minced
1 zucchini, chopped
1 tomato, diced
1 bell pepper, any color, deseeded and
diced
1 (14-ounce / 397-g) can blackeye peas
2 teaspoons chili powder
Sea salt, to taste
6 whole-grain tortillas

1. Preheat the oven to 325ºF (160ºC).
2. Heat the olive oil in a nonstick skillet over medium heat or until shimmering.
3. Add the onion and sauté for 5 minutes or until translucent.
4. Add the garlic and sauté for 30 seconds or until fragrant.
5. Add the zucchini and sauté for 5 minutes or until tender.
6. Add the tomato and bell pepper and sauté for 2 minutes or until soft.
7. Fold in the black peas and sprinkle them with chili powder and salt. Stir to mix well.
8. Place the tortillas on a clean work surface, then top them with sautéed vegetables mix.
9. Fold one ends of tortillas over the vegetable mix, then tuck and roll them into burritos.
10. Arrange the burritos in a baking dish, seam side down, then pour the juice remains in the skillet over the burritos.
11. Bake in the preheated oven for 25 minutes or until golden brown.
12. Serve immediately.

Tip: If you want to remove as much salt that contains in the canned peas as possible, drain the canned peas in a colander and rinse under running cold water, then pat dry with paper towels.

Per Serving
calories: 335 | fat: 16.2g | protein: 12.1g
carbs: 8.3g | fiber: 8.0g | sodium: 214mg

Red Pepper Coques with Pine Nuts

Prep time: 1 day 40 minutes | Cook time: 45 minutes | Makes 4 coques

Dough:

3 cups almond flour
½ teaspoon instant or rapid-rise yeast
2 teaspoons raw honey
1⅓ cups ice water
3 tablespoons extra-virgin olive oil
1½ teaspoons sea salt

Red Pepper Topping:

4 tablespoons extra-virgin olive oil, divided
2 cups jarred roasted red peppers, patted dry and sliced thinly
2 large onions, halved and sliced thin
3 garlic cloves, minced
¼ teaspoon red pepper flakes
2 bay leaves
3 tablespoons maple syrup
1½ teaspoons sea salt
3 tablespoons red whine vinegar

For Garnish:

¼ cup pine nuts (optional)
1 tablespoon minced fresh parsley

Make the Dough:

1. Combine the flour, yeast, and honey in a food processor, pulse to combine well. Gently add water while pulsing. Let the dough sit for 10 minutes.
2. Mix the olive oil and salt in the dough and knead the dough until smooth. Wrap in plastic and refrigerate for at least 1 day.

Make the Topping:

1. Heat 1 tablespoon of olive oil in a nonstick skillet over medium heat until shimmering.
2. Add the red peppers, onions, garlic, red pepper flakes, bay leaves, maple syrup, and salt. Sauté for 20 minutes or until the onion is caramelized.
3. Turn off the heat and discard the bay leaves. Remove the onion from the skillet and baste with wine vinegar. Let them sit until ready to use.

Make the Coques:

1. Preheat the oven to 500ºF (260ºC). Grease two baking sheets with 1 tablespoon of olive oil.
2. Divide the dough ball into four balls, then press and shape them into equal-sized oval. Arrange the ovals on the baking sheets and pierce each dough about 12 times.
3. Rub the ovals with 2 tablespoons of olive oil and bake for 7 minutes or until puffed. Flip the ovals halfway through the cooking time.
4. Spread the ovals with the topping and pine nuts, then bake for an additional 15 minutes or until well browned.
5. Remove the coques from the oven and spread with parsley. Allow to cool for 10 minutes before serving.

Tip: You can buy four whole-wheat 14 by 5-inch flatbread so you need not make the bread by yourself.

Per Serving (1 coque)
calories: 658 | fat: 23.1g | protein: 3.4g carbs: 112.0g | fiber: 6.2g | sodium: 1757mg

Zucchini Hummus Wraps

Prep time: 15 minutes | Cook time: 6 minutes | Serves 2

1 zucchini, ends removed, thinly sliced lengthwise
½ teaspoon dried oregano
¼ teaspoon freshly ground black pepper
¼ teaspoon garlic powder
¼ cup hummus
2 whole wheat tortillas
2 Roma tomatoes, cut lengthwise into slices
1 cup chopped kale
2 tablespoons chopped red onion
½ teaspoon ground cumin

1. In a skillet over medium heat, place the zucchini slices and cook for 3 minutes per side. Sprinkle with the oregano, pepper, and garlic powder and remove from the heat.
2. Spread 2 tablespoons of hummus on each tortilla. Lay half the zucchini in the center of each tortilla. Top with tomato slices, kale, red onion, and ¼ teaspoon of cumin. Wrap tightly and serve.

Per Serving
calories: 248 | fat: 8.1g | protein: 9.1g carbs: 37.1g | fiber: 8.1g | sodium: mg

Falafel Balls with Tahini Sauce

Prep time: 2 hours 20 minutes | Cook time: 20 minutes | Serves 4

Tahini Sauce:

½ cup tahini
2 tablespoons lemon juice
¼ cup finely chopped flat-leaf parsley
2 cloves garlic, minced
½ cup cold water, as needed

Falafel:

1 cup dried chickpeas, soaked overnight, drained
¼ cup chopped flat-leaf parsley
¼ cup chopped cilantro
1 large onion, chopped
1 teaspoon cumin
½ teaspoon chili flakes
4 cloves garlic
1 teaspoon sea salt
5 tablespoons almond flour
1½ teaspoons baking soda, dissolved in 1 teaspoon water
2 cups peanut oil
1 medium bell pepper, chopped
1 medium tomato, chopped
4 whole-wheat pita breads

Make the Tahini Sauce:

1. Combine the ingredients for the tahini sauce in a small bowl. Stir to mix well until smooth.
2. Wrap the bowl in plastic and refrigerate until ready to serve.

Make the Falafel:

1. Put the chickpeas, parsley, cilantro, onion, cumin, chili flakes, garlic, and salt in a food processor. Pulse to mix well but not puréed.
2. Add the flour and baking soda to the food processor, then pulse to form a smooth and tight dough.
3. Put the dough in a large bowl and wrap in plastic. Refrigerate for at least 2 hours to let it rise.
4. Divide and shape the dough into walnut-sized small balls.
5. Pour the peanut oil in a large pot and heat over high heat until the temperature of the oil reaches 375ºF (190ºC).
6. Drop 6 balls into the oil each time, and fry for 5 minutes or until golden brown and crispy. Turn the balls with a strainer to make them fried evenly.
7. Transfer the balls on paper towels with the strainer, then drain the oil from the balls.
8. Roast the pita breads in the oven for 5 minutes or until golden brown, if needed, then stuff the pitas with falafel balls and top with bell peppers and tomatoes. Drizzle with tahini sauce and serve immediately.

Tip: When you fry the falafel balls, if a ball falls apart after you drop it into the oil, then knead more flour into the dough to make it more stable.

Per Serving
calories: 574 | fat: 27.1g | protein: 19.8g carbs: 69.7g | fiber: 13.4g | sodium: 1246mg

Mushroom-Pesto Baked Pizza

Prep time: 5 minutes | Cook time: 15 minutes | Serves 2

1 teaspoon extra-virgin olive oil
½ cup sliced mushrooms
½ red onion, sliced
Salt and freshly ground black pepper
¼ cup store-bought pesto sauce
2 whole-wheat flatbreads
¼ cup shredded Mozzarella cheese

1. Preheat the oven to 350ºF (180ºC).
2. In a small skillet, heat the oil over medium heat. Add the mushrooms and onion, and season with salt and pepper. Sauté for 3 to 5 minutes until the onion and mushrooms begin to soften.
3. Spread 2 tablespoons of pesto on each flatbread.
4. Divide the mushroom-onion mixture between the two flatbreads. Top each with 2 tablespoons of cheese.
5. Place the flatbreads on a baking sheet and bake for 10 to 12 minutes until the cheese is melted and bubbly. Serve warm.

Per Serving
calories: 348 | fat: 23.5g | protein: 14.2g carbs: 28.1g | fiber: 7.1g | sodium: 792mg

Easy Pizza Pockets

Prep time: 10 minutes | Cook time: 0 minutes | Serves 2

½ cup tomato sauce
½ teaspoon oregano
½ teaspoon garlic powder
½ cup chopped black olives
2 canned artichoke hearts, drained and

chopped
2 ounces (57 g) pepperoni, chopped
½ cup shredded Mozzarella cheese
1 whole-wheat pita, halved

1. In a medium bowl, stir together the tomato sauce, oregano, and garlic powder.
2. Add the olives, artichoke hearts, pepperoni, and cheese. Stir to mix.
3. Spoon the mixture into the pita halves and serve.

Per Serving
calories: 375 | fat: 23.5g | protein: 17.1g carbs: 27.1g | fiber: 6.1g | sodium: 1080mg

Open-Faced Margherita Sandwiches

Prep time: 10 minutes | Cook time: 5 minutes | Serves 4

2 (6- to 7-inch) whole-wheat submarine or hoagie rolls, sliced open horizontally
1 tablespoon extra-virgin olive oil
1 garlic clove, halved
1 large ripe tomato, cut into 8 slices

¼ teaspoon dried oregano
1 cup fresh Mozzarella, sliced
¼ cup lightly packed fresh basil leaves, torn into small pieces
¼ teaspoon freshly ground black pepper

1. Preheat the broiler to High with the rack 4 inches under the heating element.
2. Put the sliced bread on a large, rimmed baking sheet and broil for 1 minute, or until the bread is just lightly toasted. Remove from the oven.
3. Brush each piece of the toasted bread with the oil, and rub a garlic half over each piece.
4. Put the toasted bread back on the baking sheet. Evenly divide the tomato slices

on each piece. Sprinkle with the oregano and top with the cheese.
5. Place the baking sheet under the broiler. Set the timer for 1½ minutes, but check after 1 minute. When the cheese is melted and the edges are just starting to get dark brown, remove the sandwiches from the oven.
6. Top each sandwich with the fresh basil and pepper before serving.

Per Serving
calories: 93 | fat: 2.0g | protein: 10.0g carbs: 8.0g | fiber: 2.0g | sodium: 313mg

Tuna and Hummus Wraps

Prep time: 10 minutes | Cook time: 0 minutes | Serves 2

Hummus:

1 cup from 1 (15-ounce / 425-g) can low-sodium chickpeas, drained and rinsed
2 tablespoons tahini

1 tablespoon extra-virgin olive oil
1 garlic clove
Juice of ½ lemon
¼ teaspoon salt
2 tablespoons water

Wraps:

4 large lettuce leaves
1 (5-ounce / 142-g) can chunk light tuna packed in water, drained

1 red bell pepper, seeded and cut into strips
1 cucumber, sliced

Make the Hummus
1. In a blender jar, combine the chickpeas, tahini, olive oil, garlic, lemon juice, salt, and water. Process until smooth. Taste and adjust with additional lemon juice or salt, as needed.

Make the Wraps
1. On each lettuce leaf, spread 1 tablespoon of hummus, and divide the tuna among the leaves. Top each with several strips of red pepper and cucumber slices.
2. Roll up the lettuce leaves, folding in the two shorter sides and rolling away from you, like a burrito. Serve immediately.

Per Serving
calories: 192 | fat: 5.1g | protein: 26.1g carbs: 15.1g | fiber: 4.1g | sodium: 352mg

Ritzy Garden Burgers

Prep time: 1 hour 30 minutes | Cook time: 30 minutes | Serves 6

1 tablespoon avocado oil
1 yellow onion, diced
½ cup shredded carrots
4 garlic cloves, halved
1 (15 ounces / 425 g) can black beans, rinsed and drained
1 cup gluten-free rolled oats
¼ cup oil-packed sun-dried tomatoes, drained and chopped
½ cup sunflower seeds, toasted
1 teaspoon chili powder
1 teaspoon paprika
1 teaspoon ground cumin
½ cup fresh parsley, stems removed
¼ teaspoon ground red pepper flakes
¾ teaspoon sea salt
¼ teaspoon ground black pepper
¼ cup olive oil

For Serving:
6 whole-wheat buns, split in half and toasted
2 ripe avocados, sliced
1 cup kaiware sprouts or mung bean sprouts
1 ripe tomato, sliced

1. Line a baking sheet with parchment paper.
2. Heat 1 tablespoon of avocado oil in a nonstick skillet over medium heat.
3. Add the onion and carrots and sauté for 10 minutes or until the onion is caramelized.
4. Add the garlic and sauté for 30 seconds or until fragrant.
5. Transfer them into a food processor, then add the remaining ingredients, except for the olive oil. Pulse until chopped fine and the mixture holds together. Make sure not to purée the mixture.
6. Divide and form the mixture into six 4-inch diameter and ½-inch thick patties.
7. Arrange the patties on the baking sheet and wrap the sheet in plastic. Put the baking sheet in the refrigerator and freeze for at least an hour until firm.
8. Remove the baking sheet from the refrigerator, let them sit under room temperature for 10 minutes.
9. Heat the olive oil in a nonstick skillet over medium-high heat until shimmering.
10. Fry the patties in the skillet for 15 minutes or until lightly browned and crispy. Flip the patties halfway through the cooking time. You may need to work in batches to avoid overcrowding.
11. Assemble the buns with patties, avocados, sprouts, and tomato slices to make the burgers.

Tip: You can use 6 large romaine lettuce leaves to replace the whole wheat buns to gift your burger with freshness.

Per Serving
calories: 613 | fat: 23.1g | protein: 26.2g
carbs: 88.3g | fiber: 22.9g | sodium: 456mg

Dulse, Avocado, and Tomato Pitas

Prep time: 10 minutes | Cook time: 30 minutes | Makes 4 pitas

2 teaspoons coconut oil
½ cup dulse, picked through and separated
Ground black pepper, to taste
2 avocados, sliced
2 tablespoons lime juice
¼ cup chopped cilantro
2 scallions, white and light green parts, sliced
Sea salt, to taste
4 (8-inch) whole wheat pitas, sliced in half
4 cups chopped romaine
4 plum tomatoes, sliced

1. Heat the coconut oil in a nonstick skillet over medium heat until melted.
2. Add the dulse and sauté for 5 minutes or until crispy. Sprinkle with ground black pepper and turn off the heat. Set aside.
3. Put the avocado, lime juice, cilantro, and scallions in a food processor and sprinkle with salt and ground black pepper. Pulse to combine well until smooth.
4. Toast the pitas in a baking pan in the oven for 1 minute until soft.
5. Transfer the pitas to a clean work surface and open. Spread the avocado mixture over the pitas, then top with dulse, romaine, and tomato slices.
6. Serve immediately.

Tip: You can use another lettuce, such as iceberg lettuce, Bibb lettuce, kale, or arugula, to replace the romaine for this recipe.

Per Serving (1 pita)
calories: 412 | fat: 18.7g | protein: 9.1g
carbs: 56.1g | fiber: 12.5g | sodium: 695mg

Glazed Mushroom and Vegetable Fajitas

Prep time: 20 minutes | Cook time: 20 minutes | Makes 6

Spicy Glazed Mushrooms:

1 teaspoon olive oil
1 (10- to 12-ounce / 284- to 340-g) package cremini mushrooms, rinsed and drained, cut into thin slices

½ to 1 teaspoon chili powder
Sea salt and freshly ground black pepper, to taste
1 teaspoon maple syrup

Fajitas:

2 teaspoons olive oil
1 onion, chopped
Sea salt, to taste
1 bell pepper, any color, deseeded and sliced into long strips
1 zucchini, cut into

large matchsticks
6 whole-grain tortilla
2 carrots, grated
3 to 4 scallions, sliced
½ cup fresh cilantro, finely chopped

Make the Spicy Glazed Mushrooms:

1. Heat the olive oil in a nonstick skillet over medium heat until shimmering.
2. Add the mushrooms and sauté for 10 minutes or until tender.
3. Sprinkle the mushrooms with chili powder, salt, and ground black pepper. Drizzle with maple syrup. Stir to mix well and cook for 5 to 7 minutes or until the mushrooms are glazed. Set aside until ready to use.

Make the Fajitas:

1. Heat the olive oil in the same skillet over medium heat until shimmering.
2. Add the onion and sauté for 5 minutes or until translucent. Sprinkle with salt.
3. Add the bell pepper and zucchini and sauté for 7 minutes or until tender.
4. Meanwhile, toast the tortilla in the oven for 5 minutes or until golden brown.
5. Allow the tortilla to cool for a few minutes until they can be handled, then assemble the tortilla with glazed mushrooms, sautéed vegetables and remaining vegetables to make the fajitas. Serve immediately.

Tip: For more flavor, you can top the fajitas with homemade guacamole or salsa to serve.

Per Serving
calories: 403 | fat: 14.8g | protein: 11.2g
carbs: 7.9g | fiber: 7.0g | sodium: 230mg

Artichoke and Cucumber Hoagies

Prep time: 10 minutes | Cook time: 15 minutes | Makes 1

1 (12-ounce / 340-g) whole grain baguette, sliced in half horizontally
1 cup frozen and thawed artichoke hearts, roughly chopped
1 cucumber, sliced
2 tomatoes, sliced
1 red bell pepper,

sliced
⅓ cup Kalamata olives, pitted and chopped
¼ small red onion, thinly sliced
Sea salt and ground black pepper, to taste
2 tablespoons pesto
Balsamic vinegar, to taste

1. Arrange the baguette halves on a clean work surface, then cut off the top third from each half. Scoop some insides of the bottom half out and reserve as breadcrumbs.
2. Toast the baguette in a baking pan in the oven for 1 minute to brown lightly.
3. Put the artichokes, cucumber, tomatoes, bell pepper, olives, and onion in a large bowl. Sprinkle with salt and ground black pepper. Toss to combine well.
4. Spread the bottom half of the baguette with the vegetable mixture and drizzle with balsamic vinegar, then smear the cut side of the baguette top with pesto. Assemble the two baguette halves.
5. Wrap the hoagies in parchment paper and let sit for at least an hour before serving.

Tip: You can make your own pesto by combining the minced garlic, crushed pine nuts, dried basil, Parmesan, and salt in a small bowl. Stir to mix well.

Per Serving (1 hoagies)
calories: 1263 | fat: 37.7g | protein: 56.3g
carbs: 180.1g | fiber: 37.8g | sodium: 2137mg

Mediterranean Greek Salad Wraps

Prep time: 15 minutes | Cook time: 0 minutes | Serves 4

1½ cups seedless cucumber, peeled and chopped
1 cup chopped tomato
½ cup finely chopped fresh mint
¼ cup diced red onion
1 (2.25-ounce / 64-g) can sliced black olives, drained
2 tablespoons extra-virgin olive oil
1 tablespoon red wine vinegar
¼ teaspoon kosher salt
¼ teaspoon freshly ground black pepper
½ cup crumbled goat cheese
4 whole-wheat flatbread wraps or soft whole-wheat tortillas

1. In a large bowl, stir together the cucumber, tomato, mint, onion and olives.
2. In a small bowl, whisk together the oil, vinegar, salt, and pepper. Spread the dressing over the salad. Toss gently to combine.
3. On a clean work surface, lay the wraps. Divide the goat cheese evenly among the wraps. Scoop a quarter of the salad filling down the center of each wrap.
4. Fold up each wrap: Start by folding up the bottom, then fold one side over and fold the other side over the top. Repeat with the remaining wraps.
5. Serve immediately.

Per Serving
calories: 225 | fat: 12.0g | protein: 12.0g
carbs: 18.0g | fiber: 4.0g | sodium: 349mg

Spicy Tofu Tacos with Cherry Tomato Salsa

Prep time: 20 minutes | Cook time: 11 minutes | Makes 4 tacos

Cherry Tomato Salsa:
¼ cup sliced cherry tomatoes
½ jalapeño, deseeded and sliced
Juice of 1 lime
1 garlic clove, minced
Sea salt and freshly ground black pepper, to taste
2 teaspoons extra-virgin olive oil

Spicy Tofu Taco Filling:
4 tablespoons water, divided
½ cup canned black beans, rinsed and drained
2 teaspoons fresh chopped chives, divided
¾ teaspoon ground cumin, divided
¾ teaspoon smoked paprika, divided
Dash cayenne pepper
(optional)
¼ teaspoon sea salt
¼ teaspoon freshly ground black pepper
1 teaspoon extra-virgin olive oil
6 ounces (170 g) firm tofu, drained, rinsed, and pressed
4 corn tortillas
¼ avocado, sliced
¼ cup fresh cilantro

Make the Cherry Tomato Salsa:
1. Combine the ingredients for the salsa in a small bowl. Stir to mix well. Set aside until ready to use.

Make the Spicy Tofu Taco Filling:
1. Add 2 tablespoons of water into a saucepan, then add the black beans and sprinkle with 1 teaspoon of chives, ½ teaspoon of cumin, ¼ teaspoon of smoked paprika, and cayenne. Stir to mix well.
2. Cook for 5 minutes over medium heat until heated through, then mash the black beans with the back of a spoon. Turn off the heat and set aside.
3. Add remaining water into a bowl, then add the remaining chives, cumin, and paprika. Sprinkle with cayenne, salt, and black pepper. Stir to mix well. Set aside.
4. Heat the olive oil in a nonstick skillet over medium heat until shimmering.
5. Add the tofu and drizzle with taco sauce, then sauté for 5 minutes or until the seasoning is absorbed. Remove the tofu from the skillet and set aside.
6. Warm the tortillas in the skillet for 1 minutes or until heated through.
7. Transfer the tortillas onto a large plate and top with tofu, mashed black beans, avocado, cilantro, then drizzle the tomato salsa over. Serve immediately.

Tip: If you don't like black beans, you can replace it with chickpeas, remember soak the chickpeas in water overnight before using.

Per Serving (1 taco)
calories: 240 | fat: 9.0g | protein: 11.6g
carbs: 31.6g | fiber: 6.7g | sodium: 195mg

Super Cheeses and Mushroom Tart

Prep time: 30 minutes | Cook time: 1 hour 30 minutes | Serves 4 to 6

Crust:

1¾ cups almond flour
1 tablespoon raw honey
¾ teaspoon sea salt
¼ cup extra-virgin olive oil
1/3 cup water

Filling:

2 tablespoons extra-virgin olive oil, divided
1 pound (454 g) white mushrooms, trimmed and sliced thinly
Sea salt, to taste
1 garlic clove, minced
2 teaspoons minced fresh thyme
¼ cup shredded Mozzarella cheese
½ cup grated Parmesan cheese
4 ounces (113 g) part-skim ricotta cheese
Ground black pepper, to taste
2 tablespoons ground basil

Make the Crust:

1. Preheat the oven to 350ºF (180ºC).
2. Combine the flour, honey, salt and olive oil in a large bowl. Stir to mix well. Gently mix in the water until a smooth dough forms.
3. Drop walnut-size clumps from the dough in the single layer on a tart pan. Press the clumps to coat the bottom of the pan.
4. Bake the crust in the preheated oven for 50 minutes or until firm and browned. Rotate the pan halfway through.

Make the Filling:

1. While baking the crust, heat 1 tablespoon of olive oil in a nonstick skillet over medium-high heat until shimmering.
2. Add the mushrooms and sprinkle with ½ teaspoon of salt. Sauté for 15 minutes or until tender.
3. Add the garlic and thyme and sauté for 30 seconds or until fragrant.

Make the Tart:

1. Meanwhile, combine the cheeses, salt, ground black pepper, and 1 tablespoon of olive oil in a bowl. Stir to mix well.
2. Spread the cheese mixture over the crust, then top with the mushroom mixture.
3. Bake in the oven for 20 minutes or until the cheeses are frothy and the tart is heated through. Rotate the pan halfway through the baking time.

4. Remove the tart from the oven. Allow to cool for at least 10 minutes, then sprinkle with basil. Slice to serve.

Tip: You can replace the raw honey with the same amount of maple syrup, if needed.

Per Serving

calories: 530 | fat: 26.6g | protein: 11.7g
carbs: 63.5g | fiber: 4.6g | sodium: 785mg

Roasted Tomato Panini

Prep time: 15 minutes | Cook time: 3 hours 6 minutes | Serves 2

2 teaspoons olive oil
4 Roma tomatoes, halved
4 cloves garlic
1 tablespoon Italian seasoning
Sea salt and freshly
ground pepper, to taste
4 slices whole-grain bread
4 basil leaves
2 slices fresh Mozzarella cheese

1. Preheat the oven to 250ºF (121ºC). Grease a baking pan with olive oil.
2. Place the tomatoes and garlic in the baking pan, then sprinkle with Italian seasoning, salt, and ground pepper. Toss to coat well.
3. Roast in the preheated oven for 3 hours or until the tomatoes are lightly wilted.
4. Preheat the panini press.
5. Make the panini: Place two slices of bread on a clean work surface, then top them with wilted tomatoes. Sprinkle with basil and spread with Mozzarella cheese. Top them with remaining two slices of bread.
6. Cook the panini for 6 minutes or until lightly browned and the cheese melts. Flip the panini halfway through the cooking.
7. Serve immediately.

Tip: Method to make the panini without panini press: Heat a grill pan over medium-high heat, then put the panini in the pan. Press another grill pan over the panini and cook for 6 minutes. Flip the panini halfway through the cooking time.

Per Serving

calories: 323 | fat: 12.0g | protein: 17.4g
carbs: 37.5g | fiber: 7.5g | sodium: 603mg

Roasted Vegetable Panini

Prep time: 10 minutes | Cook time: 15 minutes | Serves 4

2 tablespoons extra-virgin olive oil, divided
1½ cups diced broccoli
1 cup diced zucchini
¼ cup diced onion
¼ teaspoon dried oregano
⅛ teaspoon kosher or sea salt
⅛ teaspoon freshly ground black pepper
1 (12-ounce / 340-g) jar roasted red peppers, drained and finely chopped
2 tablespoons grated Parmesan or Asiago cheese
1 cup fresh Mozzarella (about 4 ounces / 113 g), sliced
1 (2-foot-long) whole-grain Italian loaf, cut into 4 equal lengths
Cooking spray

1. Place a large, rimmed baking sheet in the oven. Preheat the oven to 450ºF (235ºC) with the baking sheet inside.
2. In a large bowl, stir together 1 tablespoon of the oil, broccoli, zucchini, onion, oregano, salt and pepper.
3. Remove the baking sheet from the oven and spritz the baking sheet with cooking spray. Spread the vegetable mixture on the baking sheet and roast for 5 minutes, stirring once halfway through cooking.
4. Remove the baking sheet from the oven. Stir in the red peppers and Parmesan cheese.
5. In a large skillet over medium-high heat, heat the remaining 1 tablespoon of the oil.
6. Cut open each section of bread horizontally, but don't cut all the way through. Fill each with the vegetable mix (about ½ cup), and layer 1 ounce (28 g) of sliced Mozzarella cheese on top. Close the sandwiches, and place two of them on the skillet. Place a heavy object on top and grill for 2½ minutes. Flip the sandwiches and grill for another 2½ minutes.
7. Repeat the grilling process with the remaining two sandwiches.
8. Serve hot.

Per Serving
calories: 116 | fat: 4.0g | protein: 12.0g
carbs: 9.0g | fiber: 3.0g | sodium: 569mg

White Pizzas with Arugula and Spinach

Prep time: 10 minutes | Cook time: 20 minutes | Serves 4

1 pound (454 g) refrigerated fresh pizza dough
2 tablespoons extra-virgin olive oil, divided
½ cup thinly sliced onion
2 garlic cloves, minced
3 cups baby spinach
3 cups arugula
1 tablespoon water
¼ teaspoon freshly ground black pepper
1 tablespoon freshly squeezed lemon juice
½ cup shredded Parmesan cheese
½ cup crumbled goat cheese
Cooking spray

1. Preheat the oven to 500ºF (260ºC). Spritz a large, rimmed baking sheet with cooking spray.
2. Take the pizza dough out of the refrigerator.
3. Heat 1 tablespoon of the oil in a large skillet over medium heat. Add the onion to the skillet and cook for 4 minutes, stirring constantly. Add the garlic and cook for 1 minute, stirring constantly.
4. Stir in the spinach, arugula, water and pepper. Cook for about 2 minutes, stirring constantly, or until all the greens are coated with oil and they start to cook down. Remove the skillet from the heat and drizzle with the lemon juice.
5. On a lightly floured work surface, form the pizza dough into a 12-inch circle or a 10-by-12-inch rectangle, using a rolling pin or by stretching with your hands.
6. Place the dough on the prepared baking sheet. Brush the dough with the remaining 1 tablespoon of the oil. Spread the cooked greens on top of the dough to within ½ inch of the edge. Top with the Parmesan cheese and goat cheese.
7. Bake in the preheated oven for 10 to 12 minutes, or until the crust starts to brown around the edges.
8. Remove from the oven and transfer the pizza to a cutting board. Cut into eight pieces before serving.

Per Serving
calories: 521 | fat: 31.0g | protein: 23.0g
carbs: 38.0g | fiber: 4.0g | sodium: 1073mg

Green Veggie Sandwiches

Prep time: 20 minutes | Cook time: 0 minutes | Serves 2

Spread:
1 (15-ounce / 425-g) can cannellini beans, drained and rinsed
1/3 cup packed fresh basil leaves
1/3 cup packed fresh parsley
1/3 cup chopped fresh

chives
2 garlic cloves, chopped
Zest and juice of 1/2 lemon
1 tablespoon apple cider vinegar

Sandwiches:
4 whole-grain bread slices, toasted
8 English cucumber slices
1 large beefsteak tomato, cut into slices
1 large avocado,

halved, pitted, and cut into slices
1 small yellow bell pepper, cut into slices
2 handfuls broccoli sprouts
2 handfuls fresh spinach

Make the Spread
1. In a food processor, combine the cannellini beans, basil, parsley, chives, garlic, lemon zest and juice, and vinegar. Pulse a few times, scrape down the sides, and purée until smooth. You may need to scrape down the sides again to incorporate all the basil and parsley. Refrigerate for at least 1 hour to allow the flavors to blend.
2. Assemble the Sandwiches
3. Build your sandwiches by spreading several tablespoons of spread on each slice of bread. Layer two slices of bread with the cucumber, tomato, avocado, bell pepper, broccoli sprouts, and spinach. Top with the remaining bread slices and press down lightly.
4. Serve immediately.

Per Serving
calories: 617 | fat: 21.1g | protein: 28.1g
carbs: 86.1g | fiber: 25.6g | sodium: 593mg

Turkish Eggplant and Tomatoes Pide with Mint

Prep time: 1 day 40 minutes | Cook time: 20 minutes | Makes 6 pides

Dough:
3 cups almond flour
2 teaspoons raw honey
1/2 teaspoon instant or rapid-rise yeast

1 1/3 cups ice water
1 tablespoon extra-virgin olive oil
1 1/2 teaspoons sea salt

Eggplant and Tomato Toppings:
28 ounces (794 g) whole tomatoes, peeled and puréed
5 tablespoons extra-virgin olive oil, divided
1 pound (454 g) eggplant, cut into 1/2-inch pieces
1/2 red bell pepper, chopped
Sea salt and ground

black pepper, to taste
3 garlic cloves, minced
1/4 teaspoon red pepper flakes
1/2 teaspoon smoked paprika
6 tablespoons minced fresh mint, divided
1 1/2 cups crumbled feta cheese

Make the Dough:
Combine the flour, yeast, and honey in a food processor, pulse to combine well. Gently add water while pulsing. Let the dough sit for 10

minutes.
Mix the olive oil and salt in the dough and knead the dough until smooth. Wrap in plastic and refrigerate for at least 1 day.

Make the Toppings:
1. Heat 2 tablespoons of olive oil in a nonstick skillet over medium-high heat until shimmering.
2. Add the bell pepper, eggplant, and 1/2 teaspoon of salt. Sauté for 6 minutes or until the eggplant is lightly browned.
3. Add the red pepper flakes, paprika, and garlic. Sauté for 1 minute or until fragrant.
4. Pour in the puréed tomatoes. Bring to a simmer, then cook for 10 minutes or until the mixture is thickened into about 3 1/2 cups.
5. Turn off the heat and mix in 4 tablespoons of mint, salt, and ground black pepper. Set them aside until ready to use.

Make the Turkish Pide:
1. Preheat the oven to 500ºF (260ºC). Line three baking sheets with parchment papers.
2. On a clean work surface, divide and shape the dough into six 14 by 5-inch ovals. Transfer the dough to the baking sheets.
3. Brush them with 3 tablespoons of olive oil and spread the eggplant mixture and feta cheese on top.
4. Bake in the preheated oven for 12 minutes or until golden brown. Rotate the pide halfway through the baking time.
5. Remove the pide from the oven and spread with remaining mint and serve immediately.

Tip: You can buy four whole-wheat 14 by 5-inch flatbread so you need not make the bread by yourself.

Per Serving (1 pide)
calories: 500 | fat: 22.1g | protein: 8.0g
carbs: 69.7g | fiber: 5.8g | sodium: 1001mg

Baked Parmesan Chicken Wraps

Prep time: 10 minutes | Cook time: 18 minutes | Serves 6

1 pound (454 g) boneless, skinless chicken breasts
1 large egg
¼ cup unsweetened almond milk
⅔ cup whole-wheat bread crumbs
½ cup grated Parmesan cheese
¾ teaspoon garlic powder, divided
1 cup canned low-sodium or no-salt-added crushed tomatoes
1 teaspoon dried oregano
6 (8-inch) whole-wheat tortillas, or whole-grain spinach wraps
1 cup fresh Mozzarella cheese, sliced
1½ cups loosely packed fresh flat-leaf (Italian) parsley, chopped
Cooking spray

1. Preheat the oven to 425ºF (220ºC). Line a large, rimmed baking sheet with aluminum foil. Place a wire rack on the aluminum foil, and spritz the rack with nonstick cooking spray. Set aside.
2. Place the chicken breasts into a large plastic bag. With a rolling pin, pound the chicken so it is evenly flattened, about ¼ inch thick. Slice the chicken into six portions.
3. In a bowl, whisk together the egg and milk. In another bowl, stir together the bread crumbs, Parmesan cheese and ½ teaspoon of the garlic powder.
4. Dredge each chicken breast portion into the egg mixture, and then into the Parmesan crumb mixture, pressing the crumbs into the chicken so they stick. Arrange the chicken on the prepared wire rack.
5. Bake in the preheated oven for 15 to 18 minutes, or until the internal temperature of the chicken reads 165ºF (74ºC) on a meat thermometer and any juices run clear.
6. Transfer the chicken to a cutting board, and cut each portion diagonally into ½-inch pieces.
7. In a small, microwave-safe bowl, stir together the tomatoes, oregano, and the remaining ¼ teaspoon of the garlic powder. Cover the bowl with a paper towel and microwave for about 1 minute on high, until very hot. Set aside.
8. Wrap the tortillas in a damp paper towel and microwave for 30 to 45 seconds on high, or until warmed through.
9. Assemble the wraps: Divide the chicken slices evenly among the six tortillas and top with the sliced Mozzarella cheese. Spread 1 tablespoon of the warm tomato sauce over the cheese on each tortilla, and top each with about ¼ cup of the parsley.
10. Wrap the tortilla: Fold up the bottom of the tortilla, then fold one side over and fold the other side over the top.
11. Serve the wraps warm with the remaining sauce for dipping.

Per Serving
calories: 358 | fat: 12.0g | protein: 21.0g
carbs: 41.0g | fiber: 7.0g | sodium: 755mg

Chapter 5 Beans, Grains, and Pastas

Quinoa and Chickpea Vegetable Bowls

Prep time: 20 minutes | Cook time: 15 minutes | Serves 4

1 cup red dry quinoa, rinsed and drained
2 cups low-sodium vegetable soup
2 cups fresh spinach
2 cups finely shredded red cabbage
1 (15-ounce / 425-g) can chickpeas, drained and rinsed

1 ripe avocado, thinly sliced
1 cup shredded carrots
1 red bell pepper, thinly sliced
4 tablespoons Mango Sauce
½ cup fresh cilantro, chopped

Mango Sauce:

1 mango, diced
¼ cup fresh lime juice
½ teaspoon ground turmeric
1 teaspoon finely minced fresh ginger

¼ teaspoon sea salt
Pinch of ground red pepper
1 teaspoon pure maple syrup
2 tablespoons extra-virgin olive oil

1. Pour the quinoa and vegetable soup in a saucepan. Bring to a boil. Reduce the heat to low. Cover and cook for 15 minutes or until tender. Fluffy with a fork.
2. Meanwhile, combine the ingredients for the mango sauce in a food processor. Pulse until smooth.
3. Divide the quinoa, spinach, and cabbage into 4 serving bowls, then top with chickpeas, avocado, carrots, and bell pepper. Dress them with the mango sauce and spread with cilantro. Serve immediately.

Tip: Instead of maple syrup, you can use the same amount of raw honey for making the mango sauce.

Per Serving
calories: 366 | fat: 11.1g | protein: 15.5g
carbs: 55.6g | fiber: 17.7g | sodium: 746mg

Lentil and Vegetable Curry Stew

Prep time: 20 minutes | Cook time: 4 hours 7 minutes | Serves 8

1 tablespoon coconut oil
1 yellow onion, diced
¼ cup yellow Thai curry paste
2 cups unsweetened coconut milk
2 cups dry red lentils, rinsed well and drained
3 cups bite-sized cauliflower florets
2 golden potatoes, cut into chunks

2 carrots, peeled and diced
8 cups low-sodium vegetable soup, divided
1 bunch kale, stems removed and roughly chopped
Sea salt, to taste
½ cup fresh cilantro, chopped
Pinch crushed red pepper flakes

1. Heat the coconut oil in a nonstick skillet over medium-high heat until melted.
2. Add the onion and sauté for 5 minutes or until translucent.
3. Pour in the curry paste and sauté for another 2 minutes, then fold in the coconut milk and stir to combine well. Bring to a simmer and turn off the heat.
4. Put the lentils, cauliflower, potatoes, and carrot in the slow cooker. Pour in 6 cups of vegetable soup and the curry mixture. Stir to combine well.
5. Cover and cook on high for 4 hours or until the lentils and vegetables are soft. Stir periodically.
6. During the last 30 minutes, fold the kale in the slow cooker and pour in the remaining vegetable soup. Sprinkle with salt.
7. Pour the stew in a large serving bowl and spread the cilantro and red pepper flakes on top before serving hot.

Tip: To make this a complete meal, you can baste it over cooked brown rice.

Per Serving
calories: 530 | fat: 19.2g | protein: 20.3g
carbs: 75.2g | fiber: 15.5g | sodium: 562mg

Lush Moroccan Chickpea, Vegetable, and Fruit Stew

Prep time: 20 minutes | Cook time: 6 hours 4 minutes | Serves 6

1 large bell pepper, any color, chopped
6 ounces (170 g) green beans, trimmed and cut into bite-size pieces
3 cups canned chickpeas, rinsed and drained
1 (15-ounce / 425-g) can diced tomatoes, with the juice
1 large carrot, cut into ¼-inch rounds
2 large potatoes, peeled and cubed
1 large yellow onion, chopped
1 teaspoon grated fresh ginger
2 garlic cloves, minced
1¾ cups low-sodium vegetable soup
1 teaspoon ground cumin
1 tablespoon ground coriander
¼ teaspoon ground red pepper flakes
Sea salt and ground black pepper, to taste
8 ounces (227 g) fresh baby spinach
¼ cup diced dried figs
¼ cup diced dried apricots
1 cup plain Greek yogurt

1. Place the bell peppers, green beans, chicken peas, tomatoes and juice, carrot, potatoes, onion, ginger, and garlic in the slow cooker.
2. Pour in the vegetable soup and sprinkle with cumin, coriander, red pepper flakes, salt, and ground black pepper. Stir to mix well.
3. Put the slow cooker lid on and cook on high for 6 hours or until the vegetables are soft. Stir periodically.
4. Open the lid and fold in the spinach, figs, apricots, and yogurt. Stir to mix well.
5. Cook for 4 minutes or until the spinach is wilted. Pour them in a large serving bowl. Allow to cool for at least 20 minutes, then serve warm.

Tip: If you don't like the canned chickpeas, you can use the dried chickpeas and soak them in water overnight before using.

Per Serving
calories: 611 | fat: 9.0g | protein: 30.7g
carbs: 107.4g | fiber: 20.8g | sodium: 344mg

Wild Rice, Celery, and Cauliflower Pilaf

Prep time: 10 minutes | Cook time: 45 minutes | Serves 4

1 tablespoon olive oil, plus more for greasing the baking dish
1 cup wild rice
2 cups low-sodium chicken broth
1 sweet onion, chopped
2 stalks celery, chopped
1 teaspoon minced garlic
2 carrots, peeled, halved lengthwise, and sliced
½ cauliflower head, cut into small florets
1 teaspoon chopped fresh thyme
Sea salt, to taste

1. Preheat the oven to 350ºF (180ºC). Line a baking sheet with parchment paper and grease with olive oil.
2. Put the wild rice in a saucepan, then pour in the chicken broth. Bring to a boil. Reduce the heat to low and simmer for 30 minutes or until the rice is plump.
3. Meanwhile, heat the remaining olive oil in an oven-proof skillet over medium-high heat until shimmering.
4. Add the onion, celery, and garlic to the skillet and sauté for 3 minutes or until the onion is translucent.
5. Add the carrots and cauliflower to the skillet and sauté for 5 minutes. Turn off the heat and set aside.
6. Pour the cooked rice in the skillet with the vegetables. Sprinkle with thyme and salt.
7. Set the skillet in the preheated oven and bake for 15 minutes or until the vegetables are soft.
8. Serve immediately.

Tip: To make this a complete meal, you can serve it with seared tuna, or salmon casserole.

Per Serving
calories: 214 | fat: 3.9g | protein: 7.2g
carbs: 37.9g | fiber: 5.0g | sodium: 122mg

Slow Cooked Turkey and Brown Rice

Prep time: 20 minutes | Cook time: 3 hours 10 minutes | Serves 6

1 tablespoon extra-virgin olive oil
1½ pounds (680 g) ground turkey
2 tablespoons chopped fresh sage, divided
2 tablespoons chopped fresh thyme, divided
1 teaspoon sea salt
½ teaspoon ground black pepper
2 cups brown rice
1 (14-ounce / 397-g) can stewed tomatoes, with the juice
¼ cup pitted and sliced Kalamata olives
3 medium zucchini, sliced thinly
¼ cup chopped fresh flat-leaf parsley
1 medium yellow onion, chopped
1 tablespoon plus 1 teaspoon balsamic vinegar
2 cups low-sodium chicken stock
2 garlic cloves, minced
½ cup grated Parmesan cheese, for serving

1. Heat the olive oil in a nonstick skillet over medium-high heat until shimmering.
2. Add the ground turkey and sprinkle with 1 tablespoon of sage, 1 tablespoon of thyme, salt and ground black pepper.
3. Sauté for 10 minutes or until the ground turkey is lightly browned.
4. Pour them in the slow cooker, then pour in the remaining ingredients, except for the Parmesan. Stir to mix well.
5. Put the lid on and cook on high for 3 hours or until the rice and vegetables are tender.
6. Pour them in a large serving bowl, then spread with Parmesan cheese before serving.

Tip: There are four types of brown rice, long grain, medium grain, short grain, and light brown rice. I prefer the long-grain brown rice, because it has a chewy texture and nutty flavor which is perfect for this dish.

Per Serving
calories: 499 | fat: 16.4g | protein: 32.4g
carbs: 56.5g | fiber: 4.7g | sodium: 758mg

Pearl Barley Risotto with Parmesan Cheese

Prep time: 5 minutes | Cook time: 20 minutes | Serves 6

4 cups low-sodium or no-salt-added vegetable broth
1 tablespoon extra-virgin olive oil
1 cup chopped yellow onion
2 cups uncooked pearl barley
½ cup dry white wine
1 cup freshly grated Parmesan cheese, divided
¼ teaspoon kosher or sea salt
¼ teaspoon freshly ground black pepper
Fresh chopped chives and lemon wedges, for serving (optional)

1. Pour the broth into a medium saucepan and bring to a simmer.
2. Heat the olive oil in a large stockpot over medium-high heat. Add the onion and cook for about 4 minutes, stirring occasionally.
3. Add the barley and cook for 2 minutes, stirring, or until the barley is toasted. Pour in the wine and cook for about 1 minute, or until most of the liquid evaporates. Add 1 cup of the warm broth into the pot and cook, stirring, for about 2 minutes, or until most of the liquid is absorbed.
4. Add the remaining broth, 1 cup at a time, cooking until each cup is absorbed (about 2 minutes each time) before adding the next. The last addition of broth will take a bit longer to absorb, about 4 minutes.
5. Remove the pot from the heat, and stir in ½ cup of the cheese, and the salt and pepper.
6. Serve with the remaining ½ cup of the cheese on the side, along with the chives and lemon wedges (if desired).

Per Serving
calories: 421 | fat: 11.0g | protein: 15.0g
carbs: 67.0g | fiber: 11.0g | sodium: 641mg

Spicy Italian Bean Balls with Marinara

Prep time: 20 minutes | Cook time: 30 minutes | Serves 2 to 4

Bean Balls:

1 tablespoon extra-virgin olive oil
½ yellow onion, minced
1 teaspoon fennel seeds
2 teaspoons dried oregano
½ teaspoon crushed red pepper flakes
1 teaspoon garlic powder
1 (15-ounce / 425-g) can white beans (cannellini or navy), drained and rinsed
½ cup whole-grain bread crumbs
Sea salt and ground black pepper, to taste

Marinara:

1 tablespoon extra-virgin olive oil
3 garlic cloves, minced
Handful basil leaves
1 (28-ounce / 794-g) can chopped tomatoes with juice reserved
Sea salt, to taste

Make the Bean Balls

1. Preheat the oven to 350°F (180°C). Line a baking sheet with parchment paper.
2. Heat the olive oil in a nonstick skillet over medium heat until shimmering.
3. Add the onion and sauté for 5 minutes or until translucent.
4. Sprinkle with fennel seeds, oregano, red pepper flakes, and garlic powder, then cook for 1 minute or until aromatic.
5. Pour the sautéed mixture in a food processor and add the beans and bread crumbs. Sprinkle with salt and ground black pepper, then pulse to combine well and the mixture holds together.
6. Shape the mixture into balls with a 2-ounce (57-g) cookie scoop, then arrange the balls on the baking sheet.
7. Bake in the preheated oven for 30 minutes or until lightly browned. Flip the balls halfway through the cooking time.

Make the Marinara

1. While baking the bean balls, heat the olive oil in a saucepan over medium-high heat until shimmering.
2. Add the garlic and basil and sauté for 2 minutes or until fragrant.
3. Fold in the tomatoes and juice. Bring to a boil. Reduce the heat to low. Put the lid on and simmer for 15 minutes. Sprinkle with salt.
4. Transfer the bean balls on a large plate and baste with marinara before serving.

Tips: Wet your hands while shaping the bean balls to avoid sticking.
To make this a complete meal, you can serve the balls and the sauce with all kinds of cooked pasta, such as pappardelle pasta, corkscrew pasta, farfalle pasta, or shell pasta.

Per Serving

calories: 351 | fat: 16.4g | protein: 11.5g carbs: 42.9g | fiber: 10.3g | sodium: 377mg

Italian Sautéd Cannellini Beans

Prep time: 10 minutes | Cook time: 15 minutes | Serves 6

2 teaspoons extra-virgin olive oil
½ cup minced onion
¼ cup red wine vinegar
1 (12-ounce / 340-g) can no-salt-added tomato paste
2 tablespoons raw honey
½ cup water
¼ teaspoon ground cinnamon
2 (15-ounce / 425-g) cans cannellini beans

1. Heat the olive oil in a saucepan over medium heat until shimmering.
2. Add the onion and sauté for 5 minutes or until translucent.
3. Pour in the red wine vinegar, tomato paste, honey, and water. Sprinkle with cinnamon. Stir to mix well.
4. Reduce the heat to low, then pour all the beans into the saucepan. Cook for 10 more minutes. Stir constantly.
5. Serve immediately.

Tip: If you want to remove as much salt that contains in the canned beans as possible, drain the canned beans in a colander and rinse under running cold water, then pat dry with paper towels.

Per Serving

calories: 435 | fat: 2.1g | protein: 26.2g carbs: 80.3g | fiber: 24.0g | sodium: 72mg

Baked Rolled Oat with Pears and Pecans

Prep time: 15 minutes | Cook time: 30 minutes | Serves 6

2 tablespoons coconut oil, melted, plus more for greasing the pan
3 ripe pears, cored and diced
2 cups unsweetened almond milk
1 tablespoon pure vanilla extract
¼ cup pure maple syrup
2 cups gluten-free rolled oats
½ cup raisins
¾ cup chopped pecans
¼ teaspoon ground nutmeg
1 teaspoon ground cinnamon
½ teaspoon ground ginger
¼ teaspoon sea salt

1. Preheat the oven to 350ºF (180ºC). Grease a baking dish with melted coconut oil, then spread the pears in a single layer on the baking dish evenly.
2. Combine the almond milk, vanilla extract, maple syrup, and coconut oil in a bowl. Stir to mix well.
3. Combine the remaining ingredients in a separate large bowl. Stir to mix well. Fold the almond milk mixture in the bowl, then pour the mixture over the pears.
4. Place the baking dish in the preheated oven and bake for 30 minutes or until lightly browned and set.
5. Serve immediately.

Tip: Instead of raisins, you can also use dried berries, apricots, or currants.

Per Serving
calories: 479 | fat: 34.9g | protein: 8.8g
carbs: 50.1g | fiber: 10.8g | sodium: 113mg

Rich Cauliflower Alfredo

Prep time: 35 minutes | Cook time: 30 minutes | Serves 4

Cauliflower Alfredo Sauce:
1 tablespoon avocado oil
½ yellow onion, diced
2 cups cauliflower florets
2 garlic cloves, minced
1½ teaspoons miso
1 teaspoon Dijon mustard
Pinch of ground nutmeg
½ cup unsweetened almond milk
1½ tablespoons fresh lemon juice
2 tablespoons nutritional yeast
Sea salt and ground black pepper, to taste

Fettuccine:
1 tablespoon avocado oil
½ yellow onion, diced
1 cup broccoli florets
1 zucchini, halved lengthwise and cut into ¼-inch-thick half-moons
Sea salt and ground black pepper, to taste
½ cup sun-dried tomatoes, drained if packed in oil
8 ounces (227 g) cooked whole-wheat fettuccine
½ cup fresh basil, cut into ribbons

Make the Sauce:
1. Heat the avocado oil in a nonstick skillet over medium-high heat until shimmering.
2. Add half of the onion to the skillet and sauté for 5 minutes or until translucent.
3. Add the cauliflower and garlic to the skillet. Reduce the heat to low and cook for 8 minutes or until the cauliflower is tender.
4. Pour them in a food processor, add the remaining ingredients for the sauce and pulse to combine well. Set aside.

Make the Fettuccine:
1. Heat the avocado oil in a nonstick skillet over medium-high heat.
2. Add the remaining half of onion and sauté for 5 minutes or until translucent.
3. Add the broccoli and zucchini. Sprinkle with salt and ground black pepper, then sauté for 5 minutes or until tender.
4. Add the sun-dried tomatoes, reserved sauce, and fettuccine. Sauté for 3 minutes or until well-coated and heated through.
5. Serve the fettuccine on a large plate and spread with basil before serving.

Tip: How to cook the fettuccine: Bring a large pot of water to a boil, then add the fettuccine and cook for 8 minutes or until al dente. Drain the fettuccine in a colander before using.

Per Serving
calories: 288 | fat: 15.9g | protein: 10.1g
carbs: 32.5g | fiber: 8.1g | sodium: 185mg

Black Bean Chili with Mangoes

Prep time: 10 minutes | Cook time: 10 minutes | Serves 4

2 tablespoons coconut oil
1 onion, chopped
2 (15-ounce / 425-g) cans black beans, drained and rinsed
1 tablespoon chili powder
1 teaspoon sea salt
¼ teaspoon freshly ground black pepper
1 cup water
2 ripe mangoes, sliced thinly
¼ cup chopped fresh cilantro, divided
¼ cup sliced scallions, divided

1. Heat the coconut oil in a pot over high heat until melted.
2. Put the onion in the pot and sauté for 5 minutes or until translucent.
3. Add the black beans to the pot. Sprinkle with chili powder, salt, and ground black pepper. Pour in the water. Stir to mix well.
4. Bring to a boil. Reduce the heat to low, then simmering for 5 minutes or until the beans are tender.
5. Turn off the heat and mix in the mangoes, then garnish with scallions and cilantro before serving.

Tip: If you don't like to add the sweet taste of mango into the chili, you can replace the mango with avocado chunks, chopped tomatoes, carrots, or potato cubes.

Per Serving
calories: 430 | fat: 9.1g | protein: 20.2g
carbs: 71.9g | fiber: 22.0g | sodium: 608mg

Hearty Butternut Spinach, and Cheeses Lasagna

Prep time: 30 minutes | Cook time: 3 hours 45 minutes | Serves 4 to 6

2 tablespoons extra-virgin olive oil, divided
1 butternut squash, halved lengthwise and deseeded
½ teaspoon sage
½ teaspoon sea salt
¼ teaspoon ground black pepper
¼ cup grated Parmesan cheese
2 cups ricotta cheese
½ cup unsweetened almond milk
5 layers whole-wheat lasagna noodles (about 12 ounces / 340 g in total)
4 ounces (113 g) fresh spinach leaves, divided
½ cup shredded part skim Mozzarella, for garnish

1. Preheat the oven to 400ºF (205ºC). Line a baking sheet with parchment paper.
2. Brush 1 tablespoon of olive oil on the cut side of the butternut squash, then place the squash on the baking sheet.
3. Bake in the preheated oven for 45 minutes or until the squash is tender.
4. Allow to cool until you can handle it, then scoop the flesh out and put the flesh in a food processor to purée.
5. Combine the puréed butternut squash flesh with sage, salt, and ground black pepper in a large bowl. Stir to mix well.
6. Combine the cheeses and milk in a separate bowl, then sprinkle with salt and pepper, to taste.
7. Grease the slow cooker with 1 tablespoon of olive oil, then add a layer of lasagna noodles to coat the bottom of the slow cooker.
8. Spread half of the squash mixture on top of the noodles, then top the squash mixture with another layer of lasagna noodles.
9. Spread half of the spinach over the noodles, then top the spinach with half of cheese mixture. Repeat with remaining 3 layers of lasagna noodles, squash mixture, spinach, and cheese mixture.
10. Top the cheese mixture with Mozzarella, then put the lid on and cook on low for 3 hours or until the lasagna noodles are al dente.
11. Serve immediately.

Tip: To make this a complete meal, you can serve it with fresh cucumber soup and green leafy salad.

Per Serving
calories: 657 | fat: 37.1g | protein: 30.9g
carbs: 57.2g | fiber: 8.3g | sodium: 918mg

Israeli Style Eggplant and Chickpea Salad

Prep time: 5 minutes | Cook time: 20 minutes | Serves 6

2 tablespoons balsamic vinegar
2 tablespoons freshly squeezed lemon juice
1 teaspoon ground cumin
¼ teaspoon sea salt
2 tablespoons olive oil, divided
1 (1-pound / 454-g) medium globe eggplant, stem removed, cut into flat cubes (about ½ inch thick)
1 (15-ounce / 425-g) can chickpeas, drained and rinsed
¼ cup chopped mint leaves
1 cup sliced sweet onion
1 garlic clove, finely minced
1 tablespoon sesame seeds, toasted

1. Preheat the oven to 550ºF (288ºC) or the highest level of your oven or broiler. Grease a baking sheet with 1 tablespoon of olive oil.
2. Combine the balsamic vinegar, lemon juice, cumin, salt, and 1 tablespoon of olive oil in a small bowl. Stir to mix well.
3. Arrange the eggplant cubes on the baking sheet, then brush with 2 tablespoons of the balsamic vinegar mixture on both sides.
4. Broil in the preheated oven for 8 minutes or until lightly browned. Flip the cubes halfway through the cooking time.
5. Meanwhile, combine the chickpeas, mint, onion, garlic, and sesame seeds in a large serving bowl. Drizzle with remaining balsamic vinegar mixture. Stir to mix well.
6. Remove the eggplant from the oven. Allow to cool for 5 minutes, then slice them into ½-inch strips on a clean work surface.
7. Add the eggplant strips in the serving bowl, then toss to combine well before serving.

Tip: How to toast the sesame seeds: Before preheating the oven to 550ºF (288ºC), preheat it to 350ºF (180ºC). Pour the sesame seeds in a greased baking dish, then toast in the preheated oven for 8 minutes or until lightly browned and crispy. Stir periodically.

Per Serving
calories: 125 | fat: 2.9g | protein: 5.2g
carbs: 20.9g | fiber: 6.0g | sodium: 222mg

Caprese Pasta with Roasted Asparagus

Prep time: 5 minutes | Cook time: 25 minutes | Serves 6

8 ounces (227 g) uncooked small pasta, like orecchiette (little ears) or farfalle (bow ties)
1½ pounds (680 g) fresh asparagus, ends trimmed and stalks chopped into 1-inch pieces
1½ cups grape tomatoes, halved
2 tablespoons extra-virgin olive oil
¼ teaspoon kosher salt
¼ teaspoon freshly ground black pepper
2 cups fresh Mozzarella, drained and cut into bite-size pieces (about 8 ounces / 227 g)
⅓ cup torn fresh basil leaves
2 tablespoons balsamic vinegar

1. Preheat the oven to 400ºF (205ºC).
2. In a large stockpot of salted water, cook the pasta for about 8 to 10 minutes. Drain and reserve about ¼ cup of the cooking liquid.
3. Meanwhile, in a large bowl, toss together the asparagus, tomatoes, oil, salt and pepper. Spread the mixture onto a large, rimmed baking sheet and bake in the oven for 15 minutes, stirring twice during cooking.
4. Remove the vegetables from the oven and add the cooked pasta to the baking sheet. Mix with a few tablespoons of cooking liquid to help the sauce become smoother and the saucy vegetables stick to the pasta.
5. Gently mix in the Mozzarella and basil. Drizzle with the balsamic vinegar. Serve from the baking sheet or pour the pasta into a large bowl.

Per Serving
calories: 147 | fat: 3.0g | protein: 16.0g
carbs: 17.0g | fiber: 5.0g | sodium: 420mg

Spaghetti with Pine Nuts and Cheese

Prep time: 10 minutes | Cook time: 11 minutes | Serves 4 to 6

8 ounces (227 g) spaghetti	ground black pepper
4 tablespoons almond butter	½ cup pine nuts
1 teaspoon freshly	1 cup fresh grated Parmesan cheese, divided

1. Bring a large pot of salted water to a boil. Add the pasta and cook for 8 minutes.
2. In a large saucepan over medium heat, combine the butter, black pepper, and pine nuts. Cook for 2 to 3 minutes, or until the pine nuts are lightly toasted.
3. Reserve ½ cup of the pasta water. Drain the pasta and place it into the pan with the pine nuts.
4. Add ¾ cup of the Parmesan cheese and the reserved pasta water to the pasta and toss everything together to evenly coat the pasta.
5. Transfer the pasta to a serving dish and top with the remaining ¼ cup of the Parmesan cheese. Serve immediately.

Per Serving
calories: 542 | fat: 32.0g | protein: 20.0g
carbs: 46.0g | fiber: 2.0g | sodium: 552mg

Papaya, Jicama, and Peas Rice Bowl

Prep time: 20 minutes | Cook time: 45 minutes | Serves 4

Sauce:

Juice of ¼ lemon	honey
2 teaspoons chopped fresh basil	1 tablespoon extra-virgin olive oil
1 tablespoon raw	Sea salt, to taste

Rice:

1½ cups wild rice	julienned
2 papayas, peeled, seeded, and diced	2 cups shredded cabbage
1 jicama, peeled and shredded	1 scallion, white and green parts, chopped
1 cup snow peas,	

1. Combine the ingredients for the sauce in a bowl. Stir to mix well. Set aside until ready to use.

2. Pour the wild rice in a saucepan, then pour in enough water to cover. Bring to a boil.
3. Reduce the heat to low, then simmer for 45 minutes or until the wild rice is soft and plump. Drain and transfer to a large serving bowl.
4. Top the rice with papayas, jicama, peas, cabbage, and scallion. Pour the sauce over and stir to mix well before serving.

Tip: Instead of papaya, you can also use pineapple, peaches, apples, or cherry tomatoes.

Per Serving
calories: 446 | fat: 7.9g | protein: 13.1g
carbs: 85.8g | fiber: 16.0g | sodium: 70mg

Black-Eyed Peas Salad with Walnuts

Prep time: 10 minutes | Cook time: 0 minutes | Serves 4 to 6

3 tablespoons extra-virgin olive oil	or more to taste
3 tablespoons dukkah, divided	2 (15-ounce / 425-g) cans black-eyed peas, rinsed
2 tablespoons lemon juice	½ cup pomegranate seeds
2 tablespoons pomegranate molasses	½ cup minced fresh parsley
¼ teaspoon salt, or more to taste	½ cup walnuts, toasted and chopped
⅛ teaspoon pepper,	4 scallions, sliced thinly

1. In a large bowl, whisk together the olive oil, 2 tablespoons of the dukkah, lemon juice, pomegranate molasses, salt and pepper.
2. Stir in the remaining ingredients. Season with salt and pepper.
3. Sprinkle with the remaining 1 tablespoon of the dukkah before serving.

Per Serving
calories: 155 | fat: 11.5g | protein: 2.0g
carbs: 12.5g | fiber: 2.1g | sodium: 105mg

Turkish Canned Pinto Bean Salad

Prep time: 10 minutes | Cook time: 3 minutes | Serves 4 to 6

¼ cup extra-virgin olive oil, divided
3 garlic cloves, lightly crushed and peeled
2 (15-ounce / 425-g) cans pinto beans, rinsed
2 cups plus 1 tablespoon water
Salt and pepper, to taste
¼ cup tahini
3 tablespoons lemon juice
1 tablespoon ground dried Aleppo pepper, plus extra for serving
8 ounces (227 g) cherry tomatoes, halved
¼ red onion, sliced thinly
½ cup fresh parsley leaves
2 hard-cooked large eggs, quartered
1 tablespoon toasted sesame seeds

1. Add 1 tablespoon of the olive oil and garlic to a medium saucepan over medium heat. Cook for about 3 minutes, stirring constantly, or until the garlic turns golden but not brown.
2. Add the beans, 2 cups of the water and 1 teaspoon salt and bring to a simmer. Remove from the heat, cover and let sit for 20 minutes. Drain the beans and discard the garlic.
3. In a large bowl, whisk together the remaining 3 tablespoons of the oil, tahini, lemon juice, Aleppo, the remaining 1 tablespoon of the water and ¼ teaspoon salt. Stir in the beans, tomatoes, onion and parsley. Season with salt and pepper to taste.
4. Transfer to a serving platter and top with the eggs. Sprinkle with the sesame seeds and extra Aleppo before serving.

Per Serving
calories: 402 | fat: 18.9g | protein: 16.2g
carbs: 44.4g | fiber: 11.2g | sodium: 456mg

Minestrone Chickpeas and Macaroni Casserole

Prep time: 20 minutes | Cook time: 7 hours 20 minutes | Serves 5

1 (15-ounce / 425-g) can chickpeas, drained and rinsed
1 (28-ounce / 794-g) can diced tomatoes, with the juice
1 (6-ounce / 170-g) can no-salt-added tomato paste
3 medium carrots, sliced
3 cloves garlic, minced
1 medium yellow onion, chopped
1 cup low-sodium vegetable soup
½ teaspoon dried rosemary
1 teaspoon dried oregano
2 teaspoons maple syrup
½ teaspoon sea salt
¼ teaspoon ground black pepper
½ pound (227-g) fresh green beans, trimmed and cut into bite-size pieces
1 cup macaroni pasta
2 ounces (57 g) Parmesan cheese, grated

1. Except for the green beans, pasta, and Parmesan cheese, combine all the ingredients in the slow cooker and stir to mix well.
2. Put the slow cooker lid on and cook on low for 7 hours.
3. Fold in the pasta and green beans. Put the lid on and cook on high for 20 minutes or until the vegetable are soft and the pasta is al dente.
4. Pour them in a large serving bowl and spread with Parmesan cheese before serving.

Tip: Instead of chickpeas, you can also use kidney beans, great northern beans, or cannellini beans.

Per Serving
calories: 349 | fat: 6.7g | protein: 16.5g
carbs: 59.9g | fiber: 12.9g | sodium: 937mg

Ritzy Veggie Chili

Prep time: 15 minutes | Cook time: 5 hours | Serves 4

1 (28-ounce / 794-g) can chopped tomatoes, with the juice
1 (15-ounce / 425-g) can black beans, drained and rinsed
1 (15-ounce / 425-g) can red beans, drained and rinsed
1 medium green bell pepper, chopped
1 yellow onion, chopped

1 tablespoon onion powder
1 teaspoon paprika
1 teaspoon cayenne pepper
1 teaspoon garlic powder
½ teaspoon sea salt
½ teaspoon ground black pepper
1 tablespoon olive oil
1 large hass avocado, pitted, peeled, and chopped, for garnish

1. Combine all the ingredients, except for the avocado, in the slow cooker. Stir to mix well.
2. Put the slow cooker lid on and cook on high for 5 hours or until the vegetables are tender and the mixture has a thick consistency.
3. Pour the chili in a large serving bowl. Allow to cool for 30 minutes, then spread with chopped avocado and serve.

Tip: If you don't like the canned tomatoes, then you can replace them with the same amount of freshly chopped tomatoes and let them sit in a large bowl with their juice.

Per Serving
calories: 633 | fat: 16.3g | protein: 31.7g
carbs: 97.0g | fiber: 28.9g | sodium: 792mg

Swoodles with Almond Butter Sauce

Prep time: 20 minutes | Cook time: 20 minutes | Serves 4

Sauce:
1 garlic clove
1-inch piece fresh ginger, peeled and sliced
¼ cup chopped yellow onion
¾ cup almond butter

1 tablespoon tamari
1 tablespoon raw honey
1 teaspoon paprika
1 tablespoon fresh lemon juice
⅛ teaspoon ground

red pepper
Sea salt and ground

black pepper, to taste
¼ cup water

Swoodles:
2 large sweet potatoes, spiralized
2 tablespoons

coconut oil, melted
Sea salt and ground black pepper, to taste

For Serving:
½ cup fresh parsley, chopped
½ cup thinly sliced scallions

Make the Sauce
1. Put the garlic, ginger, and onion in a food processor, then pulse to combine well.
2. Add the almond butter, tamari, honey, paprika, lemon juice, ground red pepper, salt, and black pepper to the food processor. Pulse to combine well. Pour in the water during the pulsing until the mixture is thick and smooth.

Make the Swoodles:
1. Preheat the oven to 425ºF (220ºC). Line a baking sheet with parchment paper.
2. Put the spiralized sweet potato in a bowl, then drizzle with olive oil. Toss to coat well. Transfer them on the baking sheet. Sprinkle with salt and pepper.
3. Bake in the preheated oven for 20 minutes or until lightly browned and al dente. Check the doneness during the baking and remove any well-cooked swoodles.
4. Transfer the swoodles on a large plate and spread with sauce, parsley, and scallions. Toss to serve.

Tips: To make this a complete meal, you can serve it along with cashew slaw.
You can use the store-bought swoodles or spiralize the sweet potatoes with spiralizer yourself.

Per Serving
calories: 441 | fat: 33.6g | protein: 12.0g
carbs: 29.6g | fiber: 7.8g | sodium: 479mg

Roasted Ratatouille Pasta

Prep time: 10 minutes | Cook time: 30 minutes | Serves 2

1 small eggplant (about 8 ounces / 227 g)
1 small zucchini
1 portobello mushroom
1 Roma tomato, halved
½ medium sweet red pepper, seeded
½ teaspoon salt, plus additional for the

pasta water
1 teaspoon Italian herb seasoning
1 tablespoon olive oil
2 cups farfalle pasta (about 8 ounces / 227 g)
2 tablespoons minced sun-dried tomatoes in olive oil with herbs
2 tablespoons prepared pesto

1. Slice the ends off the eggplant and zucchini. Cut them lengthwise into ½-inch slices.
2. Place the eggplant, zucchini, mushroom, tomato, and red pepper in a large bowl and sprinkle with ½ teaspoon of salt. Using your hands, toss the vegetables well so that they're covered evenly with the salt. Let them rest for about 10 minutes.
3. While the vegetables are resting, preheat the oven to 400ºF (205ºC). Line a baking sheet with parchment paper.
4. When the oven is hot, drain off any liquid from the vegetables and pat them dry with a paper towel. Add the Italian herb seasoning and olive oil to the vegetables and toss well to coat both sides.
5. Lay the vegetables out in a single layer on the baking sheet. Roast them for 15 to 20 minutes, flipping them over after about 10 minutes or once they start to brown on the underside. When the vegetables are charred in spots, remove them from the oven.
6. While the vegetables are roasting, fill a large saucepan with water. Add salt and cook the pasta until al dente, about 8 to 10 minutes. Drain the pasta, reserving ½ cup of the pasta water.
7. When cool enough to handle, cut the vegetables into large chunks (about 2 inches) and add them to the hot pasta.
8. Stir in the sun-dried tomatoes and pesto and toss everything well. Serve immediately.

Per Serving
calories: 613 | fat: 16.0g | protein: 23.1g
carbs: 108.5g | fiber: 23.0g | sodium: 775mg

Mediterranean Lentils

Prep time: 7 minutes | Cook time: 24 minutes | Serves 2

1 tablespoon olive oil
1 small sweet or yellow onion, diced
1 garlic clove, diced
1 teaspoon dried oregano
½ teaspoon ground cumin
½ teaspoon dried parsley
½ teaspoon salt, plus

more as needed
¼ teaspoon freshly ground black pepper, plus more as needed
1 tomato, diced
1 cup brown or green lentils
2½ cups vegetable stock
1 bay leaf

1. Set your Instant Pot to Sauté and heat the olive oil until it shimmers.
2. Add the onion and cook for 3 to 4 minutes until soft. Turn off the Instant Pot and add the garlic, oregano, cumin, parsley, salt, and pepper. Cook until fragrant, about 1 minute.
3. Stir in the tomato, lentils, stock, and bay leaf.
4. Lock the lid. Select the Manual mode and set the cooking time for 18 minutes at High Pressure.
5. When the timer beeps, perform a natural pressure release for 10 minutes, then release any remaining pressure. Carefully open the lid.
6. Remove and discard the bay leaf. Taste and season with more salt and pepper, as needed. If there's too much liquid remaining, select Sauté and cook until it evaporates.
7. Serve warm.

Per Serving
calories: 426 | fat: 8.1g | protein: 26.2g
carbs: 63.8g | fiber: 31.0g | sodium: 591mg

Roasted Butternut Squash and Zucchini with Penne

Prep time: 15 minutes | Cook time: 30 minutes | Serves 6

1 large zucchini, diced
1 large butternut squash, peeled and diced
1 large yellow onion, chopped
2 tablespoons extra-virgin olive oil
1 teaspoon paprika
½ teaspoon garlic powder
½ teaspoon sea salt
½ teaspoon freshly ground black pepper
1 pound (454 g) whole-grain penne
½ cup dry white wine
2 tablespoons grated Parmesan cheese

1. Preheat the oven to 400ºF (205ºC). Line a baking sheet with aluminum foil.
2. Combine the zucchini, butternut squash, and onion in a large bowl. Drizzle with olive oil and sprinkle with paprika, garlic powder, salt, and ground black pepper. Toss to coat well.
3. Spread the vegetables in the single layer on the baking sheet, then roast in the preheated oven for 25 minutes or until the vegetables are tender.
4. Meanwhile, bring a pot of water to a boil, then add the penne and cook for 14 minutes or until al dente. Drain the penne through a colander.
5. Transfer ½ cup of roasted vegetables in a food processor, then pour in the dry white wine. Pulse until smooth.
6. Pour the puréed vegetables in a nonstick skillet and cook with penne over medium-high heat for a few minutes to heat through.
7. Transfer the penne with the purée on a large serving plate, then spread the remaining roasted vegetables and Parmesan on top before serving.

Tip: Instead of dry white wine, you can use the same amount of low-sodium chicken broth to replace it.

Per Serving
calories: 340 | fat: 6.2g | protein: 8.0g
carbs: 66.8g | fiber: 9.1g | sodium: 297mg

Brown Rice Pilaf with Pistachios and Raisins

Prep time: 5 minutes | Cook time: 15 minutes | Serves 6

1 tablespoon extra-virgin olive oil
1 cup chopped onion
½ cup shredded carrot
½ teaspoon ground cinnamon
1 teaspoon ground cumin
2 cups brown rice
1¾ cups pure orange juice
¼ cup water
½ cup shelled pistachios
1 cup golden raisins
½ cup chopped fresh chives

1. Heat the olive oil in a saucepan over medium-high heat until shimmering.
2. Add the onion and sauté for 5 minutes or until translucent.
3. Add the carrots, cinnamon, and cumin, then sauté for 1 minutes or until aromatic.
4. Pour int the brown rice, orange juice, and water. Bring to a boil. Reduce the heat to medium-low and simmer for 7 minutes or until the liquid is almost absorbed.
5. Transfer the rice mixture in a large serving bowl, then spread with pistachios, raisins, and chives. Serve immediately.

Tip: Instead of using water to cook the brown rice, you can also use unsweetened coconut milk or vegetable soup to increase the nutrition and flavor of the rice.

Per Serving
calories: 264 | fat: 7.1g | protein: 5.2g
carbs: 48.9g | fiber: 4.0g | sodium: 86mg

Garlic and Parsley Chickpeas

Prep time: 10 minutes | Cook time: 18 to 20 minutes | Serves 4 to 6

¼ cup extra-virgin olive oil, divided
4 garlic cloves, sliced thinly
⅛ teaspoon red pepper flakes
1 onion, chopped finely
¼ teaspoon salt, plus more to taste
Black pepper, to taste
2 (15-ounce / 425-g) cans chickpeas, rinsed
1 cup vegetable broth
2 tablespoons minced fresh parsley
2 teaspoons lemon juice

1. Add 3 tablespoons of the olive oil, garlic, and pepper flakes to a skillet over medium heat. Cook for about 3 minutes, stirring constantly, or until the garlic turns golden but not brown.
2. Stir in the onion and ¼ teaspoon salt and cook for 5 to 7 minutes, or until softened and lightly browned.
3. Add the chickpeas and broth to the skillet and bring to a simmer. Reduce the heat to medium-low, cover, and cook for about 7 minutes, or until the chickpeas are cooked through and flavors meld.
4. Uncover, increase the heat to high and continue to cook for about 3 minutes more, or until nearly all liquid has evaporated.
5. Turn off the heat, stir in the parsley and lemon juice. Season to taste with salt and pepper and drizzle with remaining 1 tablespoon of the olive oil.
6. Serve warm.

Per Serving
calories: 220 | fat: 11.4g | protein: 6.5g
carbs: 24.6g | fiber: 6.0g | sodium: 467mg

Tomato Sauce and Basil Pesto Fettuccine

Prep time: 15 minutes | Cook time: 15 minutes | Serves 4

4 Roma tomatoes, diced
2 teaspoons no-salt-added tomato paste
1 tablespoon chopped fresh oregano
2 garlic cloves, minced
1 cup low-sodium vegetable soup
½ teaspoon sea salt
1 packed cup fresh basil leaves
¼ cup pine nuts
¼ cup grated Parmesan cheese
2 tablespoons extra-virgin olive oil
1 pound (454 g) cooked whole-grain fettuccine

1. Put the tomatoes, tomato paste, oregano, garlic, vegetable soup, and salt in a skillet. Stir to mix well.
2. Cook over medium heat for 10 minutes or until lightly thickened.
3. Put the remaining ingredients, except for the fettuccine, in a food processor and pulse to combine until smooth.
4. Pour the puréed basil mixture into the tomato mixture, then add the fettuccine. Cook for a few minutes or until heated through and the fettuccine is well coated.
5. Serve immediately.

Tip: How to cook the fettuccine: Bring a large pot of water to a boil, then add the fettuccine and cook for 8 minutes or until al dente. Drain the fettuccine in a colander before using.

Per Serving
calories: 389 | fat: 22.7g | protein: 9.7g
carbs: 40.2g | fiber: 4.8g | sodium: 616mg

Cherry, Apricot, and Pecan Brown Rice Bowl

Prep time: 15 minutes | Cook time: 1 hour 1 minutes | Serves 2

2 tablespoons olive oil
2 green onions, sliced
½ cup brown rice
1 cup low -sodium chicken stock
2 tablespoons dried cherries
4 dried apricots, chopped
2 tablespoons pecans, toasted and chopped
Sea salt and freshly ground pepper, to taste

1. Heat the olive oil in a medium saucepan over medium-high heat until shimmering.
2. Add the green onions and sauté for 1 minutes or until fragrant.
3. Add the rice. Stir to mix well, then pour in the chicken stock.
4. Bring to a boil. Reduce the heat to low. Cover and simmer for 50 minutes or until the brown rice is soft.
5. Add the cherries, apricots, and pecans, and simmer for 10 more minutes or until the fruits are tender.
6. Pour them in a large serving bowl. Fluff with a fork. Sprinkle with sea salt and freshly ground pepper. Serve immediately.

Tip: How to toast the pecans: Put the pecans in a skillet and heat over medium heat or until golden brown and toasted. Stir constantly.

Per Serving
calories: 451 | fat: 25.9g | protein: 8.2g
carbs: 50.4g | fiber: 4.6g | sodium: 122mg

Cranberry and Almond Quinoa

Prep time: 5 minutes | Cook time: 10 minutes | Serves 2

2 cups water
1 cup quinoa, rinsed
¼ cup salted sunflower seeds
½ cup slivered almonds
1 cup dried cranberries

1. Combine water and quinoa in the Instant Pot.

2. Secure the lid. Select the Manual mode and set the cooking time for 10 minutes at High Pressure.
3. Once cooking is complete, do a quick pressure release. Carefully open the lid.
4. Add sunflower seeds, almonds, and dried cranberries and gently mix until well combined.
5. Serve hot.

Per Serving
calories: 445 | fat: 14.8g | protein: 15.1g
carbs: 64.1g | fiber: 10.2g | sodium: 113mg

Curry Apple Couscous with Leeks and Pecans

Prep time: 10 minutes | Cook time: 8 minutes | Serves 4

2 teaspoons extra-virgin olive oil
2 leeks, white parts only, sliced
1 apple, diced
2 cups cooked
couscous
2 tablespoons curry powder
½ cup chopped pecans

1. Heat the olive oil in a skillet over medium heat until shimmering.
2. Add the leeks and sauté for 5 minutes or until soft.
3. Add the diced apple and cook for 3 more minutes until tender.
4. Add the couscous and curry powder. Stir to combine.
5. Transfer them in a large serving bowl, then mix in the pecans and serve.

Tip: How to cook the couscous: Bring a pot of water to a bowl, then sprinkle with salt and olive oil, if desired. Turn off the heat and pour the couscous in the pot. Cover and let sit for 10 minutes or until the couscous is tender.

Per Serving
calories: 254 | fat: 11.9g | protein: 5.4g
carbs: 34.3g | fiber: 5.9g | sodium: 15mg

Rice and Blueberry Stuffed Sweet Potatoes

Prep time: 15 minutes | Cook time: 20 minutes | Serves 4

2 cups cooked wild rice
½ cup dried blueberries
½ cup chopped hazelnuts
½ cup shredded Swiss chard
1 teaspoon chopped fresh thyme
1 scallion, white and green parts, peeled and thinly sliced
Sea salt and freshly ground black pepper, to taste
4 sweet potatoes, baked in the skin until tender

1. Preheat the oven to 400ºF (205ºC).
2. Combine all the ingredients, except for the sweet potatoes, in a large bowl. Stir to mix well.
3. Cut the top third of the sweet potato off length wire, then scoop most of the sweet potato flesh out.
4. Fill the potato with the wild rice mixture, then set the sweet potato on a greased baking sheet.
5. Bake in the preheated oven for 20 minutes or until the sweet potato skin is lightly charred.
6. Serve immediately.

Tip: You can mix the sweet potato flesh in the bowl of wild rice mixture and fill them back in the sweet potato skin.

Per Serving
calories: 393 | fat: 7.1g | protein: 10.2g
carbs: 76.9g | fiber: 10.0g | sodium: 93mg

Mint Brown Rice

Prep time: 5 minutes | Cook time: 22 minutes | Serves 2

2 cloves garlic, minced
¼ cup chopped fresh mint, plus more for garnish
1 tablespoon chopped dried chives
1 cup short- or long-grain brown rice
1½ cups water or low-sodium vegetable broth
½ to 1 teaspoon sea salt

1. Place the garlic, mint, chives, rice, and water in the Instant Pot. Stir to combine.
2. Secure the lid. Select the Manual mode and set the cooking time for 22 minutes at High Pressure.
3. Once cooking is complete, do a natural pressure release for 10 minutes, then release any remaining pressure. Carefully open the lid.
4. Add salt to taste. Serve garnished with more mint.

Per Serving
calories: 514 | fat: 6.6g | protein: 20.7g
carbs: 80.4g | fiber: 3.3g | sodium: 786mg

Mashed Beans with Cumin

Prep time: 10 minutes | Cook time: 10 to 12 minutes | Serves 4 to 6

1 tablespoon extra-virgin olive oil, plus extra for serving
4 garlic cloves, minced
1 teaspoon ground cumin
2 (15-ounce / 425-g) cans fava beans
3 tablespoons tahini
2 tablespoons lemon juice, plus lemon
wedges for serving
Salt and pepper, to taste
1 tomato, cored and cut into ½-inch pieces
1 small onion, chopped finely
2 hard-cooked large eggs, chopped
2 tablespoons minced fresh parsley

1. Add the olive oil, garlic and cumin to a medium saucepan over medium heat. Cook for about 2 minutes, or until fragrant.
2. Stir in the beans with their liquid and tahini. Bring to a simmer and cook for 8 to 10 minutes, or until the liquid thickens slightly.
3. Turn off the heat, mash the beans to a coarse consistency with a potato masher. Stir in the lemon juice and 1 teaspoon pepper. Season with salt and pepper.
4. Transfer the mashed beans to a serving dish. Top with the tomato, onion, eggs and parsley. Drizzle with the extra olive oil.
5. Serve with the lemon wedges.

Per Serving
calories: 125 | fat: 8.6g | protein: 4.9g
carbs: 9.1g | fiber: 2.9g | sodium: 131mg

Lebanese Flavor Broken Thin Noodles

Prep time: 10 minutes | Cook time: 25 minutes | Serves 6

1 tablespoon extra-virgin olive oil
1 (3-ounce / 85-g) cup vermicelli, broken into 1- to 1½-inch pieces
3 cups shredded cabbage
1 cup brown rice
3 cups low-sodium vegetable soup
½ cup water
2 garlic cloves, mashed
¼ teaspoon sea salt
⅛ teaspoon crushed red pepper flakes
½ cup coarsely chopped cilantro
Fresh lemon slices, for serving

1. Heat the olive oil in a saucepan over medium-high heat until shimmering.
2. Add the vermicelli and sauté for 3 minutes or until toasted.
3. Add the cabbage and sauté for 4 minutes or until tender.
4. Pour in the brown rice, vegetable soup, and water. Add the garlic and sprinkle with salt and red pepper flakes.
5. Bring to a boil over high heat. Reduce the heat to medium low. Put the lid on and simmer for another 10 minutes.
6. Turn off the heat, then let sit for 5 minutes without opening the lid.
7. Pour them on a large serving platter and spread with cilantro. Squeeze the lemon slices over and serve warm.

Tip: Instead of vermicelli, you can also use thin spaghetti.

Per Serving
calories: 127 | fat: 3.1g | protein: 4.2g
carbs: 22.9g | fiber: 3.0g | sodium: 224mg

Lemony Farro and Avocado Bowl

Prep time: 5 minutes | Cook time: 25 minutes | Serves 4

1 tablespoon plus 2 teaspoons extra-virgin olive oil, divided
½ medium onion, chopped
1 carrot, shredded
2 garlic cloves, minced
1 (6-ounce / 170-g) cup pearled farro
2 cups low-sodium vegetable soup
2 avocados, peeled, pitted, and sliced
Zest and juice of 1 small lemon
¼ teaspoon sea salt

1. Heat 1 tablespoon of olive oil in a saucepan over medium-high heat until shimmering.
2. Add the onion and sauté for 5 minutes or until translucent.
3. Add the carrot and garlic and sauté for 1 minute or until fragrant.
4. Add the farro and pour in the vegetable soup. Bring to a boil over high heat. Reduce the heat to low. Put the lid on and simmer for 20 minutes or until the farro is al dente.
5. Transfer the farro in a large serving bowl, then fold in the avocado slices. Sprinkle with lemon zest and salt, then drizzle with lemon juice and 2 teaspoons of olive oil.
6. Stir to mix well and serve immediately.

Tip: You can use a citrus zester to zest the lemon, then cut the lemon into wedges and squeeze the lemon juice over the farro bowl.

Per Serving
calories: 210 | fat: 11.1g | protein: 4.2g
carbs: 27.9g | fiber: 7.0g | sodium: 152mg

Easy Walnut and Ricotta Spaghetti

Prep time: 15 minutes | Cook time: 10 minutes | Serves 6

1 pound (454 g) cooked whole-wheat spaghetti
2 tablespoons extra-virgin olive oil
4 cloves garlic, minced
¾ cup walnuts, toasted and finely chopped
2 tablespoons ricotta cheese
¼ cup flat-leaf parsley, chopped
½ cup grated Parmesan cheese
Sea salt and freshly ground pepper, to taste

1. Reserve a cup of spaghetti water while cooking the spaghetti.
2. Heat the olive oil in a nonstick skillet over medium-low heat or until shimmering.
3. Add the garlic and sauté for a minute or until fragrant.
4. Pour the spaghetti water into the skillet and cook for 8 more minutes.
5. Turn off the heat and mix in the walnuts and ricotta cheese.
6. Put the cooked spaghetti on a large serving plate, then pour the walnut sauce over. Spread with parsley and Parmesan, then sprinkle with salt and ground pepper. Toss to serve.

Tip: How to cook the spaghetti: Bring a large pot of water to a boil, then add the spaghetti and cook for 10 minutes or until al dente. Drain the spaghetti in a colander before using.

Per Serving
calories: 264 | fat: 16.8g | protein: 8.6g
carbs: 22.8g | fiber: 4.0g | sodium: 336mg

Small Pasta and Beans Pot

Prep time: 20 minutes | Cook time: 15 minutes | Serves 2 to 4

1 pound (454 g) small whole wheat pasta
1 (14.5-ounce / 411-g) can diced tomatoes, juice reserved
1 (15-ounce / 425-g) can cannellini beans, drained and rinsed
2 tablespoons no-salt-added tomato paste
1 red or yellow bell pepper, chopped
1 yellow onion, chopped
1 tablespoon Italian seasoning mix
3 garlic cloves, minced
¼ teaspoon crushed red pepper flakes, optional
1 tablespoon extra-virgin olive oil
5 cups water
1 bunch kale, stemmed and chopped
½ cup pitted Kalamata olives, chopped
1 cup sliced basil

1. Except for the kale, olives, and basil, combine all the ingredients in a pot. Stir to mix well. Bring to a boil over high heat. Stir constantly.
2. Reduce the heat to medium high and add the kale. Cook for 10 minutes or until the pasta is al dente. Stir constantly.
3. Transfer all of them on a large plate and serve with olives and basil on top.

Tip: You can use the small whole-wheat pasta like penne, farfalle, shell, corkscrew, macaroni, or alphabet pasta.

Per Serving
calories: 357 | fat: 7.6g | protein: 18.2g
carbs: 64.5g | fiber: 10.1g | sodium: 454mg

Fava and Garbanzo Bean Ful

Prep time: 10 minutes | Cook time: 10 minutes | Serves 6

1 (15-ounce / 425-g) can fava beans, rinsed and drained
1 (1-pound / 454-g) can garbanzo beans, rinsed and drained
3 cups water
½ cup lemon juice
3 cloves garlic, peeled and minced
1 teaspoon salt
3 tablespoons extra-virgin olive oil

1. In a pot over medium heat, cook the beans and water for 10 minutes.
2. Drain the beans and transfer to a bowl. Reserve 1 cup of the liquid from the cooked beans.
3. Add the reserved liquid, lemon juice, minced garlic and salt to the bowl with the beans. Mix to combine well. Using a potato masher, mash up about half the beans in the bowl.
4. Give the mixture one more stir to make sure the beans are evenly mixed.
5. Drizzle with the olive oil and serve.

Per Serving
calories: 199 | fat: 9.0g | protein: 10.0g
carbs: 25.0g | fiber: 9.0g | sodium: 395mg

Triple-Green Pasta with Cheese

Prep time: 5 minutes | Cook time: 14 to 16 minutes | Serves 4

8 ounces (227 g) uncooked penne
1 tablespoon extra-virgin olive oil
2 garlic cloves, minced
¼ teaspoon crushed red pepper
2 cups chopped fresh flat-leaf parsley, including stems
5 cups loosely packed baby spinach
¼ teaspoon ground nutmeg
¼ teaspoon kosher salt
¼ teaspoon freshly ground black pepper
⅓ cup Castelvetrano olives, pitted and sliced
⅓ cup grated Parmesan cheese

1. In a large stockpot of salted water, cook the pasta for about 8 to 10 minutes. Drain the pasta and reserve ¼ cup of the cooking liquid.
2. Meanwhile, heat the olive oil in a large skillet over medium heat. Add the garlic and red pepper and cook for 30 seconds, stirring constantly.
3. Add the parsley and cook for 1 minute, stirring constantly. Add the spinach, nutmeg, salt, and pepper, and cook for 3 minutes, stirring occasionally, or until the spinach is wilted.
4. Add the cooked pasta and the reserved ¼ cup cooking liquid to the skillet. Stir in the olives and cook for about 2 minutes, or until most of the pasta water has been absorbed.
5. Remove from the heat and stir in the cheese before serving.

Per Serving
calories: 262 | fat: 4.0g | protein: 15.0g
carbs: 51.0g | fiber: 13.0g | sodium: 1180mg

Garlic Shrimp Fettuccine

Prep time: 10 minutes | Cook time: 15 minutes | Serves 4 to 6

8 ounces (227 g) fettuccine pasta
¼ cup extra-virgin olive oil
3 tablespoons garlic, minced
1 pound (454 g) large shrimp, peeled
and deveined
⅓ cup lemon juice
1 tablespoon lemon zest
½ teaspoon salt
½ teaspoon freshly ground black pepper

1. Bring a large pot of salted water to a boil. Add the fettuccine and cook for 8 minutes. Reserve ½ cup of the cooking liquid and drain the pasta.
2. In a large saucepan over medium heat, heat the olive oil. Add the garlic and sauté for 1 minute.
3. Add the shrimp to the saucepan and cook each side for 3 minutes. Remove the shrimp from the pan and set aside.
4. Add the remaining ingredients to the saucepan. Stir in the cooking liquid. Add the pasta and toss together to evenly coat the pasta.
5. Transfer the pasta to a serving dish and serve topped with the cooked shrimp.

Per Serving
calories: 615 | fat: 17.0g | protein: 33.0g
carbs: 89.0g | fiber: 4.0g | sodium: 407mg

Easy Simple Pesto Pasta

Prep time: 10 minutes | Cook time: 8 minutes | Serves 4 to 6

1 pound (454 g) spaghetti
4 cups fresh basil leaves, stems removed
3 cloves garlic
1 teaspoon salt
½ teaspoon freshly

ground black pepper
½ cup toasted pine nuts
¼ cup lemon juice
½ cup grated Parmesan cheese
1 cup extra-virgin olive oil

1. Bring a large pot of salted water to a boil. Add the spaghetti to the pot and cook for 8 minutes.
2. In a food processor, place the remaining ingredients, except for the olive oil, and pulse.
3. While the processor is running, slowly drizzle the olive oil through the top opening. Process until all the olive oil has been added.
4. Reserve ½ cup of the cooking liquid. Drain the pasta and put it into a large bowl. Add the pesto and cooking liquid to the bowl of pasta and toss everything together.
5. Serve immediately.

Per Serving
calories: 1067 | fat: 72.0g | protein: 23.0g
carbs: 91..0g | fiber: 6.0g | sodium: 817mg

Creamy Garlic Parmesan Chicken Pasta

Prep time: 5 minutes | Cook time: 15 minutes | Serves 4

3 tablespoons extra-virgin olive oil
2 boneless, skinless chicken breasts, cut into thin strips
1 large onion, thinly sliced
3 tablespoons garlic, minced
1½ teaspoons salt

1 pound (454 g) fettuccine pasta
1 cup heavy whipping cream
¾ cup freshly grated Parmesan cheese, divided
½ teaspoon freshly ground black pepper

1. In a large skillet over medium heat, heat the olive oil. Add the chicken and cook for 3 minutes.
2. Add the onion, garlic and salt to the skillet. Cook for 7 minutes, stirring occasionally.
3. Meanwhile, bring a large pot of salted water to a boil and add the pasta, then cook for 7 minutes.
4. While the pasta is cooking, add the heavy cream, ½ cup of the Parmesan cheese and black pepper to the chicken. Simmer for 3 minutes.
5. Reserve ½ cup of the pasta water. Drain the pasta and add it to the chicken cream sauce.
6. Add the reserved pasta water to the pasta and toss together. Simmer for 2 minutes. Top with the remaining ¼ cup of the Parmesan cheese and serve warm.

Per Serving
calories: 879 | fat: 42.0g | protein: 35.0g
carbs: 90.0g | fiber: 5.0g | sodium: 1336mg

Bulgur Pilaf with Garbanzo

Prep time: 5 minutes | Cook time: 20 minutes | Serves 4 to 6

3 tablespoons extra-virgin olive oil
1 large onion, chopped
1 (1-pound / 454-g) can garbanzo beans, rinsed and drained

2 cups bulgur wheat, rinsed and drained
1½ teaspoons salt
½ teaspoon cinnamon
4 cups water

1. In a large pot over medium heat, heat the olive oil. Add the onion and cook for 5 minutes.
2. Add the garbanzo beans and cook for an additional 5 minutes.
3. Stir in the remaining ingredients.
4. Reduce the heat to low. Cover and cook for 10 minutes.
5. When done, fluff the pilaf with a fork. Cover and let sit for another 5 minutes before serving.

Per Serving
calories: 462 | fat: 13.0g | protein: 15.0g
carbs: 76.0g | fiber: 19.0g | sodium: 890mg

Israeli Couscous with Asparagus

Prep time: 5 minutes | Cook time: 25 minutes | Serves 6

1½ pounds (680 g) asparagus spears, ends trimmed and stalks chopped into 1-inch pieces
1 garlic clove, minced
1 tablespoon extra-virgin olive oil
¼ teaspoon freshly ground black pepper
1¾ cups water

1 (8-ounce / 227-g) box uncooked whole-wheat or regular Israeli couscous (about 1⅓ cups)
¼ teaspoon kosher salt
1 cup garlic-and-herb goat cheese, at room temperature

1. Preheat the oven to 425ºF (220ºC).
2. In a large bowl, stir together the asparagus, garlic, oil, and pepper. Spread the asparagus on a large, rimmed baking sheet and roast for 10 minutes, stirring a few times. Remove the pan from the oven, and spoon the asparagus into a large serving bowl. Set aside.
3. While the asparagus is roasting, bring the water to a boil in a medium saucepan. Add the couscous and season with salt, stirring well.
4. Reduce the heat to medium-low. Cover and cook for 12 minutes, or until the water is absorbed.
5. Pour the hot couscous into the bowl with the asparagus. Add the goat cheese and mix thoroughly until completely melted.
6. Serve immediately.

Per Serving
calories: 103 | fat: 2.0g | protein: 6.0g
carbs: 18.0g | fiber: 5.0g | sodium: 343mg

Freekeh Pilaf with Dates and Pistachios

Prep time: 10 minutes | Cook time: 10 minutes | Serves 4 to 6

2 tablespoons extra-virgin olive oil, plus extra for drizzling
1 shallot, minced
1½ teaspoons grated fresh ginger
¼ teaspoon ground

coriander
¼ teaspoon ground cumin
Salt and pepper, to taste
1¾ cups water
1½ cups cracked

freekeh, rinsed
3 ounces (85 g) pitted dates, chopped
¼ cup shelled pistachios, toasted

and coarsely chopped
1½ tablespoons lemon juice
¼ cup chopped fresh mint

1. Set the Instant Pot to Sauté mode and heat the olive oil until shimmering.
2. Add the shallot, ginger, coriander, cumin, salt, and pepper to the pot and cook for about 2 minutes, or until the shallot is softened. Stir in the water and freekeh.
3. Secure the lid. Select the Manual mode and set the cooking time for 4 minutes at High Pressure. Once cooking is complete, do a quick pressure release. Carefully open the lid.
4. Add the dates, pistachios and lemon juice and gently fluff the freekeh with a fork to combine. Season to taste with salt and pepper.
5. Transfer to a serving dish and sprinkle with the mint. Serve drizzled with extra olive oil.

Per Serving
calories: 280 | fat: 8.0g | protein: 8.0g
carbs: 46.0g | fiber: 9.0g | sodium: 200mg

Quinoa with Baby Potatoes and Broccoli

Prep time: 5 minutes | Cook time: 10 minutes | Serves 4

2 tablespoons olive oil
1 cup baby potatoes, cut in half
1 cup broccoli florets

2 cups cooked quinoa
Zest of 1 lemon
Sea salt and freshly ground pepper, to taste

1. Heat the olive oil in a large skillet over medium heat until shimmering.
2. Add the potatoes and cook for about 6 to 7 minutes, or until softened and golden brown. Add the broccoli and cook for about 3 minutes, or until tender.
3. Remove from the heat and add the quinoa and lemon zest. Season with salt and pepper to taste, then serve.

Per Serving
calories: 205 | fat: 8.6g | protein: 5.1g
carbs: 27.3g | fiber: 3.7g | sodium: 158mg

Black-Eyed Pea and Vegetable Stew

Prep time: 15 minutes | Cook time: 40 minutes | Serves 2

½ cup black-eyed peas, soaked in water overnight
3 cups water, plus more as needed
1 large carrot, peeled and cut into ½-inch pieces (about ¾ cup)
1 large beet, peeled and cut into ½-inch pieces (about ¾ cup)
¼ teaspoon turmeric
¼ teaspoon cayenne pepper
¼ teaspoon ground cumin seeds, toasted
¼ cup finely chopped parsley
¼ teaspoon salt (optional)
½ teaspoon fresh lime juice

1. Pour the black-eyed peas and water into a large pot, then cook over medium heat for 25 minutes.
2. Add the carrot and beet to the pot and cook for 10 minutes more, adding more water as needed.
3. Add the turmeric, cayenne pepper, cumin, and parsley to the pot and cook for another 6 minutes, or until the vegetables are softened. Stir the mixture periodically. Season with salt, if desired.
4. Serve drizzled with the fresh lime juice.

Per Serving
calories: 89 | fat: 0.7g | protein: 4.1g
carbs: 16.6g | fiber: 4.5g | sodium: 367mg

Chickpea Salad with Tomatoes and Basil

Prep time: 5 minutes | Cook time: 45 minutes | Serves 2

1 cup dried chickpeas, rinsed
1 quart water, or enough to cover the chickpeas by 3 to 4 inches
1½ cups halved grape tomatoes
1 cup chopped fresh basil leaves
2 to 3 tablespoons balsamic vinegar
½ teaspoon garlic powder
½ teaspoon salt, plus more as needed

1. In your Instant Pot, combine the chickpeas and water.
2. Secure the lid. Select the Manual mode and set the cooking time for 45 minutes at High Pressure.

3. Once cooking is complete, do a natural pressure release for 20 minutes, then release any remaining pressure. Carefully open the lid and drain the chickpeas. Refrigerate to cool (unless you want to serve this warm, which is good, too).
4. While the chickpeas cool, in a large bowl, stir together the basil, tomatoes, vinegar, garlic powder, and salt. Add the beans, stir to combine, and serve.

Per Serving
calories: 395 | fat: 6.0g | protein: 19.8g
carbs: 67.1g | fiber: 19.0g | sodium: 612mg

Bean and Veggie Pasta

Prep time: 10 minutes | Cook time: 15 minutes | Serves 2

16 ounces (454 g) small whole wheat pasta, such as penne, farfalle, or macaroni
5 cups water
1 (15-ounce / 425-g) can cannellini beans, drained and rinsed
1 (14.5-ounce / 411-g) can diced (with juice) or crushed tomatoes
1 yellow onion, chopped
1 red or yellow bell pepper, chopped
2 tablespoons tomato paste
1 tablespoon olive oil
3 garlic cloves, minced
¼ teaspoon crushed red pepper (optional)
1 bunch kale, stemmed and chopped
1 cup sliced basil
½ cup pitted Kalamata olives, chopped

1. Add the pasta, water, beans, tomatoes (with juice if using diced), onion, bell pepper, tomato paste, oil, garlic, and crushed red pepper (if desired), to a large stockpot or deep skillet with a lid. Bring to a boil over high heat, stirring often.
2. Reduce the heat to medium-high, add the kale, and cook, continuing to stir often, until the pasta is al dente, about 10 minutes.
3. Remove from the heat and let sit for 5 minutes. Garnish with the basil and olives and serve.

Per Serving
calories: 565 | fat: 17.7g | protein: 18.0g
carbs: 85.5g | fiber: 16.5g | sodium: 540mg

Lentil and Mushroom Pasta

Prep time: 10 minutes | Cook time: 50 minutes | Serves 2

2 tablespoons olive oil
1 large yellow onion, finely diced
2 portobello mushrooms, trimmed and chopped finely
2 tablespoons tomato paste
3 garlic cloves, chopped
1 teaspoon oregano
2½ cups water
1 cup brown lentils
1 (28-ounce / 794-g) can diced tomatoes with basil (with juice if diced)
1 tablespoon balsamic vinegar
8 ounces (227 g) pasta of choice, cooked
Salt and black pepper, to taste
Chopped basil, for garnish

1. Place a large stockpot over medium heat. Add the oil. Once the oil is hot, add the onion and mushrooms. Cover and cook until both are soft, about 5 minutes. Add the tomato paste, garlic, and oregano and cook 2 minutes, stirring constantly.
2. Stir in the water and lentils. Bring to a boil, then reduce the heat to medium-low and cook for 5 minutes, covered.
3. Add the tomatoes (and juice if using diced) and vinegar. Replace the lid, reduce the heat to low and cook until the lentils are tender, about 30 minutes.
4. Remove the sauce from the heat and season with salt and pepper to taste. Garnish with the basil and serve over the cooked pasta.

Per Serving
calories: 463 | fat: 15.9g | protein: 12.5g
carbs: 70.8g | fiber: 16.9g | sodium: 155mg

Mediterranean-Style Beans and Greens

Prep time: 10 minutes | Cook time: 15 minutes | Serves 2

1 (14.5-ounce / 411-g) can diced tomatoes with juice
1 (15-ounce / 425-g) can cannellini beans, drained and rinsed
2 tablespoons
chopped green olives, plus 1 or 2 sliced for garnish
¼ cup vegetable broth, plus more as needed
1 teaspoon extra-virgin olive oil
2 cloves garlic, minced
4 cups arugula
¼ cup freshly squeezed lemon juice

1. In a medium saucepan, bring the tomatoes, beans and chopped olives to a low boil, adding just enough broth to make the ingredients saucy (you may need more than ¼ cup if your canned tomatoes don't have a lot of juice). Reduce heat to low and simmer for about 5 minutes.
2. Meanwhile, in a large skillet, heat the olive oil over medium-high heat. When the oil is hot and starts to shimmer, add garlic and sauté just until it starts to turn slightly tan, about 30 seconds. Add the arugula and lemon juice, stirring to coat leaves with the olive oil and juice. Cover and reduce heat to low. Simmer for 3 to 5 minutes.
3. Serve beans over the greens and garnish with olive slices.

Per Serving
calories: 262 | fat: 5.9g | protein: 13.2g
carbs: 40.4g | fiber: 9.8g | sodium: 897mg

Broccoli and Carrot Pasta Salad

Prep time: 5 minutes | Cook time: 10 minutes | Serves 2

8 ounces (227 g) whole-wheat pasta
2 cups broccoli florets
1 cup peeled and shredded carrots
¼ cup plain Greek yogurt
Juice of 1 lemon
1 teaspoon red pepper flakes
Sea salt and freshly ground pepper, to taste

1. Bring a large pot of lightly salted water to a boil. Add the pasta to the boiling water and cook until al dente. Drain and let rest for a few minutes.
2. When cooled, combine the pasta with the veggies, yogurt, lemon juice, and red pepper flakes in a large bowl, and stir thoroughly to combine.
3. Taste and season to taste with salt and pepper. Serve immediately.

Per Serving
calories: 428 | fat: 2.9g | protein: 15.9g
carbs: 84.6g | fiber: 11.7g | sodium: 642mg

Tomato Basil Pasta

Prep time: 3 minutes | Cook time: 2 minutes | Serves 2

2 cups dried campanelle or similar pasta
1¾ cups vegetable stock
½ teaspoon salt, plus more as needed
2 tomatoes, cut into large dices
1 or 2 pinches red

pepper flakes
½ teaspoon garlic powder
½ teaspoon dried oregano
10 to 12 fresh sweet basil leaves
Freshly ground black pepper, to taste

1. In your Instant Pot, stir together the pasta, stock, and salt. Scatter the tomatoes on top (do not stir).
2. Secure the lid. Select the Manual mode and set the cooking time for 2 minutes at High Pressure.
3. Once cooking is complete, do a quick pressure release. Carefully open the lid.
4. Stir in the red pepper flakes, oregano, and garlic powder. If there's more than a few tablespoons of liquid in the bottom, select Sauté and cook for 2 to 3 minutes until it evaporates.
5. When ready to serve, chiffonade the basil and stir it in. Taste and season with more salt and pepper, as needed. Serve warm.

Per Serving
calories: 415 | fat: 2.0g | protein: 15.2g
carbs: 84.2g | fiber: 5.0g | sodium: 485mg

Simple Lentil Risotto

Prep time: 10 minutes | Cook time: 20 minutes | Serves 2

½ tablespoon olive oil
½ medium onion, chopped
½ cup dry lentils, soaked overnight
½ celery stalk, chopped

1 sprig parsley, chopped
½ cup Arborio (short-grain Italian) rice
1 garlic clove, lightly mashed
2 cups vegetable stock

1. Press the Sauté button to heat your

Instant Pot.
2. Add the oil and onion to the Instant Pot and sauté for 5 minutes.
3. Add all the remaining ingredients to the Instant Pot.
4. Secure the lid. Select the Manual mode and set the cooking time for 15 minutes at High Pressure.
5. Once cooking is complete, do a natural pressure release for 20 minutes, then release any remaining pressure. Carefully open the lid.
6. Stir and serve hot.

Per Serving
calories: 261 | fat: 3.6g | protein: 10.6g
carbs: 47.1g | fiber: 8.4g | sodium: 247mg

Bulgur Pilaf with Kale and Tomatoes

Prep time: 10 minutes | Cook time: 10 minutes | Serves 2

2 tablespoons olive oil
2 cloves garlic, minced
1 bunch kale, trimmed and cut into bite-sized pieces
Juice of 1 lemon

2 cups cooked bulgur wheat
1 pint cherry tomatoes, halved
Sea salt and freshly ground pepper, to taste

1. Heat the olive oil in a large skillet over medium heat. Add the garlic and sauté for 1 minute.
2. Add the kale leaves and stir to coat. Cook for 5 minutes until leaves are cooked through and thoroughly wilted.
3. Add the lemon juice, bulgur and tomatoes. Season with sea salt and freshly ground pepper to taste, then serve.

Per Serving
calories: 300 | fat: 14.0g | protein: 6.2g
carbs: 37.8g | fiber: 8.7g | sodium: 595mg

Cumin Quinoa Pilaf

Prep time: 5 minutes | Cook time: 5 minutes | Serves 2

2 tablespoons extra virgin olive oil
2 cloves garlic, minced
3 cups water
2 cups quinoa, rinsed
2 teaspoons ground cumin
2 teaspoons turmeric
Salt, to taste
1 handful parsley, chopped

1. Press the Sauté button to heat your Instant Pot.
2. Once hot, add the oil and garlic to the pot, stir and cook for 1 minute.
3. Add water, quinoa, cumin, turmeric, and salt, stirring well.
4. Lock the lid. Select the Manual mode and set the cooking time for 1 minute at High Pressure.
5. When the timer beeps, perform a natural pressure release for 10 minutes, then release any remaining pressure. Carefully remove the lid.
6. Fluff the quinoa with a fork. Season with more salt, if needed.
7. Sprinkle parsley on top and serve.

Per Serving
calories: 384 | fat: 12.3g | protein: 12.8g
carbs: 57.4g | fiber: 6.9g | sodium: 448mg

Chapter 6 Vegetable Mains

Fried Eggplant Rolls

Prep time: 20 minutes | Cook time: 10 minutes | Serves 4 to 6

2 large eggplants, trimmed and cut lengthwise into ¼-inch-thick slices
1 teaspoon salt
1 cup shredded ricotta cheese
4 ounces (113 g) goat cheese, shredded
¼ cup finely chopped fresh basil
½ teaspoon freshly ground black pepper
Olive oil spray

1. Add the eggplant slices to a colander and season with salt. Set aside for 15 to 20 minutes.
2. Mix together the ricotta and goat cheese, basil, and black pepper in a large bowl and stir to combine. Set aside.
3. Dry the eggplant slices with paper towels and lightly mist them with olive oil spray.
4. Heat a large skillet over medium heat and lightly spray it with olive oil spray.
5. Arrange the eggplant slices in the skillet and fry each side for 3 minutes until golden brown.
6. Remove from the heat to a paper towel-lined plate and rest for 5 minutes.
7. Make the eggplant rolls: Lay the eggplant slices on a flat work surface and top each slice with a tablespoon of the prepared cheese mixture. Roll them up and serve immediately.

Tips: The eggplant rolls can be made in advance and stored in the refrigerator. You can add 1 teaspoon of lemon zest to the filling for a punch of citrus flavor.

Per Serving
calories: 254 | fat: 14.9g | protein: 15.3g
carbs: 18.6g | fiber: 7.1g | sodium: 745mg

Roasted Veggies and Brown Rice Bowl

Prep time: 15 minutes | Cook time: 20 minutes | Serves 4

2 cups cauliflower florets
2 cups broccoli florets
1 (15-ounce / 425-g) can chickpeas, drained and rinsed
1 cup carrot slices (about 1 inch thick)
2 to 3 tablespoons extra-virgin olive oil, divided

Salt and freshly ground black pepper, to taste
Nonstick cooking spray
2 cups cooked brown rice
2 to 3 tablespoons sesame seeds, for garnish

Dressing:

3 to 4 tablespoons tahini
2 tablespoons honey
1 lemon, juiced

1 garlic clove, minced
Salt and freshly ground black pepper, to taste

1. Preheat the oven to 400ºF (205ºC). Spritz two baking sheets with nonstick cooking spray.
2. Spread the cauliflower and broccoli on the first baking sheet and the second with the chickpeas and carrot slices.
3. Drizzle each sheet with half of the olive oil and sprinkle with salt and pepper. Toss to coat well.
4. Roast the chickpeas and carrot slices in the preheated oven for 10 minutes, leaving the carrots tender but crisp, and the cauliflower and broccoli for 20 minutes until fork-tender. Stir them once halfway through the cooking time.
5. Meanwhile, make the dressing: Whisk together the tahini, honey, lemon juice, garlic, salt, and pepper in a small bowl.
6. Divide the cooked brown rice among four bowls. Top each bowl evenly with roasted vegetables and dressing. Sprinkle the sesame seeds on top for garnish before serving.

Tip: If you like the Brussels sprouts, you can add them to this dish. Slice the Brussels sprouts in half and roast them with the vegetables in the preheated oven.

Per Serving
calories: 453 | fat: 17.8g | protein: 12.1g
carbs: 61.8g | fiber: 11.2g | sodium: 60mg

Beet and Watercress Salad

Prep time: 15 minutes | Cook time: 8 minutes | Serves 4

2 pounds (907 g) beets, scrubbed, trimmed and cut into ¾-inch pieces
½ cup water
1 teaspoon caraway seeds
½ teaspoon table salt, plus more for seasoning
1 cup plain Greek yogurt
1 small garlic clove, minced
5 ounces (142 g) watercress, torn into bite-size pieces
1 tablespoon extra-

virgin olive oil, divided, plus more for drizzling
1 tablespoon white wine vinegar, divided
Black pepper, to taste
1 teaspoon grated orange zest
2 tablespoons orange juice
¼ cup coarsely chopped fresh dill
¼ cup hazelnuts, toasted, skinned and chopped
Coarse sea salt, to taste

1. Combine the beets, water, caraway seeds and table salt in the Instant Pot. Set the lid in place. Select the Manual mode and set the cooking time for 8 minutes on High Pressure. When the timer goes off, do a quick pressure release.
2. Carefully open the lid. Using a slotted spoon, transfer the beets to a plate. Set aside to cool slightly.
3. In a small bowl, combine the yogurt, garlic and 3 tablespoons of the beet cooking liquid. In a large bowl, toss the watercress with 2 teaspoons of the oil and 1 teaspoon of the vinegar. Season with table salt and pepper.
4. Spread the yogurt mixture over a serving dish. Arrange the watercress on top of the yogurt mixture, leaving 1-inch border of the yogurt mixture.
5. Add the beets to now-empty large bowl and toss with the orange zest and juice, the remaining 2 teaspoons of the vinegar and the remaining 1 teaspoon of the oil. Season with table salt and pepper.
6. Arrange the beets on top of the watercress mixture. Drizzle with the olive oil and sprinkle with the dill, hazelnuts and sea salt.
7. Serve immediately.

Per Serving
calories: 240 | fat: 15.0g | protein: 9.0g
carbs: 19.0g | fiber: 5.0g | sodium: 440mg

Eggplant and Zucchini Gratin

Prep time: 10 minutes | Cook time: 19 minutes | Serves 6

2 large zucchinis, finely chopped
1 large eggplant, finely chopped
¼ teaspoon kosher salt
¼ teaspoon freshly ground black pepper
3 tablespoons extra-virgin olive oil, divided
¾ cup unsweetened almond milk
1 tablespoon all-purpose flour
⅓ cup plus 2 tablespoons grated Parmesan cheese, divided
1 cup chopped tomato
1 cup diced fresh Mozzarella
¼ cup fresh basil leaves

1. Preheat the oven to 425ºF (220ºC).
2. In a large bowl, toss together the zucchini, eggplant, salt and pepper.
3. In a large skillet over medium-high heat, heat 1 tablespoon of the oil. Add half of the veggie mixture to the skillet. Stir a few times, then cover and cook for about 4 minutes, stirring occasionally. Pour the cooked veggies into a baking dish. Place the skillet back on the heat, add 1 tablespoon of the oil and repeat with the remaining veggies. Add the veggies to the baking dish.
4. Meanwhile, heat the milk in the microwave for 1 minute. Set aside.
5. Place a medium saucepan over medium heat. Add the remaining 1 tablespoon of the oil and flour to the saucepan. Whisk together until well blended.
6. Slowly pour the warm milk into the saucepan, whisking the entire time. Continue to whisk frequently until the mixture thickens a bit. Add ⅓ cup of the Parmesan cheese and whisk until melted. Pour the cheese sauce over the vegetables in the baking dish and mix well.
7. Fold in the tomatoes and Mozzarella cheese. Roast in the oven for 10 minutes, or until the gratin is almost set and not runny.
8. Top with the fresh basil leaves and the remaining 2 tablespoons of the Parmesan cheese before serving.

Per Serving
calories: 122 | fat: 5.0g | protein: 10.0g
carbs: 11.0g | fiber: 4.0g | sodium: 364mg

Veggie-Stuffed Portabello Mushrooms

Prep time: 5 minutes | Cook time: 24 to 25 minutes | Serves 6

3 tablespoons extra-virgin olive oil, divided
1 cup diced onion
2 garlic cloves, minced
1 large zucchini, diced
3 cups chopped mushrooms
1 cup chopped tomato
1 teaspoon dried
oregano
¼ teaspoon kosher salt
¼ teaspoon crushed red pepper
6 large portabello mushrooms, stems and gills removed
Cooking spray
4 ounces (113 g) fresh Mozzarella cheese, shredded

1. In a large skillet over medium heat, heat 2 tablespoons of the oil. Add the onion and sauté for 4 minutes. Stir in the garlic and sauté for 1 minute.
2. Stir in the zucchini, mushrooms, tomato, oregano, salt and red pepper. Cook for 10 minutes, stirring constantly. Remove from the heat.
3. Meanwhile, heat a grill pan over medium-high heat.
4. Brush the remaining 1 tablespoon of the oil over the portabello mushroom caps. Place the mushrooms, bottom-side down, on the grill pan. Cover with a sheet of aluminum foil sprayed with nonstick cooking spray. Cook for 5 minutes.
5. Flip the mushroom caps over, and spoon about ½ cup of the cooked vegetable mixture into each cap. Top each with about 2½ tablespoons of the Mozzarella.
6. Cover and grill for 4 to 5 minutes, or until the cheese is melted.
7. Using a spatula, transfer the portabello mushrooms to a plate. Let cool for about 5 minutes before serving.

Per Serving
calories: 111 | fat: 4.0g | protein: 11.0g
carbs: 11.0g | fiber: 4.0g | sodium: 314mg

Cauliflower Hash with Carrots

Prep time: 10 minutes | Cook time: 10 minutes | Serves 4

3 tablespoons extra-virgin olive oil
1 large onion, chopped
1 tablespoon minced garlic
2 cups diced carrots
4 cups cauliflower florets
½ teaspoon ground cumin
1 teaspoon salt

1. In a large skillet, heat the olive oil over medium heat.
2. Add the onion and garlic and sauté for 1 minute. Stir in the carrots and stir-fry for 3 minutes.
3. Add the cauliflower florets, cumin, and salt and toss to combine.
4. Cover and cook for 3 minutes until lightly browned. Stir well and cook, uncovered, for 3 to 4 minutes, until softened.
5. Remove from the heat and serve warm.

Tip: For an even heartier dish, serve the vegetable hash with whole-grain pasta or rice.

Per Serving
calories: 158 | fat: 10.8g | protein: 3.1g
carbs: 14.9g | fiber: 5.1g | sodium: 656mg

Zucchini and Artichokes Bowl with Farro

Prep time: 15 minutes | Cook time: 10 minutes | Serves 4 to 6

⅓ cup extra-virgin olive oil
⅓ cup chopped red onions
½ cup chopped red bell pepper
2 garlic cloves, minced
1 cup zucchini, cut into ½-inch-thick slices
½ cup coarsely chopped artichokes
½ cup canned chickpeas, drained and rinsed
3 cups cooked farro
Salt and freshly ground black pepper, to taste
½ cup crumbled feta cheese, for serving (optional)
¼ cup sliced olives, for serving (optional)
2 tablespoons fresh basil, chiffonade, for serving (optional)
3 tablespoons balsamic vinegar, for serving (optional)

1. Heat the olive oil in a large skillet over medium heat until it shimmers.
2. Add the onions, bell pepper, and garlic and sauté for 5 minutes, stirring occasionally, until softened.
3. Stir in the zucchini slices, artichokes, and chickpeas and sauté for about 5 minutes until slightly tender.
4. Add the cooked farro and toss to combine until heated through. Sprinkle the salt and pepper to season.
5. Divide the mixture into bowls. Top each bowl evenly with feta cheese, olive slices, and basil and sprinkle with the balsamic vinegar, if desired.

Tip: You can replace the farro with your favorite gluten-free base.

Per Serving
calories: 366 | fat: 19.9g | protein: 9.3g
carbs: 50.7g | fiber: 9.0g | sodium: 86mg

Garlicky Zucchini Cubes with Mint

Prep time: 5 minutes | Cook time: 10 minutes | Serves 4

3 large green zucchinis, cut into ½-inch cubes
3 tablespoons extra-virgin olive oil
1 large onion, chopped
3 cloves garlic, minced
1 teaspoon salt
1 teaspoon dried mint

1. Heat the olive oil in a large skillet over medium heat.
2. Add the onion and garlic and sauté for 3 minutes, stirring constantly, or until softened.
3. Stir in the zucchini cubes and salt and cook for 5 minutes, or until the zucchini is browned and tender.
4. Add the mint to the skillet and toss to combine, then continue cooking for 2 minutes.
5. Serve warm.

Tip: For different flavors, you can grill, fry, or even roast the zucchini. The mint can be replaced with the oregano in this recipe.

Per Serving
calories: 146 | fat: 10.6g | protein: 4.2g
carbs: 11.8g | fiber: 3.0g | sodium: 606mg

Roasted Vegetables

Prep time: 20 minutes | Cook time: 35 minutes | Serves 2

6 teaspoons extra-virgin olive oil, divided
12 to 15 Brussels sprouts, halved
1 medium sweet potato, peeled and cut into 2-inch cubes
2 cups fresh cauliflower florets
1 medium zucchini, cut into 1-inch rounds
1 red bell pepper, cut into 1-inch slices
Salt, to taste

1. Preheat the oven to 425°F (220°C).
2. Add 2 teaspoons of olive oil, Brussels sprouts, sweet potato, and salt to a large bowl and toss until they are completely coated.
3. Transfer them to a large roasting pan and roast for 10 minutes, or until the Brussels sprouts are lightly browned.
4. Meantime, combine the cauliflower florets with 2 teaspoons of olive oil and salt in a separate bowl.
5. Remove from the oven. Add the cauliflower florets to the roasting pan and roast for 10 minutes more.
6. Meanwhile, toss the zucchini and bell pepper with the remaining olive oil in a medium bowl until well coated. Season with salt.
7. Remove the roasting pan from the oven and stir in the zucchini and bell pepper. Continue roasting for 15 minutes, or until the vegetables are fork-tender.
8. Divide the roasted vegetables between two plates and serve warm.

Tip: To make this a complete meal, serve these roasted vegetables with grilled chicken, steak, or fish.

Per Serving
calories: 333 | fat: 16.8g | protein: 12.2g
carbs: 37.6g | fiber: 11.0g | sodium: 329mg

5-Ingredient Zucchini Fritters

Prep time: 15 minutes | Cook time: 5 minutes | Makes 14 fritters

4 cups grated zucchini
Salt, to taste
2 large eggs, lightly beaten
1/3 cup sliced scallions (green and white parts)
2/3 all-purpose flour
1/8 teaspoon black pepper
2 tablespoons olive oil

1. Put the grated zucchini in a colander and lightly season with salt. Set aside to rest for 10 minutes. Squeeze out as much liquid from the grated zucchini as possible.
2. Pour the grated zucchini into a bowl. Fold in the beaten eggs, scallions, flour, salt, and pepper and stir until everything is well combined.
3. Heat the olive oil in a large skillet over medium heat until hot.
4. Drop 3 tablespoons mounds of the zucchini mixture onto the hot skillet to make each fritter, pressing them lightly into rounds and spacing them about 2 inches apart.
5. Cook for 2 to 3 minutes. Flip the zucchini fritters and cook for 2 minutes more, or until they are golden brown and cooked through.
6. Remove from the heat to a plate lined with paper towels. Repeat with the remaining zucchini mixture.
7. Serve hot.

Tip: You can add any of your favorite herbs such as basil, thyme, or parsley to the zucchini mixture.

Per Serving (2 fritters)
calories: 113 | fat: 6.1g | protein: 4.0g
carbs: 12.2g | fiber: 1.0g | sodium: 25mg

Moroccan Tagine with Vegetables

Prep time: 20 minutes | Cook time: 40 minutes | Serves 2

2 tablespoons olive oil
½ onion, diced
1 garlic clove, minced
2 cups cauliflower florets
1 medium carrot, cut into 1-inch pieces
1 cup diced eggplant
1 (28-ounce / 794-g) can whole tomatoes with their juices
1 (15-ounce / 425-g) can chickpeas,

drained and rinsed
2 small red potatoes, cut into 1-inch pieces
1 cup water
1 teaspoon pure maple syrup
½ teaspoon cinnamon
½ teaspoon turmeric
1 teaspoon cumin
½ teaspoon salt
1 to 2 teaspoons harissa paste

1. In a Dutch oven, heat the olive oil over medium-high heat. Sauté the onion for 5 minutes, stirring occasionally, or until the onion is translucent.
2. Stir in the garlic, cauliflower florets, carrot, eggplant, tomatoes, and potatoes. Using a wooden spoon or spatula to break up the tomatoes into smaller pieces.
3. Add the chickpeas, water, maple syrup, cinnamon, turmeric, cumin, and salt and stir to incorporate. Bring the mixture to a boil.
4. Once it starts to boil, reduce the heat to medium-low. Stir in the harissa paste, cover, allow to simmer for about 40 minutes, or until the vegetables are softened. Taste and adjust seasoning as needed.
5. Let the mixture cool for 5 minutes before serving.

Tip: A tagine is a corn-shaped cooking vessel traditionally used in Morocco. This recipe uses the Dutch oven that works just as well for this stew.

Per Serving
calories: 293 | fat: 9.9g | protein: 11.2g
carbs: 45.5g | fiber: 12.1g | sodium: 337mg

Zoodles with Walnut Pesto

Prep time: 10 minutes | Cook time: 10 minutes | Serves 4

4 medium zucchinis, spiralized
¼ cup extra-virgin olive oil, divided
1 teaspoon minced garlic, divided
½ teaspoon crushed red pepper
¼ teaspoon freshly ground black pepper,

divided
¼ teaspoon kosher salt, divided
2 tablespoons grated Parmesan cheese, divided
1 cup packed fresh basil leaves
¾ cup walnut pieces, divided

1. In a large bowl, stir together the zoodles, 1 tablespoon of the olive oil, ½ teaspoon of the minced garlic, red pepper, ⅛ teaspoon of the black pepper and ⅛ teaspoon of the salt. Set aside.
2. Heat ½ tablespoon of the oil in a large skillet over medium-high heat. Add half of the zoodles to the skillet and cook for 5 minutes, stirring constantly. Transfer the cooked zoodles into a bowl. Repeat with another ½ tablespoon of the oil and the remaining zoodles. When done, add the cooked zoodles to the bowl.
3. Make the pesto: In a food processor, combine the remaining ½ teaspoon of the minced garlic, ⅛ teaspoon of the black pepper and ⅛ teaspoon of the salt, 1 tablespoon of the Parmesan, basil leaves and ¼ cup of the walnuts. Pulse until smooth and then slowly drizzle the remaining 2 tablespoons of the oil into the pesto. Pulse again until well combined.
4. Add the pesto to the zoodles along with the remaining 1 tablespoon of the Parmesan and the remaining ½ cup of the walnuts. Toss to coat well.
5. Serve immediately.

Per Serving
calories: 166 | fat: 16.0g | protein: 4.0g
carbs: 3.0g | fiber: 2.0g | sodium: 307mg

Potato Tortilla with Leeks and Mushrooms

Prep time: 30 minutes | Cook time: 50 minutes | Serves 2

1 tablespoon olive oil
1 cup thinly sliced leeks
4 ounces (113 g) baby bella (cremini) mushrooms, stemmed and sliced
1 small potato, peeled and sliced ¼-inch thick
5 large eggs, beaten
½ cup unsweetened almond milk
1 teaspoon Dijon mustard
½ teaspoon dried thyme
½ teaspoon salt
Pinch freshly ground black pepper
3 ounces (85 g) Gruyère cheese, shredded

1. Preheat the oven to 350ºF (180ºC).
2. Heat the olive oil in a large sauté pan (nonstick is best) over medium-high heat. Add the leeks, mushrooms, and potato slices and sauté until the leeks are golden and the potatoes start to brown, about 10 minutes.
3. Reduce the heat to medium-low, cover, and let the vegetables cook for another 10 minutes, or until the potatoes begin to soften. If the potato slices stick to the bottom of the pan, add 1 to 2 tablespoons of water to the pan, but be careful because it may splatter.
4. Meanwhile, combine the beaten eggs, milk, mustard, thyme, salt, pepper, and cheese in a medium bowl and whisk everything together.
5. When the potatoes are soft enough to pierce with a fork or knife, turn off the heat.
6. Transfer the cooked vegetables to an oiled ovenproof pan (nonstick is best) and arrange them in a nice layer along the bottom and slightly up the sides of the pan.
7. Pour the egg mixture over the vegetables and give it a light shake or tap to distribute the eggs evenly through the vegetables.
8. Bake for 25 to 30 minutes, or until the eggs are set and the top is golden and puffed.
9. Remove from the oven and cool for 5 minutes before cutting and serving.

Per Serving
calories: 541 | fat: 33.1g | protein: 32.8g carbs: 31.0g | fiber: 4.0g | sodium: 912mg

Cheesy Sweet Potato Burgers

Prep time: 10 minutes | Cook time: 19 to 20 minutes | Serves 4

1 large sweet potato (about 8 ounces / 227 g)
2 tablespoons extra-virgin olive oil, divided
1 cup chopped onion
1 large egg
1 garlic clove
1 cup old-fashioned rolled oats
1 tablespoon dried oregano
1 tablespoon balsamic vinegar
¼ teaspoon kosher salt
½ cup crumbled Gorgonzola cheese

1. Using a fork, pierce the sweet potato all over and microwave on high for 4 to 5 minutes, until softened in the center. Cool slightly before slicing in half.
2. Meanwhile, in a large skillet over medium-high heat, heat 1 tablespoon of the olive oil. Add the onion and sauté for 5 minutes.
3. Spoon the sweet potato flesh out of the skin and put the flesh in a food processor. Add the cooked onion, egg, garlic, oats, oregano, vinegar and salt. Pulse until smooth. Add the cheese and pulse four times to barely combine.
4. Form the mixture into four burgers. Place the burgers on a plate, and press to flatten each to about ¾-inch thick.
5. Wipe out the skillet with a paper towel. Heat the remaining 1 tablespoon of the oil over medium-high heat for about 2 minutes. Add the burgers to the hot oil, then reduce the heat to medium. Cook the burgers for 5 minutes per side.
6. Transfer the burgers to a plate and serve.

Per Serving
calories: 290 | fat: 12.0g | protein: 12.0g carbs: 43.0g | fiber: 8.0g | sodium: 566mg

Wilted Dandelion Greens with Sweet Onion

Prep time: 15 minutes | Cook time: 15 minutes | Serves 4

1 tablespoon extra-virgin olive oil
2 garlic cloves, minced
1 Vidalia onion, thinly sliced
½ cup low-sodium vegetable broth
2 bunches dandelion greens, roughly chopped
Freshly ground black pepper, to taste

1. Heat the olive oil in a large skillet over low heat.
2. Add the garlic and onion and cook for 2 to 3 minutes, stirring occasionally, or until the onion is translucent.
3. Fold in the vegetable broth and dandelion greens and cook for 5 to 7 minutes until wilted, stirring frequently.
4. Sprinkle with the black pepper and serve on a plate while warm.

Tip: For extra flavor and nutrition, you can add the dandelion greens to a white bean salad, soup or even stew. And the chili pepper also pairs perfectly with these greens.

Per Serving
calories: 81 | fat: 3.9g | protein: 3.2g
carbs: 10.8g | fiber: 4.0g | sodium: 72mg

Celery and Mustard Greens

Prep time: 10 minutes | Cook time: 15 minutes | Serves 4

½ cup low-sodium vegetable broth
1 celery stalk, roughly chopped
½ sweet onion, chopped
½ large red bell pepper, thinly sliced
2 garlic cloves, minced
1 bunch mustard greens, roughly chopped

1. Pour the vegetable broth into a large cast iron pan and bring it to a simmer over medium heat.
2. Stir in the celery, onion, bell pepper, and garlic. Cook uncovered for about 3 to 5

minutes, or until the onion is softened.
3. Add the mustard greens to the pan and stir well. Cover, reduce the heat to low, and cook for an additional 10 minutes, or until the liquid is evaporated and the greens are wilted.
4. Remove from the heat and serve warm.

Tips: If the mustard greens aren't available, you can use the turnip greens. For added color and flavor, serve it with a sprinkle of red pepper flakes and a squeeze of lemon before serving.

Per Serving (1 cup)
calories: 39 | fat: 0g | protein: 3.1g
carbs: 6.8g | fiber: 3.0g | sodium: 120mg

Lentil and Tomato Collard Wraps

Prep time: 15 minutes | Cook time: 0 minutes | Serves 4

2 cups cooked lentils
5 Roma tomatoes, diced
½ cup crumbled feta cheese
10 large fresh basil leaves, thinly sliced
¼ cup extra-virgin olive oil
1 tablespoon balsamic vinegar
2 garlic cloves, minced
½ teaspoon raw honey
½ teaspoon salt
¼ teaspoon freshly ground black pepper
4 large collard leaves, stems removed

1. Combine the lentils, tomatoes, cheese, basil leaves, olive oil, vinegar, garlic, honey, salt, and black pepper in a large bowl and stir until well blended.
2. Lay the collard leaves on a flat work surface. Spoon the equal-sized amounts of the lentil mixture onto the edges of the leaves. Roll them up and slice in half to serve.

Tip: If you want to make the collard leaves easier to wrap, you can steam them for 1 to 2 minutes before wrapping.

Per Serving
calories: 318 | fat: 17.6g | protein: 13.2g
carbs: 27.5g | fiber: 9.9g | sodium: 475mg

Vegetable and Tofu Scramble

Prep time: 5 minutes | Cook time: 10 minutes | Serves 2

2 tablespoons extra-virgin olive oil	tofu, cut into pieces
½ red onion, finely chopped	2 garlic cloves, minced
1 cup chopped kale	Pinch red pepper flakes
8 ounces (227 g) mushrooms, sliced	½ teaspoon sea salt
8 ounces (227 g)	⅛ teaspoon freshly ground black pepper

1. Heat the olive oil in a medium nonstick skillet over medium-high heat until shimmering.
2. Add the onion, kale, and mushrooms to the skillet and cook for about 5 minutes, stirring occasionally, or until the vegetables start to brown.
3. Add the tofu and stir-fry for 3 to 4 minutes until softened.
4. Stir in the garlic, red pepper flakes, salt, and black pepper and cook for 30 seconds.
5. Let the mixture cool for 5 minutes before serving.

Tip: If you'd like to add some carbs to this dish, you can serve the vegetable and tofu scramble over the whole-grain toast and pita bread.

Per Serving
calories: 233 | fat: 15.9g | protein: 13.4g carbs: 11.9g | fiber: 2.0g | sodium: 672mg

Simple Zoodles

Prep time: 10 minutes | Cook time: 5 minutes | Serves 2

2 tablespoons avocado oil	¼ teaspoon salt
2 medium zucchinis, spiralized	Freshly ground black pepper, to taste

1. Heat the avocado oil in a large skillet over medium heat until it shimmers.
2. Add the zucchini noodles, salt, and black pepper to the skillet and toss to coat. Cook for 1 to 2 minutes, stirring constantly, until tender.

3. Serve warm.

Tips: Don't cook the zucchini noodles too long, or they will be not al dente. You can use a spiralizer, vegetable peeler, or sharp knife to make the zoodles.

Per Serving
calories: 128 | fat: 14.0g | protein: 0.3g carbs: 0.3g | fiber: 0.1g | sodium: 291mg

Vegan Lentil Bolognese

Prep time: 15 minutes | Cook time: 50 minutes | Serves 2

1 medium celery stalk	tomatoes
1 large carrot	1 cup red wine
½ large onion	½ teaspoon salt, plus more as needed
1 garlic clove	½ teaspoon pure maple syrup
2 tablespoons olive oil	1 cup cooked lentils (prepared from ½ cup dry)
1 (28-ounce / 794-g) can crushed	

1. Add the celery, carrot, onion, and garlic to a food processor and process until everything is finely chopped.
2. In a Dutch oven, heat the olive oil over medium-high heat. Add the chopped mixture and sauté for about 10 minutes, stirring occasionally, or until the vegetables are lightly browned.
3. Stir in the tomatoes, wine, salt, and maple syrup and bring to a boil.
4. Once the sauce starts to boil, cover, and reduce the heat to medium-low. Simmer for 30 minutes, stirring occasionally, or until the vegetables are softened.
5. Stir in the cooked lentils and cook for an additional 5 minutes until warmed through.
6. Taste and add additional salt, if needed. Serve warm.

Tip: You can use 1 cup of cooked bulgur wheat or minced mushrooms to substitute for the lentils.

Per Serving
calories: 367 | fat: 15.0g | protein: 13.7g carbs: 44.5g | fiber: 17.6g | sodium: 1108mg

Vegetable and Red Lentil Stew

Prep time: 10 minutes | Cook time: 35 minutes | Serves 6

1 tablespoon extra-virgin olive oil	4 celery stalks, finely diced
2 onions, peeled and finely diced	3 cups red lentils
6½ cups water	1 teaspoon dried oregano
2 zucchinis, finely diced	1 teaspoon salt, plus more as needed

1. Heat the olive oil in a large pot over medium heat.
2. Add the onions and sauté for about 5 minutes, stirring constantly, or until the onions are softened.
3. Stir in the water, zucchini, celery, lentils, oregano, and salt and bring the mixture to a boil.
4. Reduce the heat to low and let simmer covered for 30 minutes, stirring occasionally, or until the lentils are tender.
5. Taste and adjust the seasoning as needed.

Tip: You can try this recipe with different lentils such as brown and green lentils, but they need additional cooking time, about 20 minutes.

Per Serving
calories: 387 | fat: 4.4g | protein: 24.0g
carbs: 63.7g | fiber: 11.7g | sodium: 418mg

Cauliflower Rice Risotto with Mushrooms

Prep time: 5 minutes | Cook time: 10 minutes | Serves 4

1 teaspoon extra-virgin olive oil	rice
½ cup chopped portobello mushrooms	½ cup half-and-half
	¼ cup low-sodium vegetable broth
4 cups cauliflower	1 cup shredded Parmesan cheese

1. In a medium skillet, heat the olive oil over medium-low heat until shimmering.
2. Add the mushrooms and stir-fry for 3 minutes.
3. Stir in the cauliflower rice, half-and-half, and vegetable broth. Cover and bring

to a boil over high heat for 5 minutes, stirring occasionally.
4. Add the Parmesan cheese and stir to combine. Continue cooking for an additional 3 minutes until the cheese is melted.
5. Divide the mixture into four bowls and serve warm.

Tip: This risotto uses the cauliflower rice different from the traditional risotto. The cauliflower rice is low-carb and it saves your cooking time.

Per Serving
calories: 167 | fat: 10.7g | protein: 12.1g
carbs: 8.1g | fiber: 3.0g | sodium: 326mg

Sautéed Green Beans with Tomatoes

Prep time: 10 minutes | Cook time: 20 minutes | Serves 4

¼ cup extra-virgin olive oil	or frozen, cut into 2-inch pieces
1 large onion, chopped	1½ teaspoons salt, divided
4 cloves garlic, finely chopped	1 (15-ounce / 425-g) can diced tomatoes
1 pound (454 g) green beans, fresh	½ teaspoon freshly ground black pepper

1. Heat the olive oil in a large skillet over medium heat.
2. Add the onion and garlic and sauté for 1 minute until fragrant.
3. Stir in the green beans and sauté for 3 minutes. Sprinkle with ½ teaspoon of salt.
4. Add the tomatoes, remaining salt, and pepper and stir to mix well. Cook for an additional 12 minutes, stirring occasionally, or until the green beans are crisp and tender.
5. Remove from the heat and serve warm.

Tips: To add more flavors to this meal, top the green beans with a sprinkle of toasted pine nuts or almonds before serving. For a spicy kick, you can sprinkle with ½ teaspoon red pepper flakes.

Per Serving
calories: 219 | fat: 13.9g | protein: 4.0g
carbs: 17.7g | fiber: 6.2g | sodium: 843mg

Creamy Cauliflower Chickpea Curry

Prep time: 5 minutes | Cook time: 15 minutes | Serves 4

3 cups fresh or frozen cauliflower florets
2 cups unsweetened almond milk
1 (15-ounce / 425-g) can low-sodium chickpeas, drained and rinsed
1 (15-ounce / 425-g) can coconut milk

1 tablespoon curry powder
¼ teaspoon garlic powder
¼ teaspoon ground ginger
⅛ teaspoon onion powder
¼ teaspoon salt

1. Add the cauliflower florets, almond milk, chickpeas, coconut milk, curry powder, garlic powder, ginger, and onion powder to a large stockpot and stir to combine.
2. Cover and cook over medium-high heat for 10 minutes, stirring occasionally.
3. Reduce the heat to low and continue cooking uncovered for 5 minutes, or until the cauliflower is tender.
4. Sprinkle with the salt and stir well. Serve warm.

Tip: For added protein, you can serve the curry with a side salad. For added flavor, sprinkle with some chopped fresh cilantro.

Per Serving
calories: 409 | fat: 29.6g | protein: 10.0g
carbs: 29.8g | fiber: 9.1g | sodium: 117mg

Grilled Vegetable Skewers

Prep time: 15 minutes | Cook time: 10 minutes | Serves 4

4 medium red onions, peeled and sliced into 6 wedges
4 medium zucchini, cut into 1-inch-thick slices
2 beefsteak tomatoes, cut into quarters
4 red bell peppers, cut into 2-inch

squares
2 orange bell peppers, cut into 2-inch squares
2 yellow bell peppers, cut into 2-inch squares
2 tablespoons plus 1 teaspoon olive oil, divided

SPECIAL EQUIPMENT:
4 wooden skewers, soaked in water for at least 30 minutes

1. Preheat the grill to medium-high heat.
2. Skewer the vegetables by alternating between red onion, zucchini, tomatoes, and the different colored bell peppers. Brush them with 2 tablespoons of olive oil.
3. Oil the grill grates with 1 teaspoon of olive oil and grill the vegetable skewers for 5 minutes. Flip the skewers and grill for 5 minutes more, or until they are cooked to your liking.
4. Let the skewers cool for 5 minutes before serving.

Tip: You can add any leftover vegetables to a pita with a dollop of hummus for a quick and easy lunch or dinner.

Per Serving
calories: 115 | fat: 3.0g | protein: 3.5g
carbs: 18.7g | fiber: 4.7g | sodium: 12mg

Chickpea Lettuce Wraps with Celery

Prep time: 10 minutes | Cook time: 0 minutes | Serves 4

1 (15-ounce / 425-g) can low-sodium chickpeas, drained and rinsed
1 celery stalk, thinly sliced
2 tablespoons finely chopped red onion

2 tablespoons unsalted tahini
3 tablespoons honey mustard
1 tablespoon capers, undrained
12 butter lettuce leaves

1. In a bowl, mash the chickpeas with a potato masher or the back of a fork until mostly smooth.
2. Add the celery, red onion, tahini, honey mustard, and capers to the bowl and stir until well incorporated.
3. For each serving, place three overlapping lettuce leaves on a plate and top with ¼ of the mashed chickpea filling, then roll up. Repeat with the remaining lettuce leaves and chickpea mixture.

Tips: To make this a complete meal, serve the wraps with ¼ cup baby carrots topped with 1 to 2 tablespoon hummus or 1 to 2 hard-boiled eggs. And you can try this recipe with romaine or green leaf lettuce.

Per Serving
calories: 182 | fat: 7.1g | protein: 10.3g
carbs: 19.6g | fiber: 3.0g | sodium: 171mg

Stuffed Portobello Mushroom with Tomatoes

Prep time: 10 minutes | Cook time: 15 minutes | Serves 4

4 large portobello mushroom caps
3 tablespoons extra-virgin olive oil
Salt and freshly ground black pepper, to taste
4 sun-dried tomatoes
1 cup shredded mozzarella cheese, divided
½ to ¾ cup low-sodium tomato sauce

1. Preheat the broiler on high.
2. Arrange the mushroom caps on a baking sheet and drizzle with olive oil. Sprinkle with salt and pepper.
3. Broil for 1o minutes, flipping the mushroom caps halfway through, until browned on the top.
4. Remove from the broil. Spoon 1 tomato, 2 tablespoons of cheese, and 2 to 3 tablespoons of sauce onto each mushroom cap.
5. Return the mushroom caps to the broiler and continue broiling for 2 to 3 minutes.
6. Cool for 5 minutes before serving.

Tips: You can make a caprese mushroom cap by substituting your favorite jarred pesto sauce for the tomato sauce. And if you are a meat lover, add ½ pound (227 g) cooked, ground chicken to the filling.

Per Serving
calories: 217 | fat: 15.8g | protein: 11.2g
carbs: 11.7g | fiber: 2.0g | sodium: 243mg

Stir-Fry Baby Bok Choy

Prep time: 12 minutes | Cook time: 10 to 13 minutes | Serves 6

2 tablespoons coconut oil
1 large onion, finely diced
2 teaspoons ground cumin
1-inch piece fresh ginger, grated
1 teaspoon ground turmeric
½ teaspoon salt
12 baby bok choy heads, ends trimmed and sliced lengthwise
Water, as needed
3 cups cooked brown rice

1. Heat the coconut oil in a large pan over medium heat.
2. Sauté the onion for 5 minutes, stirring occasionally, or until the onion is translucent.
3. Fold in the cumin, ginger, turmeric, and salt and stir to coat well.
4. Add the bok choy and cook for 5 to 8 minutes, stirring occasionally, or until the bok choy is tender but crisp. You can add 1 tablespoon of water at a time, if the skillet gets dry until you finish sautéing.
5. Transfer the bok choy to a plate and serve over the cooked brown rice.

Tip: To add more flavors to this meal, you can serve this stir-fired bok choy with a simple grilled steak or harissa chicken.

Per Serving
calories: 443 | fat: 8.8g | protein: 30.3g
carbs: 75.7g | fiber: 19.0g | sodium: 1289mg

Parmesan Stuffed Zucchini Boats

Prep time: 5 minutes | Cook time: 15 minutes | Serves 4

1 cup canned low-sodium chickpeas, drained and rinsed
1 cup no-sugar-added spaghetti
sauce
2 zucchinis
¼ cup shredded Parmesan cheese

1. Preheat the oven to 425ºF (220ºC).
2. In a medium bowl, stir together the chickpeas and spaghetti sauce.
3. Cut the zucchini in half lengthwise and scrape a spoon gently down the length of each half to remove the seeds.
4. Fill each zucchini half with the chickpea sauce and top with one-quarter of the Parmesan cheese.
5. Place the zucchini halves on a baking sheet and roast in the oven for 15 minutes.
6. Transfer to a plate. Let rest for 5 minutes before serving.

Per Serving
calories: 139 | fat: 4.0g | protein: 8.0g
carbs: 20.0g | fiber: 5.0g | sodium: 344mg

Sweet Pepper Stew

Prep time: 20 minutes | Cook time: 50 minutes | Serves 2

2 tablespoons olive oil
2 sweet peppers, diced (about 2 cups)
½ large onion, minced
1 garlic clove, minced
1 tablespoon gluten-free Worcestershire

sauce
1 teaspoon oregano
1 cup low-sodium tomato juice
1 cup low-sodium vegetable stock
¼ cup brown rice
¼ cup brown lentils
Salt, to taste

1. In a Dutch oven, heat the olive oil over medium-high heat.
2. Sauté the sweet peppers and onion for 10 minutes, stirring occasionally, or until the onion begins to turn golden and the peppers are wilted.
3. Stir in the garlic, Worcestershire sauce, and oregano and cook for 30 seconds more. Add the tomato juice, vegetable stock, rice, and lentils to the Dutch oven and stir to mix well.
4. Bring the mixture to a boil and then reduce the heat to medium-low. Let it simmer covered for about 45 minutes, or until the rice is cooked through and the lentils are tender.
5. Sprinkle with salt and serve warm.

Tips: If you'd like to use the meat in place of lentils, try adding lean ground turkey, beef, or lamb, and substitute the beef stock for vegetable stock. If the stew gets too thick, you can thin it with extra water to reach your preferred preference.

Per Serving
calories: 378 | fat: 15.6g | protein: 11.4g
carbs: 52.8g | fiber: 7.0g | sodium: 391mg

Sautéed Spinach and Leeks

Prep time: 5 minutes | Cook time: 8 minutes | Serves 2

3 tablespoons olive oil
2 garlic cloves, crushed
2 leeks, chopped
2 red onions, chopped

9 ounces (255 g) fresh spinach
1 teaspoon kosher salt
½ cup crumbled goat cheese

1. Coat the bottom of the Instant Pot with the olive oil.
2. Add the garlic, leek, and onions and stir-fry for about 5 minutes, on Sauté mode.
3. Stir in the spinach. Sprinkle with the salt and sauté for an additional 3 minutes, stirring constantly.
4. Transfer to a plate and scatter with the goat cheese before serving.

Per Serving
calories: 447 | fat: 31.2g | protein: 14.6g
carbs: 28.7g | fiber: 6.3g | sodium: 937mg

Baked Tomatoes and chickpeas

Prep time: 15 minutes | Cook time: 40 to 45 minutes | Serves 4

1 tablespoon extra-virgin olive oil
½ medium onion, chopped
3 garlic cloves, chopped
¼ teaspoon ground cumin
2 teaspoons smoked paprika

2 (15-ounce / 425-g) cans chickpeas, drained and rinsed
4 cups halved cherry tomatoes
½ cup plain Greek yogurt, for serving
1 cup crumbled feta cheese, for serving

1. Preheat the oven to 425ºF (220ºC).
2. Heat the olive oil in an ovenproof skillet over medium heat.
3. Add the onion and garlic and sauté for about 5 minutes, stirring occasionally, or until tender and fragrant.
4. Add the paprika and cumin and cook for 2 minutes. Stir in the chickpeas and tomatoes and allow to simmer for 5 to 10 minutes.
5. Transfer the skillet to the preheated oven and roast for 25 to 30 minutes, or until the mixture bubbles and thickens.
6. Remove from the oven and serve topped with yogurt and crumbled feta cheese.

Tips: If you want to make it a vegan dish, you can skip the plain Greek yogurt and feta cheese topping. To add more flavors to this dish, serve the chickpeas and tomatoes over the cauliflower rice or quinoa.

Per Serving
calories: 411 | fat: 14.9g | protein: 20.2g
carbs: 50.7g | fiber: 13.3g | sodium: 443mg

Stuffed Portobello Mushrooms with Spinach

Prep time: 5 minutes | Cook time: 20 minutes | Serves 4

8 large portobello mushrooms, stems removed
3 teaspoons extra-virgin olive oil, divided

1 medium red bell pepper, diced
4 cups fresh spinach
¼ cup crumbled feta cheese

1. Preheat the oven to 450ºF (235ºC).
2. Using a spoon to scoop out the gills of the mushrooms and discard them. Brush the mushrooms with 2 teaspoons of olive oil.
3. Arrange the mushrooms (cap-side down) on a baking sheet. Roast in the preheated oven for 20 minutes.
4. Meantime, in a medium skillet, heat the remaining olive oil over medium heat until it shimmers.
5. Add the bell pepper and spinach and sauté for 8 to 10 minutes, stirring occasionally, or until the spinach is wilted.
6. Remove the mushrooms from the oven to a paper towel-lined plate. Using a spoon to stuff each mushroom with the bell pepper and spinach mixture. Scatter the feta cheese all over.
7. Serve immediately.

Tip: For more bulk and flavor, you can add a green or yellow bell pepper to this filling.

Per Serving (2 mushrooms)
calories: 115 | fat: 5.9g | protein: 7.2g
carbs: 11.5g | fiber: 4.0g | sodium: 125mg

Creamy Polenta with Mushrooms

Prep time: 20 minutes | Cook time: 30 minutes | Serves 2

½ ounce (14 g) dried porcini mushrooms (optional but recommended)
2 tablespoons olive oil
1 pound (454 g) baby bella (cremini) mushrooms, quartered
1 large shallot, minced
1 garlic clove, minced
1 tablespoon flour
2 teaspoons tomato paste

½ cup red wine
1 cup mushroom stock (or reserved liquid from soaking the porcini mushrooms, if using)
½ teaspoon dried thyme
1 fresh rosemary sprig
1½ cups water
½ teaspoon salt
$1/_3$ cup instant polenta
2 tablespoons grated Parmesan cheese

1. If using the dried porcini mushrooms, soak them in 1 cup of hot water for about 15 minutes to soften them. When they're softened, scoop them out of the water, reserving the soaking liquid. Mince the porcini mushrooms.
2. Heat the olive oil in a large sauté pan over medium-high heat. Add the mushrooms, shallot, and garlic, and sauté for 10 minutes, or until the vegetables are wilted and starting to caramelize.
3. Add the flour and tomato paste, and cook for another 30 seconds. Add the red wine, mushroom stock or porcini soaking liquid, thyme, and rosemary. Bring the mixture to a boil, stirring constantly until it thickens. Reduce the heat and let it simmer for 10 minutes.
4. Meanwhile, bring the water to a boil in a saucepan and add salt.
5. Add the instant polenta and stir quickly while it thickens. Stir in the Parmesan cheese. Taste and add additional salt, if needed. Serve warm.

Per Serving
calories: 450 | fat: 16.0g | protein: 14.1g
carbs: 57.8g | fiber: 5.0g | sodium: 165mg

Ratatouille

Prep time: 10 minutes | Cook time: 30 minutes | Serves 4

4 tablespoons extra-virgin olive oil, divided
1 cup diced zucchini
2 cups diced eggplant
1 cup diced onion
1 cup chopped green bell pepper
1 (15-ounce / 425-g) can no-salt-added diced tomatoes
½ teaspoon garlic powder
1 teaspoon ground thyme
Salt and freshly ground black pepper, to taste

1. Heat 2 tablespoons of olive oil in a large saucepan over medium heat until it shimmers.
2. Add the zucchini and eggplant and sauté for 10 minutes, stirring occasionally. If necessary, add the remaining olive oil.
3. Stir in the onion and bell pepper and sauté for 5 minutes until softened.
4. Add the diced tomatoes with their juice, garlic powder, and thyme and stir to combine. Continue cooking for 15 minutes until the vegetables are cooked through, stirring occasionally. Sprinkle with salt and black pepper.
5. Remove from the heat and serve on a plate.

Tips: For added protein, serve topped with shredded Parmesan cheese. To save time, you can use the frozen chopped green bell peppers.

Per Serving
calories: 189 | fat: 13.7g | protein: 3.1g
carbs: 14.8g | fiber: 4.0g | sodium: 27mg

Brussels Sprouts Linguine

Prep time: 5 minutes | Cook time: 25 minutes | Serves 4

8 ounces (227 g) whole-wheat linguine
$1/_3$ cup plus 2 tablespoons extra-virgin olive oil, divided
1 medium sweet onion, diced
2 to 3 garlic cloves, smashed
8 ounces (227 g) Brussels sprouts, chopped
½ cup chicken stock
$1/_3$ cup dry white wine
½ cup shredded Parmesan cheese
1 lemon, quartered

1. Bring a large pot of water to a boil and cook the pasta for about 5 minutes, or until al dente. Drain the pasta and reserve 1 cup of the pasta water. Mix the cooked pasta with 2 tablespoons of the olive oil. Set aside.
2. In a large skillet, heat the remaining $1/_3$ cup of the olive oil over medium heat. Add the onion to the skillet and sauté for about 4 minutes, or until tender. Add the smashed garlic cloves and sauté for 1 minute, or until fragrant.
3. Stir in the Brussels sprouts and cook covered for 10 minutes. Pour in the chicken stock to prevent burning. Once the Brussels sprouts have wilted and are fork-tender, add white wine and cook for about 5 minutes, or until reduced.
4. Add the pasta to the skillet and add the pasta water as needed.
5. Top with the Parmesan cheese and squeeze the lemon over the dish right before eating.

Per Serving
calories: 502 | fat: 31.0g | protein: 15.0g
carbs: 50.0g | fiber: 9.0g | sodium: 246mg

Garlicky Broccoli Rabe

Prep time: 10 minutes | Cook time: 5 to 6 minutes | Serves 4

14 ounces (397 g) broccoli rabe, trimmed and cut into 1-inch pieces
2 teaspoons salt, plus more for seasoning
Black pepper, to taste
2 tablespoons extra-virgin olive oil
3 garlic cloves, minced
¼ teaspoon red pepper flakes

1. Bring 3 quarts water to a boil in a large saucepan. Add the broccoli rabe and 2 teaspoons of the salt to the boiling water and cook for 2 to 3 minutes, or until wilted and tender.
2. Drain the broccoli rabe. Transfer to ice water and let sit until chilled. Drain again and pat dry.
3. In a skillet over medium heat, heat the oil and add the garlic and red pepper flakes. Sauté for about 2 minutes, or until the garlic begins to sizzle.
4. Increase the heat to medium-high. Stir in the broccoli rabe and cook for about 1 minute, or until heated through, stirring constantly. Season with salt and pepper.
5. Serve immediately.

Per Serving
calories: 87 | fat: 7.3g | protein: 3.4g
carbs: 4.0g | fiber: 2.9g | sodium: 1196mg

Quick Steamed Broccoli

Prep time: 5 minutes | Cook time: 0 minutes | Serves 2

¼ cup water
3 cups broccoli florets
Salt and ground black pepper, to taste

1. Pour the water into the Instant Pot and insert a steamer basket. Place the broccoli florets in the basket.
2. Secure the lid. Select the Manual mode and set the cooking time for 0 minutes at High Pressure.
3. Once cooking is complete, do a quick pressure release. Carefully open the lid.
4. Transfer the broccoli florets to a bowl with cold water to keep bright green color.

5. Season the broccoli with salt and pepper to taste, then serve.

Per Serving
calories: 16 | fat: 0.2g | protein: 1.9g
carbs: 1.7g | fiber: 1.6g | sodium: 292mg

Sautéed Cabbage with Parsley

Prep time: 10 minutes | Cook time: 12 to 14 minutes | Serves 4 to 6

1 small head green cabbage (about 1¼ pounds / 567 g), cored and sliced thin
2 tablespoons extra-virgin olive oil, divided
1 onion, halved and sliced thin
¾ teaspoon salt, divided
¼ teaspoon black pepper
¼ cup chopped fresh parsley
1½ teaspoons lemon juice

1. Place the cabbage in a large bowl with cold water. Let sit for 3 minutes. Drain well.
2. Heat 1 tablespoon of the oil in a skillet over medium-high heat until shimmering. Add the onion and ¼ teaspoon of the salt and cook for 5 to 7 minutes, or until softened and lightly browned. Transfer to a bowl.
3. Heat the remaining 1 tablespoon of the oil in now-empty skillet over medium-high heat until shimmering. Add the cabbage and sprinkle with the remaining ½ teaspoon of the salt and black pepper. Cover and cook for about 3 minutes, without stirring, or until cabbage is wilted and lightly browned on bottom.
4. Stir and continue to cook for about 4 minutes, uncovered, or until the cabbage is crisp-tender and lightly browned in places, stirring once halfway through cooking. Off heat, stir in the cooked onion, parsley and lemon juice.
5. Transfer to a plate and serve.

Per Serving
calories: 117 | fat: 7.0g | protein: 2.7g
carbs: 13.4g | fiber: 5.1g | sodium: 472mg

Braised Cauliflower with White Wine

Prep time: 10 minutes | Cook time: 12 to 16 minutes | Serves 4 to 6

3 tablespoons plus 1 teaspoon extra-virgin olive oil, divided
3 garlic cloves, minced
⅛ teaspoon red pepper flakes
1 head cauliflower (2 pounds / 907 g), cored and cut into
1½-inch florets
¼ teaspoon salt, plus more for seasoning
Black pepper, to taste
⅓ cup vegetable broth
⅓ cup dry white wine
2 tablespoons minced fresh parsley

1. Combine 1 teaspoon of the oil, garlic and pepper flakes in small bowl.
2. Heat the remaining 3 tablespoons of the oil in a skillet over medium-high heat until shimmering. Add the cauliflower and ¼ teaspoon of the salt and cook for 7 to 9 minutes, stirring occasionally, or until florets are golden brown.
3. Push the cauliflower to sides of the skillet. Add the garlic mixture to the center of the skillet. Cook for about 30 seconds, or until fragrant. Stir the garlic mixture into the cauliflower.
4. Pour in the broth and wine and bring to simmer. Reduce the heat to medium-low. Cover and cook for 4 to 6 minutes, or until the cauliflower is crisp-tender. Off heat, stir in the parsley and season with salt and pepper.
5. Serve immediately.

Per Serving
calories: 143 | fat: 11.7g | protein: 3.1g
carbs: 8.7g | fiber: 3.1g | sodium: 263mg

Cauliflower Steaks with Arugula

Prep time: 5 minutes | Cook time: 20 minutes | Serves 4

Cauliflower:
1 head cauliflower
Cooking spray
½ teaspoon garlic
powder
4 cups arugula

Dressing:
1½ tablespoons extra-virgin olive oil
1½ tablespoons
honey mustard
1 teaspoon freshly squeezed lemon juice

1. Preheat the oven to 425ºF (220ºC).
2. Remove the leaves from the cauliflower head, and cut it in half lengthwise. Cut 1½-inch-thick steaks from each half.
3. Spritz both sides of each steak with cooking spray and season both sides with the garlic powder.
4. Place the cauliflower steaks on a baking sheet, cover with foil, and roast in the oven for 10 minutes.
5. Remove the baking sheet from the oven and gently pull back the foil to avoid the steam. Flip the steaks, then roast uncovered for 10 minutes more.
6. Meanwhile, make the dressing: Whisk together the olive oil, honey mustard and lemon juice in a small bowl.
7. When the cauliflower steaks are done, divide into four equal portions. Top each portion with one-quarter of the arugula and dressing.
8. Serve immediately.

Per Serving
calories: 115 | fat: 6.0g | protein: 5.0g
carbs: 14.0g | fiber: 4.0g | sodium: 97mg

Baby Kale and Cabbage Salad

Prep time: 10 minutes | Cook time: 0 minutes | Serves 6

2 bunches baby kale, thinly sliced
½ head green savoy cabbage, cored and thinly sliced
1 medium red bell pepper, thinly sliced
1 garlic clove, thinly sliced
1 cup toasted
peanuts
Dressing:
Juice of 1 lemon
¼ cup apple cider vinegar
1 teaspoon ground cumin
¼ teaspoon smoked paprika

1. In a large mixing bowl, toss together the kale and cabbage.
2. Make the dressing: Whisk together the lemon juice, vinegar, cumin and paprika in a small bowl.
3. Pour the dressing over the greens and gently massage with your hands.
4. Add the pepper, garlic and peanuts to the mixing bowl. Toss to combine.
5. Serve immediately.

Per Serving
calories: 199 | fat: 12.0g | protein: 10.0g
carbs: 17.0g | fiber: 5.0g | sodium: 46mg

Grilled Romaine Lettuce

Prep time: 5 minutes | Cook time: 3 to 5 minutes | Serves 4

Romaine:
2 heads romaine lettuce, halved lengthwise
2 tablespoons extra-virgin olive oil

Dressing:
½ cup unsweetened almond milk
1 tablespoon extra-virgin olive oil
¼ bunch fresh chives,
thinly chopped
1 garlic clove, pressed
1 pinch red pepper flakes

1. Heat a grill pan over medium heat.
2. Brush each lettuce half with the olive oil. Place the lettuce halves, flat-side down, on the grill. Grill for 3 to 5 minutes, or until the lettuce slightly wilts and develops light grill marks.

3. Meanwhile, whisk together all the ingredients for the dressing in a small bowl.
4. Drizzle 2 tablespoons of the dressing over each romaine half and serve.

Per Serving
calories: 126 | fat: 11.0g | protein: 2.0g
carbs: 7.0g | fiber: 1.0g | sodium: 41mg

Mini Crustless Spinach Quiches

Prep time: 10 minutes | Cook time: 20 minutes | Serves 6

2 tablespoons extra-virgin olive oil
1 onion, finely chopped
2 cups baby spinach
2 garlic cloves, minced
8 large eggs, beaten
¼ cup unsweetened almond milk
½ teaspoon sea salt
¼ teaspoon freshly ground black pepper
1 cup shredded Swiss cheese
Cooking spray

1. Preheat the oven to 375ºF (190ºC). Spritz a 6-cup muffin tin with cooking spray. Set aside.
2. In a large skillet over medium-high heat, heat the olive oil until shimmering. Add the onion and cook for about 4 minutes, or until soft. Add the spinach and cook for about 1 minute, stirring constantly, or until the spinach softens. Add the garlic and sauté for 30 seconds. Remove from the heat and let cool.
3. In a medium bowl, whisk together the eggs, milk, salt and pepper.
4. Stir the cooled vegetables and the cheese into the egg mixture. Spoon the mixture into the prepared muffin tins. Bake for about 15 minutes, or until the eggs are set.
5. Let rest for 5 minutes before serving.

Per Serving
calories: 218 | fat: 17.0g | protein: 14.0g
carbs: 4.0g | fiber: 1.0g | sodium: 237mg

Veggie Rice Bowls with Pesto Sauce

Prep time: 15 minutes | Cook time: 1 minute | Serves 2

2 cups water
1 cup arborio rice, rinsed
Salt and ground black pepper, to taste
2 eggs
1 cup broccoli florets
½ pound (227 g)

Brussels sprouts
1 carrot, peeled and chopped
1 small beet, peeled and cubed
¼ cup pesto sauce
Lemon wedges, for serving

1. Combine the water, rice, salt, and pepper in the Instant Pot. Insert a trivet over rice and place a steamer basket on top. Add the eggs, broccoli, Brussels sprouts, carrots, beet cubes, salt, and pepper to the steamer basket.
2. Lock the lid. Select the Manual mode and set the cooking time for 1 minute at High Pressure.
3. When the timer beeps, perform a natural pressure release for 10 minutes, then release any remaining pressure. Carefully open the lid.
4. Remove the steamer basket and trivet from the pot and transfer the eggs to a bowl of ice water. Peel and halve the eggs. Use a fork to fluff the rice.
5. Divide the rice, broccoli, Brussels sprouts, carrot, beet cubes, and eggs into two bowls. Top with a dollop of pesto sauce and serve with the lemon wedges.

Per Serving
calories: 590 | fat: 34.1g | protein: 21.9g
carbs: 50.0g | fiber: 19.6g | sodium: 670mg

Butternut Noodles with Mushrooms

Prep time: 10 minutes | Cook time: 12 minutes | Serves 4

¼ cup extra-virgin olive oil
1 pound (454 g) cremini mushrooms, sliced
½ red onion, finely chopped
1 teaspoon dried thyme
½ teaspoon sea salt

3 garlic cloves, minced
½ cup dry white wine
Pinch of red pepper flakes
4 cups butternut noodles
4 ounces (113 g) grated Parmesan cheese

1. In a large skillet over medium-high heat, heat the olive oil until shimmering. Add the mushrooms, onion, thyme, and salt to the skillet. Cook for about 6 minutes, stirring occasionally, or until the mushrooms start to brown. Add the garlic and sauté for 30 seconds. Stir in the white wine and red pepper flakes.
2. Fold in the noodles. Cook for about 5 minutes, stirring occasionally, or until the noodles are tender.
3. Serve topped with the grated Parmesan.

Per Serving
calories: 244 | fat: 14.0g | protein: 4.0g
carbs: 22.0g | fiber: 4.0g | sodium: 159mg

Zoodles with Beet Pesto

Prep time: 10 minutes | Cook time: 50 minutes | Serves 2

1 medium red beet, peeled, chopped
½ cup walnut pieces
½ cup crumbled goat cheese
3 garlic cloves
2 tablespoons freshly squeezed lemon juice

2 tablespoons plus 2 teaspoons extra-virgin olive oil, divided
¼ teaspoon salt
4 small zucchinis, spiralized

1. Preheat the oven to 375ºF (190ºC).
2. Wrap the chopped beet in a piece of aluminum foil and seal well.
3. Roast in the preheated oven for 30 to 40 minutes until tender.
4. Meanwhile, heat a skillet over medium-high heat until hot. Add the walnuts and toast for 5 to 7 minutes, or until fragrant and lightly browned.
5. Remove the cooked beets from the oven and place in a food processor. Add the toasted walnuts, goat cheese, garlic, lemon juice, 2 tablespoons of olive oil, and salt. Pulse until smoothly blended. Set aside.
6. Heat the remaining 2 teaspoons of olive oil in a large skillet over medium heat. Add the zucchini and toss to coat in the oil. Cook for 2 to 3 minutes, stirring gently, or until the zucchini is softened.
7. Transfer the zucchini to a serving plate and toss with the beet pesto, then serve.

Per Serving
calories: 423 | fat: 38.8g | protein: 8.0g
carbs: 17.1g | fiber: 6.0g | sodium: 338mg

Roasted Vegetables and Chickpeas

Prep time: 10 minutes | Cook time: 30 minutes | Serves 2

4 cups cauliflower florets (about ½ small head)
2 medium carrots, peeled, halved, and then sliced into quarters lengthwise
2 tablespoons olive oil, divided
½ teaspoon garlic powder, divided
½ teaspoon salt, divided
2 teaspoons za'atar spice mix, divided
1 (15-ounce / 425-g) can chickpeas, drained, rinsed, and patted dry
¾ cup plain Greek yogurt
1 teaspoon harissa spice paste

1. Preheat the oven to 400ºF (205ºC). Line a sheet pan with foil or parchment paper.
2. Place the cauliflower and carrots in a large bowl. Drizzle with 1 tablespoon olive oil and sprinkle with ¼ teaspoon of garlic powder, ¼ teaspoon of salt, and 1 teaspoon of za'atar. Toss well to combine.
3. Spread the vegetables onto one half of the sheet pan in a single layer.
4. Place the chickpeas in the same bowl and season with the remaining 1 tablespoon of oil, ¼ teaspoon of garlic powder, and ¼ teaspoon of salt, and the remaining za'atar. Toss well to combine.
5. Spread the chickpeas onto the other half of the sheet pan.
6. Roast for 30 minutes, or until the vegetables are tender and the chickpeas start to turn golden. Flip the vegetables halfway through the cooking time, and give the chickpeas a stir so they cook evenly.
7. The chickpeas may need an extra few minutes if you like them crispy. If so, remove the vegetables and leave the chickpeas in until they're cooked to desired crispiness.
8. Meanwhile, combine the yogurt and harissa in a small bowl. Taste and add additional harissa as desired, then serve.

Per Serving
calories: 468 | fat: 23.0g | protein: 18.1g
carbs: 54.1g | fiber: 13.8g | sodium: 631mg

Sweet Potato Chickpea Buddha Bowl

Prep time: 10 minutes | Cook time: 10 to 15 minutes | Serves 2

Sauce:
1 tablespoon tahini
2 tablespoons plain Greek yogurt
2 tablespoons hemp seeds
1 garlic clove, minced
Pinch salt
Freshly ground black pepper, to taste

Bowl:
1 small sweet potato, peeled and finely diced
1 teaspoon extra-virgin olive oil
1 cup from 1
(15-ounce / 425-g) can low-sodium chickpeas, drained and rinsed
2 cups baby kale

Make the Sauce
1. Whisk together the tahini and yogurt in a small bowl.
2. Stir in the hemp seeds and minced garlic. Season with salt pepper. Add 2 to 3 tablespoons water to create a creamy yet pourable consistency and set aside.
3. Make the Bowl
4. Preheat the oven to 425ºF (220ºC). Line a baking sheet with parchment paper.
5. Place the sweet potato on the prepared baking sheet and drizzle with the olive oil. Toss well
6. Roast in the preheated oven for 10 to 15 minutes, stirring once during cooking, or until fork-tender and browned.
7. In each of 2 bowls, place ½ cup of chickpeas, 1 cup of baby kale, and half of the cooked sweet potato. Serve drizzled with half of the prepared sauce.

Per Serving
calories: 323 | fat: 14.1g | protein: 17.0g
carbs: 36.0 g | fiber: 7.9g | sodium: 304mg

Easy Zucchini Patties

Prep time: 15 minutes | Cook time: 5 minutes | Serves 2

2 medium zucchinis, shredded	chickpea flour
1 teaspoon salt, divided	1 tablespoon chopped fresh mint
2 eggs	1 scallion, chopped
2 tablespoons	2 tablespoons extra-virgin olive oil

1. Put the shredded zucchini in a fine-mesh strainer and season with ½ teaspoon of salt. Set aside.
2. Beat together the eggs, chickpea flour, mint, scallion, and remaining ½ teaspoon of salt in a medium bowl.
3. Squeeze the zucchini to drain as much liquid as possible. Add the zucchini to the egg mixture and stir until well incorporated.
4. Heat the olive oil in a large skillet over medium-high heat.
5. Drop the zucchini mixture by spoonful into the skillet. Gently flatten the zucchini with the back of a spatula.
6. Cook for 2 to 3 minutes or until golden brown. Flip and cook for an additional 2 minutes.
7. Remove from the heat and serve on a plate.

Per Serving
calories: 264 | fat: 20.0g | protein: 9.8g
carbs: 16.1g | fiber: 4.0g | sodium: 1780mg

Garlic-Butter Asparagus with Parmesan

Prep time: 5 minutes | Cook time: 8 minutes | Serves 2

1 cup water	butter
1 pound (454 g) asparagus, trimmed	Salt and ground black pepper, to taste
2 cloves garlic, chopped	3 tablespoons grated Parmesan cheese
3 tablespoons almond	

1. Pour the water into the Instant Pot and insert a trivet.
2. Put the asparagus on a tin foil add the butter and garlic. Season to taste with salt and pepper.
3. Fold over the foil and seal the asparagus inside so the foil doesn't come open. Arrange the asparagus on the trivet.
4. Secure the lid. Select the Manual mode and set the cooking time for 8 minutes at High Pressure.
5. Once cooking is complete, do a quick pressure release. Carefully open the lid.
6. Unwrap the foil packet and serve sprinkled with the Parmesan cheese.

Per Serving
calories: 243 | fat: 15.7g | protein: 12.3g
carbs: 15.3g | fiber: 7.3g | sodium: 435mg

Simple Honey-Glazed Baby Carrots

Prep time: 5 minutes | Cook time: 6 minutes | Serves 2

⅔ cup water	1 teaspoon dried thyme
1½ pounds (680 g) baby carrots	1½ teaspoons dried dill
4 tablespoons almond butter	Salt, to taste
½ cup honey	

1. Pour the water into the Instant Pot and add a steamer basket. Place the baby carrots in the basket.
2. Secure the lid. Select the Manual mode and set the cooking time for 4 minutes at High Pressure.
3. Once cooking is complete, do a quick pressure release. Carefully open the lid.
4. Transfer the carrots to a plate and set aside.
5. Pour the water out of the Instant Pot and dry it.
6. Press the Sauté button on the Instant Pot and heat the almond butter.
7. Stir in the honey, thyme, and dill.
8. Return the carrots to the Instant Pot and stir until well coated. Sauté for another 1 minute.
9. Taste and season with salt as needed. Serve warm.

Per Serving
calories: 575 | fat: 23.5g | protein: 2.8g
carbs: 90.6g | fiber: 10.3g | sodium: 547mg

Zucchini Crisp

Prep time: 10 minutes | Cook time: 20 minutes | Serves 2

4 zucchinis, sliced into ½-inch rounds
½ cup unsweetened almond milk
1 teaspoon fresh lemon juice
1 teaspoon arrowroot powder
½ teaspoon salt, divided
½ cup whole wheat bread crumbs
¼ cup nutritional yeast
¼ cup hemp seeds
½ teaspoon garlic powder
¼ teaspoon crushed red pepper
¼ teaspoon black pepper

1. Preheat the oven to 375ºF (190ºC). Line two baking sheets with parchment paper and set aside.
2. Put the zucchini in a medium bowl with the almond milk, lemon juice, arrowroot powder, and ¼ teaspoon of salt. Stir to mix well.
3. In a large bowl with a lid, thoroughly combine the bread crumbs, nutritional yeast, hemp seeds, garlic powder, crushed red pepper and black pepper. Add the zucchini in batches and shake until the slices are evenly coated.
4. Arrange the zucchini on the prepared baking sheets in a single layer.
5. Bake in the preheated oven for about 20 minutes, or until the zucchini slices are golden brown.
6. Season with the remaining ¼ teaspoon of salt before serving.

Per Serving
calories: 255 | fat: 11.3g | protein: 8.6g
carbs: 31.9g | fiber: 3.8g | sodium: 826mg

Creamy Sweet Potatoes and Collards

Prep time: 20 minutes | Cook time: 35 minutes | Serves 2

1 tablespoon avocado oil
3 garlic cloves, chopped
1 yellow onion, diced
½ teaspoon crushed red pepper flakes
1 large sweet potato, peeled and diced
2 bunches collard greens (about 2 pounds/907 g), stemmed, leaves chopped into 1-inch squares
1 (14.5-ounce / 411-g) can diced tomatoes with juice
1 (15-ounce / 425-g) can red kidney beans or chickpeas, drained and rinsed
1½ cups water
½ cup unsweetened coconut milk
Salt and black pepper, to taste

1. In a large, deep skillet over medium heat, melt the avocado oil.
2. Add the garlic, onion, and red pepper flakes and cook for 3 minutes. Stir in the sweet potato and collards.
3. Add the tomatoes with their juice, beans, water, and coconut milk and mix well. Bring the mixture just to a boil.
4. Reduce the heat to medium-low, cover, and simmer for about 30 minutes, or until softened.
5. Season to taste with salt and pepper and serve.

Per Serving
calories: 445 | fat: 9.6g | protein: 18.1g
carbs: 73.1g | fiber: 22.1g | sodium: 703mg

Paprika Cauliflower Steaks with Walnut Sauce

Prep time: 5 minutes | Cook time: 30 minutes | Serves 2

Walnut Sauce:

½ cup raw walnut halves
2 tablespoons virgin olive oil, divided
1 clove garlic, chopped
1 small yellow onion, chopped
½ cup unsweetened almond milk
2 tablespoons fresh lemon juice
Salt and pepper, to taste

Paprika Cauliflower:

1 medium head cauliflower
1 teaspoon sweet paprika
1 teaspoon minced fresh thyme leaves (about 2 sprigs)

1. Preheat the oven to 350ºF (180ºC).
2. Make the walnut sauce: Toast the walnuts in a large, ovenproof skillet over medium heat until fragrant and slightly darkened, about 5 minutes. Transfer the walnuts to a blender.
3. Heat 1 tablespoon of olive oil in the skillet. Add the garlic and onion and sauté for about 2 minutes, or until slightly softened. Transfer the garlic and onion into the blender, along with the almond milk, lemon juice, salt, and pepper. Blend the ingredients until smooth and creamy. Keep the sauce warm while you prepare the cauliflower.
4. Make the paprika cauliflower: Cut two 1-inch-thick "steaks" from the center of the cauliflower. Lightly moisten the steaks with water and season both sides with paprika, thyme, salt, and pepper.
5. Heat the remaining 1 tablespoon of olive oil in the skillet over medium-high heat. Add the cauliflower steaks and sear for about 3 minutes until evenly browned. Flip the cauliflower steaks and transfer the skillet to the oven.
6. Roast in the preheated oven for about 20 minutes until crisp-tender.
7. Serve the cauliflower steaks warm with the walnut sauce on the side.

Per Serving

calories: 367 | fat: 27.9g | protein: 7.0g
carbs: 22.7g | fiber: 5.8g | sodium: 173mg

Stir-Fried Eggplant

Prep time: 25 minutes | Cook time: 15 minutes | Serves 2

1 cup water, plus more as needed
½ cup chopped red onion
1 tablespoon finely chopped garlic
1 tablespoon dried Italian herb seasoning
1 teaspoon ground cumin
1 small eggplant (about 8 ounces / 227 g), peeled and cut into ½-inch cubes
1 medium carrot, sliced
2 cups green beans, cut into 1-inch pieces
2 ribs celery, sliced
1 cup corn kernels
2 tablespoons almond butter
2 medium tomatoes, chopped

1. Heat 1 tablespoon of water in a large soup pot over medium-high heat until it sputters.
2. Cook the onion for 2 minutes, adding a little more water as needed.
3. Add the garlic, Italian seasoning, cumin, and eggplant and stir-fry for 2 to 3 minutes, adding a little more water as needed.
4. Add the carrot, green beans, celery, corn kernels, and ½ cup of water and stir well. Reduce the heat to medium, cover, and cook for 8 to 10 minutes, stirring occasionally, or until the vegetables are tender.
5. Meanwhile, in a bowl, stir together the almond butter and ½ cup of water.
6. Remove the vegetables from the heat and stir in the almond butter mixture and chopped tomatoes. Cool for a few minutes before serving.

Per Serving

calories: 176 | fat: 5.5g | protein: 5.8g
carbs: 25.4g | fiber: 8.6g | sodium: 198mg

Chapter 7 Poultry and Meats

Grilled Lemon Chicken

Prep time: 10 minutes | Cook time: 12 to 14 minutes | Serves 2

Marinade:

4 tablespoons freshly squeezed lemon juice
2 tablespoons olive oil, plus more for greasing the grill grates
1 teaspoon dried basil
1 teaspoon paprika
½ teaspoon dried thyme
¼ teaspoon salt
¼ teaspoon garlic powder

2 (4-ounce / 113-g) boneless, skinless chicken breasts

1. Make the marinade: Whisk together the lemon juice, olive oil, basil, paprika, thyme, salt, and garlic powder in a large bowl until well combined.
2. Add the chicken breasts to the bowl and let marinate for at least 30 minutes.
3. When ready to cook, preheat the grill to medium-high heat. Lightly grease the grill grates with the olive oil.
4. Discard the marinade and arrange the chicken breasts on the grill grates.
5. Grill for 12 to 14 minutes, flipping the chicken halfway through, or until a meat thermometer inserted in the center of the chicken reaches 165ºF (74ºC).
6. Let the chicken cool for 5 minutes and serve warm.

Tip: You can add any of your favorite spices or herbs to this marinade. To make this a complete meal, you can serve it with sautéed green beans and mashed potatoes.

Per Serving
calories: 251 | fat: 15.5g | protein: 27.3g
carbs: 1.9g | fiber: 1.0g | sodium: 371mg

Quick Chicken Salad Wraps

Prep time: 15 minutes | Cook time: 0 minutes | Serves 2

Tzatziki Sauce:

½ cup plain Greek yogurt
1 tablespoon freshly squeezed lemon juice
Pinch garlic powder
1 teaspoon dried dill
Salt and freshly ground black pepper, to taste

Salad Wraps:

2 (8-inch) whole-grain pita bread
1 cup shredded chicken meat
2 cups mixed greens
2 roasted red bell peppers, thinly sliced
½ English cucumber, peeled if desired and thinly sliced
¼ cup pitted black olives
1 scallion, chopped

1. Make the tzatziki sauce: In a bowl, whisk together the yogurt, lemon juice, garlic powder, dill, salt, and pepper until creamy and smooth.
2. Make the salad wraps: Place the pita bread on a clean work surface and spoon ¼ cup of the tzatziki sauce onto each piece of pita bread, spreading it all over. Top with the shredded chicken, mixed greens, red pepper slices, cucumber slices, black olives, finished by chopped scallion.
3. Roll the salad wraps and enjoy.

Tips: You can cover the bottom half of each salad wrap in foil, for it's easier to eat. If you cannot find the pita bread, whole-grain naan bread will work, too.

Per Serving
calories: 428 | fat: 10.6g | protein: 31.1g
carbs: 50.9g | fiber: 6.0g | sodium: 675mg

Roasted Chicken Thighs With Basmati Rice

Prep time: 15 minutes | Cook time: 50 to 55 minutes | Serves 2

Chicken:

½ teaspoon cumin
½ teaspoon cinnamon
½ teaspoon paprika
¼ teaspoon ginger powder
¼ teaspoon garlic powder
¼ teaspoon coriander
¼ teaspoon salt
⅛ teaspoon cayenne pepper
10 ounces (284 g) boneless, skinless chicken thighs (about 4 pieces)

Rice:

1 tablespoon olive oil
½ small onion, minced
½ cup basmati rice
2 pinches saffron
1 cup low-sodium chicken stock
¼ teaspoon salt

Make the Chicken

1. Preheat the oven to 350ºF (180ºC).
2. Combine the cumin, cinnamon, paprika, ginger powder, garlic powder, coriander, salt, and cayenne pepper in a small bowl.
3. Using your hands to rub the spice mixture all over the chicken thighs.
4. Transfer the chicken thighs to a baking dish. Roast in the preheated oven for 35 to 40 minutes, or until the internal temperature reaches 165ºF (74ºC) on a meat thermometer.

Make the Rice

1. Meanwhile, heat the olive oil in a skillet over medium-high heat.
2. Sauté the onion for 5 minutes until fragrant, stirring occasionally.
3. Stir in the basmati rice, saffron, chicken stock, and salt. Reduce the heat to low, cover, and bring to a simmer for 15 minutes, until light and fluffy.
4. Remove the chicken from the oven to a plate and serve with the rice.

Tip: You can substitute the boneless or bone-in chicken breasts for chicken thighs.

Per Serving

calories: 400 | fat: 9.6g | protein: 37.2g carbs: 40.7g | fiber: 2.1g | sodium: 714mg

Slow Cook Lamb Shanks with Cannellini Beans Stew

Prep time: 20 minutes | Cook time: 10 hours 15 minutes | Serves 12

1 (19-ounce / 539-g) can cannellini beans, rinsed and drained
1 large yellow onion, chopped
2 medium-sized carrots, diced
1 large stalk celery, chopped
2 cloves garlic, thinly sliced
4 (1½-pound / 680-g) lamb shanks, fat trimmed
2 teaspoons tarragon
½ teaspoon sea salt
¼ teaspoon ground black pepper
1 (28-ounce / 794-g) can diced tomatoes, with the juice

1. Combine the beans, onion, carrots, celery, and garlic in the slow cooker. Stir to mix well.
2. Add the lamb shanks and sprinkle with tarragon, salt, and ground black pepper.
3. Pour in the tomatoes with juice, then cover the lid and cook on high for an hour.
4. Reduce the heat to low and cook for 9 hours or until the lamb is super tender.
5. Transfer the lamb on a plate, then pour the bean mixture in a colander over a separate bowl to reserve the liquid.
6. Let the liquid sit for 5 minutes until set, then skim the fat from the surface of the liquid. Pour the bean mixture back to the liquid.
7. Remove the bones from the lamb heat and discard the bones. Put the lamb meat and bean mixture back to the slow cooker. Cover and cook to reheat for 15 minutes or until heated through.
8. Pour them on a large serving plate and serve immediately.

Tip: If you want to remove as much salt that contains in the canned beans as possible, drain the canned beans in a colander and rinse under running cold water, then pat dry with paper towels.

Per Serving

calories: 317 | fat: 9.7g | protein: 52.1g carbs: 7.0g | fiber: 2.1g | sodium: 375mg

Lamb Tagine with Couscous and Almonds

Prep time: 15 minutes | Cook time: 7 hours 7 minutes | Serves 6

2 tablespoons almond flour
Juice and zest of 1 navel orange
2 tablespoons extra-virgin olive oil
2 pounds (907 g) boneless lamb leg, fat trimmed and cut into 1½-inch cubes
½ cup low-sodium chicken stock
2 large white onions, chopped
1 teaspoon pumpkin pie spice
¼ teaspoon crushed saffron threads
1 teaspoon ground cumin
¼ teaspoon ground red pepper flakes
½ teaspoon sea salt
2 tablespoons raw honey
1 cup pitted dates
3 cups cooked couscous, for serving
2 tablespoons toasted slivered almonds, for serving

1. Combine the almond flour with orange juice in a large bowl. Stir until smooth, then mix in the orange zest. Set aside.
2. Heat the olive oil in a nonstick skillet over medium-high heat until shimmering.
3. Add the lamb cubes and sauté for 7 minutes or until lightly browned.
4. Pour in the flour mixture and chicken stock, then add the onions, pumpkin pie spice, saffron, cumin, ground red pepper flakes, and salt. Stir to mix well.
5. Pour them in the slow cooker. Cover and cook on low for 6 hours or until the internal temperature of the lamb reaches at least 145ºF (63ºC).
6. When the cooking is complete, mix in the honey and dates, then cook for another an hour.
7. Put the couscous in a tagine bowl or a simple large bowl, then top with lamb mixture. Scatter with slivered almonds and serve immediately.

Tip: How to cook the couscous: Bring a saucepan of salted water to a boil. Turn off the heat, then add the couscous and cover the pan. Stream the couscous for 5 minutes or until tender. Fluff with a fork.

Per Serving
calories: 447 | fat: 10.2g | protein: 36.3g
carbs: 53.5g | fiber: 4.9g | sodium: 329mg

Grilled Chicken and Zucchini Kebabs

Prep time: 10 minutes | Cook time: 20 minutes | Serves 4

¼ cup extra-virgin olive oil
2 tablespoons balsamic vinegar
1 teaspoon dried oregano, crushed between your fingers
1 pound (454 g) boneless, skinless chicken breasts, cut into 1½-inch pieces
2 medium zucchinis, cut into 1-inch pieces
½ cup Kalamata olives, pitted and halved
2 tablespoons olive brine
¼ cup torn fresh basil leaves
Nonstick cooking spray

Special Equipment:
14 to 15 (12-inch) wooden skewers, soaked for at least 30 minutes

1. Spray the grill grates with nonstick cooking spray. Preheat the grill to medium-high heat.
2. In a small bowl, whisk together the olive oil, vinegar, and oregano. Divide the marinade between two large plastic zip-top bags.
3. Add the chicken to one bag and the zucchini to another. Seal and massage the marinade into both the chicken and zucchini.
4. Thread the chicken onto 6 wooden skewers. Thread the zucchini onto 8 or 9 wooden skewers.
5. Cook the kebabs in batches on the grill for 5 minutes, flip, and grill for 5 minutes more, or until any chicken juices run clear.
6. Remove the chicken and zucchini from the skewers to a large serving bowl. Toss with the olives, olive brine, and basil and serve.

Per Serving
calories: 283 | fat: 15.0g | protein: 11.0g
carbs: 26.0g | fiber: 3.0g | sodium: 575mg

Panko Grilled Chicken Patties

Prep time: 10 minutes | Cook time: 8 to 10 minutes | Serves 4

1 pound (454 g) ground chicken
3 tablespoons crumbled feta cheese
3 tablespoons finely chopped red pepper
¼ cup finely chopped red onion
3 tablespoons panko
bread crumbs
1 garlic clove, minced
1 teaspoon chopped fresh oregano
¼ teaspoon salt
⅛ teaspoon freshly ground black pepper
Cooking spray

1. Mix together the ground chicken, feta cheese, red pepper, red onion, bread crumbs, garlic, oregano, salt, and black pepper in a large bowl, and stir to incorporate.
2. Divide the chicken mixture into 8 equal portions and form each portion into a patty with your hands.
3. Preheat a grill to medium-high heat and oil the grill grates with cooking spray.
4. Arrange the patties on the grill grates and grill each side for 4 to 5 minutes, or until the patties are cooked through.
5. Rest for 5 minutes before serving.

Tip: Use any leftovers to your favorite salad. You can cook the patties in a nonstick skillet over medium-high, 4 to 5 minutes per side, until cooked through.

Per Serving
calories: 241 | fat: 13.5g | protein: 23.2g
carbs:6.7g | fiber: 1.1g | sodium: 321mg

Coconut Chicken Tenders

Prep time: 10 minutes | Cook time: 15 to 20 minutes | Serves 6

4 chicken breasts, each cut lengthwise into 3 strips
½ teaspoon salt
¼ teaspoon freshly ground black pepper
½ cup coconut flour
2 eggs
2 tablespoons unsweetened plain almond milk
1 cup unsweetened coconut flakes

1. Preheat the oven to 400ºF (205ºC). Line a baking sheet with parchment paper.
2. On a clean work surface, season the chicken with salt and pepper.
3. In a small bowl, add the coconut flour. In a separate bowl, whisk the eggs with almond milk until smooth. Place the coconut flakes on a plate.
4. One at a time, roll the chicken strips in the coconut flour, then dredge them in the egg mixture, shaking off any excess, and finally in the coconut flakes to coat.
5. Arrange the coated chicken pieces on the baking skeet. Bake in the preheated oven for 15 to 20 minutes, flipping the chicken halfway through, or until the chicken is golden brown and cooked through.
6. Remove from the oven and serve on plates.

Tip: The chicken tenders can be served with anything you like. They taste great with a small potato with a green salad.

Per Serving
calories: 215 | fat: 12.6g | protein: 20.2g
carbs: 8.9g | fiber: 6.1g | sodium: 345mg

Easy Grilled Pork Chops

Prep time: 20 minutes | Cook time: 10 minutes | Serves 4

¼ cup extra-virgin olive oil
2 tablespoons fresh thyme leaves
1 teaspoon smoked
paprika
1 teaspoon salt
4 pork loin chops, ½-inch-thick

1. In a small bowl, mix together the olive oil, thyme, paprika, and salt.
2. Put the pork chops in a plastic zip-top bag or a bowl and coat them with the spice mix. Let them marinate for 15 minutes.
3. Preheat the grill to high heat. Cook the pork chops for 4 minutes on each side until cooked through.
4. Serve warm.

Per Serving
calories: 282 | fat: 23.0g | protein: 21.0g
carbs: 1.0g | fiber: 0g | sodium: 832mg

Gyro Burgers with Tahini Sauce

Prep time: 15 minutes | Cook time: 10 minutes | Serves 4

2 tablespoons extra-virgin olive oil
1 tablespoon dried oregano
1¼ teaspoons garlic powder, divided
1 teaspoon ground cumin
½ teaspoon freshly ground black pepper
¼ teaspoon kosher or sea salt
1 pound (454 g) beef flank steak, top round steak, or lamb leg steak, center cut, about 1 inch thick
1 medium green bell pepper, halved and seeded
2 tablespoons tahini or peanut butter
1 tablespoon hot water (optional)
½ cup plain Greek yogurt
1 tablespoon freshly squeezed lemon juice
1 cup thinly sliced red onion
4 (6-inch) whole-wheat pita breads, warmed
Nonstick cooking spray

1. Set an oven rack about 4 inches below the broiler element. Preheat the oven broiler to high. Line a large, rimmed baking sheet with aluminum foil. Place a wire cooling rack on the foil, and spray the rack with nonstick cooking spray. Set aside.
2. In a small bowl, whisk together the olive oil, oregano, 1 teaspoon of garlic powder, cumin, pepper, and salt. Rub the oil mixture on all sides of the steak, reserving 1 teaspoon of the mixture. Place the steak on the prepared rack. Rub the remaining oil mixture on the bell pepper, and place on the rack, cut-side down. Press the pepper with the heel of your hand to flatten.
3. Broil for 5 minutes. Flip the steak and the pepper pieces, and broil for 2 to 5 minutes more, until the pepper is charred and the internal temperature of the meat measures 145ºF (63ºC) on a meat thermometer. Put the pepper and steak on a cutting board to rest for 5 minutes.
4. Meanwhile, in a small bowl, whisk the tahini until smooth (adding 1 tablespoon of hot water if your tahini is sticky). Add the remaining ¼ teaspoon of garlic powder and the yogurt and lemon juice, and whisk thoroughly.
5. Slice the steak crosswise into ¼-inch-thick strips. Slice the bell pepper into strips. Divide the steak, bell pepper, and onion among the warm pita breads. Drizzle with tahini sauce and serve.

Per Serving
calories: 348 | fat: 15.0g | protein: 33.0g
carbs: 20.0g | fiber: 3.0g | sodium: 530mg

Yogurt Chicken Breasts

Prep time: 10 minutes | Cook time: 10 minutes | Serves 4

Yogurt Sauce:
½ cup plain Greek yogurt
2 tablespoons water
Pinch saffron (3 or 4 threads)
3 garlic cloves, minced
½ onion, chopped
2 tablespoons chopped fresh
cilantro
Juice of ½ lemon
½ teaspoon salt
1 pound (454 g) boneless, skinless chicken breasts, cut into 2-inch strips
1 tablespoon extra-virgin olive oil

1. Make the yogurt sauce: Place the yogurt, water, saffron, garlic, onion, cilantro, lemon juice, and salt in a blender, and pulse until completely mixed.
2. Transfer the yogurt sauce to a large bowl, along with the chicken strips. Toss to coat well.
3. Cover with plastic wrap and marinate in the refrigerator for at least 1 hour, or up to overnight.
4. When ready to cook, heat the olive oil in a large skillet over medium heat.
5. Add the chicken strips to the skillet, discarding any excess marinade. Cook each side for 5 minutes, or until cooked through.
6. Let the chicken cool for 5 minutes before serving.

Tips: If the saffron isn't available, you can use ½ teaspoon of turmeric to replace it.
To make this a complete meal, serve it with your favorite salad or cooked brown rice.

Per Serving
calories: 154 | fat: 4.8g | protein: 26.3g
carbs: 2.9g | fiber: 0g | sodium: 500mg

Potato Lamb and Olive Stew

Prep time: 20 minutes | Cook time: 3 hours 42 minutes | Serves 10

4 tablespoons almond flour
¾ cup low-sodium chicken stock
1¼ pounds (567 g) small potatoes, halved
3 cloves garlic, minced
4 large shallots, cut into ½-inch wedges
3 sprigs fresh rosemary
1 tablespoon lemon zest

Coarse sea salt and black pepper, to taste
3½ pounds (1.6 kg) lamb shanks, fat trimmed and cut crosswise into 1½-inch pieces
2 tablespoons extra-virgin olive oil
½ cup dry white wine
1 cup pitted green olives, halved
2 tablespoons lemon juice

1. Combine 1 tablespoon of almond flour with chicken stock in a bowl. Stir to mix well.
2. Put the flour mixture, potatoes, garlic, shallots, rosemary, and lemon zest in the slow cooker. Sprinkle with salt and black pepper. Stir to mix well. Set aside.
3. Combine the remaining almond flour with salt and black pepper in a large bowl, then dunk the lamb shanks in the flour and toss to coat.
4. Heat the olive oil in a nonstick skillet over medium-high heat until shimmering.
5. Add the well-coated lamb and cook for 10 minutes or until golden brown. Flip the lamb pieces halfway through the cooking time. Transfer the cooked lamb to the slow cooker.
6. Pour the wine in the same skillet, then cook for 2 minutes or until it reduces in half. Pour the wine in the slow cooker.
7. Put the slow cooker lid on and cook on high for 3 hours and 30 minutes or until the lamb is very tender.
8. In the last 20 minutes of the cooking, open the lid and fold in the olive halves to cook.
9. Pour the stew on a large plate, let them sit for 5 minutes, then skim any fat remains over the face of the liquid.
10. Drizzle with lemon juice and sprinkle with salt and pepper. Serve warm.

Tip: To make this a complete meal, you can serve it with roasted root vegetables and mushroom soup.

Per Serving
calories: 309 | fat: 10.3g | protein: 36.9g
carbs: 16.1g | fiber: 2.2g | sodium: 239mg

Spiced Roast Chicken

Prep time: 10 minutes | Cook time: 35 minutes | Serves 6

1 teaspoon garlic powder
1 teaspoon ground paprika
½ teaspoon ground cumin
½ teaspoon ground

coriander
½ teaspoon salt
¼ teaspoon ground cayenne pepper
6 chicken legs
1 teaspoon extra-virgin olive oil

1. Preheat the oven to 400ºF (205ºC).
2. Combine the garlic powder, paprika, cumin, coriander, salt, and cayenne pepper in a small bowl.
3. On a clean work surface, rub the spices all over the chicken legs until completely coated.
4. Heat the olive oil in an ovenproof skillet over medium heat.
5. Add the chicken thighs and sear each side for 8 to 10 minutes, or until the skin is crispy and browned.
6. Transfer the skillet to the preheated oven and continue cooking for 10 to 15 minutes, or until the juices run clear and it registers an internal temperature of 165ºF (74ºC).
7. Remove from the heat and serve on plates.

Tip: The skin-on, bone-in chicken breasts would work just as well as chicken legs with this spice rub. The chicken breasts take longer to cook. Bake for 45 minutes until cooked through, flipping halfway through.

Per Serving
calories: 275 | fat: 15.6g | protein: 30.3g
carbs: 0.9g | fiber: 0g | sodium: 255mg

Parsley-Dijon Chicken and Potatoes

Prep time: 5 minutes | Cook time: 22 minutes | Serves 6

1 tablespoon extra-virgin olive oil
1½ pounds (680 g) boneless, skinless chicken thighs, cut into 1-inch cubes, patted dry
1½ pounds (680 g) Yukon Gold potatoes, unpeeled, cut into ½-inch cubes
2 garlic cloves, minced
¼ cup dry white wine
1 cup low-sodium or no-salt-added chicken broth
1 tablespoon Dijon mustard
¼ teaspoon freshly ground black pepper
¼ teaspoon kosher or sea salt
1 cup chopped fresh flat-leaf (Italian) parsley, including stems
1 tablespoon freshly squeezed lemon juice

1. In a large skillet over medium-high heat, heat the oil. Add the chicken and cook for 5 minutes, stirring only after the chicken has browned on one side. Remove the chicken and reserve on a plate.
2. Add the potatoes to the skillet and cook for 5 minutes, stirring only after the potatoes have become golden and crispy on one side. Push the potatoes to the side of the skillet, add the garlic, and cook, stirring constantly, for 1 minute. Add the wine and cook for 1 minute, until nearly evaporated. Add the chicken broth, mustard, salt, pepper, and reserved chicken. Turn the heat to high and bring to a boil.
3. Once boiling, cover, reduce the heat to medium-low, and cook for 10 to 12 minutes, until the potatoes are tender and the internal temperature of the chicken measures 165°F (74°C) on a meat thermometer and any juices run clear.
4. During the last minute of cooking, stir in the parsley. Remove from the heat, stir in the lemon juice, and serve.

Per Serving
calories: 324 | fat: 9.0g | protein: 16.0g
carbs: 45.0g | fiber: 5.0g | sodium: 560mg

Chicken Cacciatore

Prep time: 15 minutes | Cook time: 1 hour and 30 minutes | Serves 2

1½ pounds (680 g) bone-in chicken thighs, skin removed and patted dry
Salt, to taste
2 tablespoons olive oil
½ large onion, thinly sliced
4 ounces (113 g) baby bella mushrooms, sliced
1 red sweet pepper, cut into 1-inch pieces
1 (15-ounce / 425-g) can crushed fire-roasted tomatoes
1 fresh rosemary sprig
½ cup dry red wine
1 teaspoon Italian herb seasoning
½ teaspoon garlic powder
3 tablespoons flour

1. Season the chicken thighs with a generous pinch of salt.
2. Heat the olive oil in a Dutch oven over medium-high heat. Add the chicken and brown for 5 minutes per side.
3. Add the onion, mushrooms, and sweet pepper to the Dutch oven and sauté for another 5 minutes.
4. Add the tomatoes, rosemary, wine, Italian seasoning, garlic powder, and salt, stirring well.
5. Bring the mixture to a boil, then reduce the heat to low. Allow to simmer slowly for at least 1 hour, stirring occasionally, or until the chicken is tender and easily pulls away from the bone.
6. Measure out 1 cup of the sauce from the pot and put it into a bowl. Add the flour and whisk well to make a slurry.
7. Increase the heat to medium-high and slowly whisk the slurry into the pot. Stir until it comes to a boil and cook until the sauce is thickened.
8. Remove the chicken from the bones and shred it, and add it back to the sauce before serving, if desired.

Per Serving
calories: 520 | fat: 23.1g | protein: 31.8g
carbs: 37.0g | fiber: 6.0g | sodium: 484mg

Sautéed Ground Turkey with Brown Rice

Prep time: 20 minutes | Cook time: 45 minutes | Serves 2

1 tablespoon olive oil
½ medium onion, minced
2 garlic cloves, minced
8 ounces (227 g) ground turkey breast
½ cup chopped roasted red peppers, (about 2 jarred peppers)
¼ cup sun-dried tomatoes, minced
1¼ cups low-sodium chicken stock
½ cup brown rice
1 teaspoon dried oregano
Salt, to taste
2 cups lightly packed baby spinach

1. In a skillet, heat the olive oil over medium heat. Sauté the onion for 5 minutes, stirring occasionally.
2. Stir in the garlic and sauté for 30 seconds more until fragrant.
3. Add the turkey breast and cook for about 7 minutes, breaking apart with a wooden spoon, until the turkey is no longer pink.
4. Stir in the roasted red peppers, tomatoes, chicken stock, brown rice, and oregano and bring to a boil.
5. When the mixture starts to boil, cover, and reduce the heat to medium-low. Bring to a simmer until the rice is tender, stirring occasionally, about 30 minutes. Sprinkle with the salt.
6. Add the baby spinach and keep stirring until wilted.
7. Remove from the heat and serve warm.

Per Serving
calories: 445 | fat: 16.8g | protein: 30.2g
carbs: 48.9g | fiber: 5.1g | sodium: 662mg

Beef Stew with Beans and Zucchini

Prep time: 20 minutes | Cook time: 6 to 8 hours | Serves 2

1 (15-ounce / 425-g) can diced or crushed tomatoes with basil
1 teaspoon beef base
2 tablespoons olive oil, divided
8 ounces (227 g) baby bella (cremini) mushrooms, quartered
2 garlic cloves, minced
½ large onion, diced
1 pound (454 g) cubed beef stew meat
3 tablespoons flour
¼ teaspoon salt
Pinch freshly ground black pepper
¾ cup dry red wine
¼ cup minced brined olives
1 fresh rosemary sprig
1 (15-ounce / 425-g) can white cannellini beans, drained and rinsed
1 medium zucchini, cut in half lengthwise and then cut into 1-inch pieces.

1. Place the tomatoes into a slow cooker and set it to low heat. Add the beef base and stir to incorporate.
2. Heat 1 tablespoon of olive oil in a large sauté pan over medium heat.
3. Add the mushrooms and onion and sauté for 10 minutes, stirring occasionally, or until they're golden.
4. Add the garlic and cook for 30 seconds more. Transfer the vegetables to the slow cooker.
5. In a plastic food storage bag, combine the stew meat with the flour, salt, and pepper. Seal the bag and shake well to combine.
6. Heat the remaining 1 tablespoon of olive oil in the sauté pan over high heat.
7. Add the floured meat and sear to get a crust on the outside edges. Deglaze the pan by adding about half of the red wine and scraping up any browned bits on the bottom. Stir so the wine thickens a bit and transfer to the slow cooker along with any remaining wine.
8. Stir the stew to incorporate the ingredients. Stir in the olives and rosemary, cover, and cook for 6 to 8 hours on Low.
9. About 30 minutes before the stew is finished, add the beans and zucchini to let them warm through. Serve warm.

Per Serving
calories: 389 | fat: 15.1g | protein: 30.8g
carbs: 25.0g | fiber: 8.0g | sodium: 582mg

Baked Teriyaki Turkey Meatballs

Prep time: 20 minutes | Cook time: 20 minutes | Serves 6

1 pound (454 g) lean ground turkey
1 egg, whisked
¼ cup finely chopped scallions, both white and green parts
2 garlic cloves, minced
2 tablespoons

reduced-sodium tamari or gluten-free soy sauce
1 teaspoon grated fresh ginger
1 tablespoon honey
2 teaspoons mirin
1 teaspoon olive oil

1. Preheat the oven to 400ºF (205ºC). Line a baking sheet with parchment paper and set aside.
2. Mix together the ground turkey, whisked egg, scallions, garlic, tamari, ginger, honey, mirin, and olive oil in a large bowl, and stir until well blended.
3. Using a tablespoon to scoop out rounded heaps of the turkey mixture, and then roll them into balls with your hands. Transfer the balls to the prepared baking sheet.
4. Bake in the preheated oven for 20 minutes, flipping the balls with a spatula halfway through, or until the meatballs are browned and cooked through.
5. Serve warm.

Tip: Teriyaki is a cooking technique used in Japanese cuisine where foods are broiled or grilled with a glaze of soy sauce, mirin, and sugar. In this recipe, the sugar is replaced with honey, and it is still packed with teriyaki flavor.

Per Serving
calories: 158 | fat: 8.6g | protein: 16.2g
carbs: 4.0g | fiber: 0.2g | sodium: 269mg

Beef, Tomato, and Lentils Stew

Prep time: 10 minutes | Cook time: 10 minutes | Serves 4

1 tablespoon extra-virgin olive oil
1 pound (454 g) extra-lean ground beef
1 onion, chopped
1 (14-ounce / 397-g) can chopped

tomatoes with garlic and basil, drained
1 (14-ounce / 397-g) can lentils, drained
½ teaspoon sea salt
⅛ teaspoon freshly ground black pepper

1. Heat the olive oil in a pot over medium-high heat until shimmering.
2. Add the beef and onion to the pot and sauté for 5 minutes or until the beef is lightly browned.
3. Add the remaining ingredients. Bring to a boil. Reduce the heat to medium and cook for 4 more minutes or until the lentils are tender. Keep stirring during the cooking.
4. Pour them in a large serving bowl and serve immediately.

Tip: If you want to remove as much salt that contains in the canned beans as possible, drain the canned beans in a colander and rinse under running cold water, then pat dry with paper towels.

Per Serving
calories: 460 | fat: 14.8g | protein: 44.2g
carbs: 36.9g | fiber: 17.0g | sodium: 320mg

Ground Beef, Tomato, and Kidney Bean Chili

Prep time: 10 minutes | Cook time: 15 minutes | Serves 4

1 tablespoon extra-virgin olive oil
1 pound (454 g) extra-lean ground beef
1 onion, chopped
2 (14-ounce / 397-g) cans kidney beans
2 (28-ounce / 794-g) cans chopped tomatoes, juice reserved

Simple Chili Spice:
1 teaspoon garlic powder
1 tablespoon chili powder
½ teaspoon sea salt

1. Heat the olive oil in a pot over medium-high heat until shimmering.
2. Add the beef and onion to the pot and sauté for 5 minutes or until the beef is lightly browned and the onion is translucent.
3. Add the remaining ingredients. Bring to a boil. Reduce the heat to medium and cook for 10 more minutes. Keep stirring during the cooking.
4. Pour them in a large serving bowl and serve immediately.

Tip: You can make your own chili spice for this recipe by mixing chili powder, dried oregano, onion powder, cumin, garlic powder, ground coriander, and sea salt in a 4:2:1:1:1:1:1 ratio.

Per Serving
calories: 891 | fat: 20.1g | protein: 116.3g
carbs: 62.9g | fiber: 17.0g | sodium: 561mg

Herbed-Mustard-Coated Pork Tenderloin

Prep time: 10 minutes | Cook time: 15 minutes | Serves 4

3 tablespoons fresh rosemary leaves
¼ cup Dijon mustard
½ cup fresh parsley leaves
6 garlic cloves
½ teaspoon sea salt
¼ teaspoon freshly ground black pepper
1 tablespoon extra-virgin olive oil
1 (1½-pound / 680-g) pork tenderloin

1. Preheat the oven to 400ºF (205ºC).
2. Put all the ingredients, except for the pork tenderloin, in a food processor. Pulse until it has a thick consistency.
3. Put the pork tenderloin on a baking sheet, then rub with the mixture to coat well.
4. Put the sheet in the preheated oven and bake for 15 minutes or until the internal temperature of the pork reaches at least 165ºF (74ºC). Flip the tenderloin halfway through the cooking time.
5. Transfer the cooked pork tenderloin to a large plate and allow to cool for 5 minutes before serving.

Tip: If you want to make your pork hotter, you can add a touch of crushed jalapeño to the mixture in the food processor.

Per Serving
calories: 363 | fat: 18.1g | protein: 2.2g
carbs: 4.9g | fiber: 2.0g | sodium: 514mg

Macadamia Pork

Prep time: 10 minutes | Cook time: 10 minutes | Serves 4

1 (1-pound / 454-g) pork tenderloin, cut into ½-inch slices and pounded thin
1 teaspoon sea salt, divided
¼ teaspoon freshly ground black pepper, divided
½ cup macadamia nuts
1 cup unsweetened coconut milk
1 tablespoon extra-virgin olive oil

1. Preheat the oven to 400ºF (205ºC).
2. On a clean work surface, rub the pork with ½ teaspoon of the salt and ⅛ teaspoon of the ground black pepper. Set aside.
3. Ground the macadamia nuts in a food processor, then combine with remaining salt and black pepper in a bowl. Stir to mix well and set aside.
4. Combine the coconut milk and olive oil in a separate bowl. Stir to mix well.
5. Dredge the pork chops into the bowl of coconut milk mixture, then dunk into the bowl of macadamia nut mixture to coat well. Shake the excess off.
6. Put the well-coated pork chops on a baking sheet, then bake for 10 minutes or until the internal temperature of the pork reaches at least 165ºF (74ºC).
7. Transfer the pork chops to a serving plate and serve immediately.

Tip: To make this a complete meal, you can serve it with roasted cauliflower. Or you can use it as a snack to serve during the brunch time. Or you can use it as the filling to make the burgers.

Per Serving
calories: 436 | fat: 32.8g | protein: 33.1g
carbs: 5.9g | fiber: 3.0g | sodium: 310mg

Almond-Crusted Chicken Tenders with Honey

Prep time: 10 minutes | Cook time: 20 minutes | Serves 4

1 tablespoon honey
1 tablespoon whole-grain or Dijon mustard
¼ teaspoon freshly ground black pepper
¼ teaspoon kosher or sea salt
1 pound (454 g) boneless, skinless chicken breast tenders or tenderloins
1 cup almonds, roughly chopped
Nonstick cooking spray

1. Preheat the oven to 425ºF (220ºC). Line a large, rimmed baking sheet with parchment paper. Place a wire cooling rack on the parchment-lined baking sheet, and spray the rack well with nonstick cooking spray.
2. In a large bowl, combine the honey, mustard, pepper, and salt. Add the chicken and toss gently to coat. Set aside.
3. Dump the almonds onto a large sheet of parchment paper and spread them out. Press the coated chicken tenders into the nuts until evenly coated on all sides. Place the chicken on the prepared wire rack.
4. Bake in the preheated oven for 15 to 20 minutes, or until the internal temperature of the chicken measures 165ºF (74ºC) on a meat thermometer and any juices run clear.
5. Cool for 5 minutes before serving.

Per Serving
calories: 222 | fat: 7.0g | protein: 11.0g
carbs: 29.0g | fiber: 2.0g | sodium: 448mg

Beef Kebabs with Onion and Pepper

Prep time: 15 minutes | Cook time: 10 minutes | Serves 6

2 pounds (907 g) beef fillet
1½ teaspoons salt
1 teaspoon freshly ground black pepper
½ teaspoon ground nutmeg
½ teaspoon ground allspice
⅓ cup extra-virgin olive oil
1 large onion, cut into 8 quarters
1 large red bell pepper, cut into 1-inch cubes

1. Preheat the grill to high heat.
2. Cut the beef into 1-inch cubes and put them in a large bowl.
3. In a small bowl, mix together the salt, black pepper, allspice, and nutmeg.
4. Pour the olive oil over the beef and toss to coat. Evenly sprinkle the seasoning over the beef and toss to coat all pieces.
5. Skewer the beef, alternating every 1 or 2 pieces with a piece of onion or bell pepper.
6. To cook, place the skewers on the preheated grill, and flip every 2 to 3 minutes until all sides have cooked to desired doneness, 6 minutes for medium-rare, 8 minutes for well done. Serve hot.

Per Serving
calories: 485 | fat: 36.0g | protein: 35.0g
carbs: 4.0g | fiber: 1.0g | sodium: 1453mg

Greek-Style Lamb Burgers

Prep time: 10 minutes | Cook time: 10 minutes | Serves 4

1 pound (454 g) ground lamb
½ teaspoon salt
½ teaspoon freshly ground black pepper
4 tablespoons crumbled feta cheese
Buns, toppings, and tzatziki, for serving (optional)

1. Preheat the grill to high heat.
2. In a large bowl, using your hands, combine the lamb with the salt and pepper.
3. Divide the meat into 4 portions. Divide each portion in half to make a top and a bottom. Flatten each half into a 3-inch circle. Make a dent in the center of one of the halves and place 1 tablespoon of the feta cheese in the center. Place the second half of the patty on top of the feta cheese and press down to close the 2 halves together, making it resemble a round burger.
4. Grill each side for 3 minutes, for medium-well. Serve on a bun with your favorite toppings and tzatziki sauce, if desired.

Per Serving
calories: 345 | fat: 29.0g | protein: 20.0g
carbs: 1.0g | fiber: 0g | sodium: 462mg

Chicken Bruschetta Burgers

Prep time: 10 minutes | Cook time: 16 minutes | Serves 2

1 tablespoon olive oil
2 garlic cloves, minced
3 tablespoons finely minced onion
1 teaspoon dried basil
3 tablespoons minced sun-dried tomatoes
packed in olive oil
8 ounces (227 g) ground chicken breast
¼ teaspoon salt
3 pieces small Mozzarella balls, minced

1. Heat the olive oil in a nonstick skillet over medium-high heat. Add the garlic and onion and sauté for 5 minutes until tender. Stir in the basil.
2. Remove from the skillet to a medium bowl.
3. Add the tomatoes, ground chicken, and salt and stir until incorporated. Mix in the Mozzarella balls.
4. Divide the chicken mixture in half and form into two burgers, each about ¾-inch thick.
5. Heat the same skillet over medium-high heat and add the burgers. Cook each side for 5 to 6 minutes, or until they reach an internal temperature of 165ºF (74ºC).
6. Serve warm.

Per Serving
calories: 300 | fat: 17.0g | protein: 32.2g
carbs: 6.0g | fiber: 1.1g | sodium: 724mg

Chicken Gyros with Tzatziki Sauce

Prep time: 15 minutes | Cook time: 10 minutes | Serves 2

2 tablespoons freshly squeezed lemon juice
2 tablespoons olive oil, divided, plus more for oiling the grill
1 teaspoon minced fresh oregano
½ teaspoon garlic powder
Salt, to taste
8 ounces (227 g) chicken tenders
1 small eggplant, cut into 1-inch strips lengthwise
1 small zucchini, cut into ½-inch strips lengthwise
½ red pepper, seeded and cut in half lengthwise
½ English cucumber, peeled and minced
¾ cup plain Greek yogurt
1 tablespoon minced fresh dill
2 (8-inch) pita breads

1. Combine the lemon juice, 1 tablespoon of olive oil, oregano, garlic powder, and salt in a medium bowl. Add the chicken and let marinate for 30 minutes.
2. Place the eggplant, zucchini, and red pepper in a large mixing bowl and sprinkle with salt and the remaining 1 tablespoon of olive oil. Toss well to coat. Let the vegetables rest while the chicken is marinating.
3. Make the tzatziki sauce: Combine the cucumber, yogurt, salt, and dill in a medium bowl. Stir well to incorporate and set aside in the refrigerator.
4. When ready, preheat the grill to medium-high heat and oil the grill grates.
5. Drain any liquid from the vegetables and put them on the grill.
6. Remove the chicken tenders from the marinade and put them on the grill.
7. Grill the chicken and vegetables for 3 minutes per side, or until the chicken is no longer pink inside.
8. Remove the chicken and vegetables from the grill and set aside. On the grill, heat the pitas for about 30 seconds, flipping them frequently.
9. Divide the chicken tenders and vegetables between the pitas and top each with ¼ cup of the prepared sauce. Roll the pitas up like a cone and serve.

Per Serving
calories: 586 | fat: 21.9g | protein: 39.0g
carbs: 62.0g | fiber: 11.8g | sodium: 955mg

Crispy Pesto Chicken

Prep time: 15 minutes | Cook time: 50 minutes | Serves 2

12 ounces (340 g) small red potatoes (3 or 4 potatoes), scrubbed and diced into 1-inch pieces
1 tablespoon olive oil
½ teaspoon garlic powder
¼ teaspoon salt
1 (8-ounce / 227-g) boneless, skinless chicken breast
3 tablespoons prepared pesto

1. Preheat the oven to 425ºF (220ºC). Line a baking sheet with parchment paper.
2. Combine the potatoes, olive oil, garlic powder, and salt in a medium bowl. Toss well to coat.
3. Arrange the potatoes on the parchment paper and roast for 10 minutes. Flip the potatoes and roast for an additional 10 minutes.
4. Meanwhile, put the chicken in the same bowl and toss with the pesto, coating the chicken evenly.
5. Check the potatoes to make sure they are golden brown on the top and bottom. Toss them again and add the chicken breast to the pan.
6. Turn the heat down to 350ºF (180ºC) and roast the chicken and potatoes for 30 minutes. Check to make sure the chicken reaches an internal temperature of 165ºF (74ºC) and the potatoes are fork-tender.
7. Let cool for 5 minutes before serving.

Per Serving
calories: 378 | fat: 16.0g | protein: 29.8g
carbs: 30.1g | fiber: 4.0g | sodium: 425mg

Greek Beef Kebabs

Prep time: 15 minutes | Cook time: 20 minutes | Serves 2

6 ounces (170 g) beef sirloin tip, trimmed of fat and cut into 2-inch pieces
3 cups of any mixture of vegetables: mushrooms, summer squash, zucchini, onions, red peppers, cherry tomatoes
½ cup olive oil
¼ cup freshly

squeezed lemon juice
2 tablespoons balsamic vinegar
2 teaspoons dried oregano
1 teaspoon garlic powder
1 teaspoon salt
1 teaspoon minced fresh rosemary
Cooking spray

1. Put the beef in a plastic freezer bag.
2. Slice the vegetables into similar-size pieces and put them in a second freezer bag.
3. Make the marinade: Mix the olive oil, lemon juice, balsamic vinegar, oregano, garlic powder, salt, and rosemary in a measuring cup. Whisk well to combine. Pour half of the marinade over the beef, and the other half over the vegetables.
4. Put the beef and vegetables in the refrigerator to marinate for 4 hours.
5. When ready, preheat the grill to medium-high heat and spray the grill grates with cooking spray.
6. Thread the meat onto skewers and the vegetables onto separate skewers.
7. Grill the meat for 3 minutes per side. They should only take 10 to 12 minutes to cook, depending on the thickness of the meat.
8. Grill the vegetables for about 3 minutes per side, or until they have grill marks and are softened. Serve hot.

Per Serving
calories: 284 | fat: 18.2g | protein: 21.0g
carbs: 9.0g | fiber: 3.9g | sodium: 122mg

Chermoula Roasted Pork Tenderloin

Prep time: 15 minutes | Cook time: 20 minutes | Serves 2

½ cup fresh cilantro
½ cup fresh parsley
6 small garlic cloves
3 tablespoons olive oil, divided
3 tablespoons freshly squeezed lemon juice
2 teaspoons cumin

1 teaspoon smoked paprika
½ teaspoon salt, divided
Pinch freshly ground black pepper
1 (8-ounce / 227-g) pork tenderloin

1. Preheat the oven to 425ºF (220ºC).
2. In a food processor, combine the cilantro, parsley, garlic, 2 tablespoons of olive oil, lemon juice, cumin, paprika, and ¼ teaspoon of salt. Pulse 15 to 20 times, or until the mixture is fairly smooth. Scrape the sides down as needed to incorporate all the ingredients. Transfer the sauce to a small bowl and set aside.
3. Season the pork tenderloin on all sides with the remaining ¼ teaspoon of salt and a generous pinch of black pepper.
4. Heat the remaining 1 tablespoon of olive oil in a sauté pan.
5. Sear the pork for 3 minutes, turning often, until golden brown on all sides.
6. Transfer the pork to a baking dish and roast in the preheated oven for 15 minutes, or until the internal temperature registers 145ºF (63ºC).
7. Cool for 5 minutes before serving.

Per Serving
calories: 169 | fat: 13.1g | protein: 11.0g
carbs: 2.9g | fiber: 1.0g | sodium: 332mg

Lamb Kofta (Spiced Meatballs)

Prep time: 15 minutes | Cook time: 30 minutes | Serves 2

¼ cup walnuts
1 garlic clove
½ small onion
1 roasted piquillo pepper
2 tablespoons fresh mint
2 tablespoons fresh parsley
¼ teaspoon cumin
¼ teaspoon allspice
¼ teaspoon salt
Pinch cayenne pepper
8 ounces (227 g) lean ground lamb

1. Preheat the oven to 350ºF (180ºC). Line a baking sheet with aluminum foil.
2. In a food processor, combine the walnuts, garlic, onion, roasted pepper, mint, parsley, cumin, allspice, salt, and cayenne pepper. Pulse about 10 times to combine everything.
3. Transfer the spice mixture to a large bowl and add the ground lamb. With your hands or a spatula, mix the spices into the lamb.
4. Roll the lamb into 1½-inch balls (about the size of golf balls).
5. Arrange the meatballs on the prepared baking sheet and bake for 30 minutes, or until cooked to an internal temperature of 165ºF (74ºC).
6. Serve warm.

Per Serving
calories: 409 | fat: 22.9g | protein: 22.0g
carbs: 7.1g | fiber: 3.0g | sodium: 428mg

Chapter 8 Fish and Seafood

Mediterranean Grilled Sea Bass

Prep time: 20 minutes | Cook time: 20 minutes | Serves 6

¼ teaspoon onion powder
¼ teaspoon garlic powder
¼ teaspoon paprika
Lemon pepper and sea salt to taste
2 pounds (907 g) sea bass
3 tablespoons extra-virgin olive oil, divided
2 large cloves garlic, chopped
1 tablespoon chopped Italian flat leaf parsley

1. Preheat the grill to high heat.
2. Place the onion powder, garlic powder, paprika, lemon pepper, and sea salt in a large bowl and stir to combine.
3. Dredge the fish in the spice mixture, turning until well coated.
4. Heat 2 tablespoon of olive oil in a small skillet. Add the garlic and parsley and cook for 1 to 2 minutes, stirring occasionally. Remove the skillet from the heat and set aside.
5. Brush the grill grates lightly with remaining 1 tablespoon olive oil.
6. Grill the fish for about 7 minutes. Flip the fish and drizzle with the garlic mixture and cook for an additional 7 minutes, or until the fish flakes when pressed lightly with a fork.
7. Serve hot.

Tip: To make this a complete meal, serve the grilled sea bass with rice and grilled or steamed vegetables.

Per Serving
calories: 200 | fat: 10.3g | protein: 26.9g
carbs: 0.6g | fiber: 0.1g | sodium: 105mg

Air-Fried Flounder Fillets

Prep time: 5 minutes | Cook time: 12 minutes | Serves 4

2 cups unsweetened almond milk
½ teaspoon onion powder
½ teaspoon garlic powder
4 (4-ounce / 113-g) flounder fillets
½ cup chickpea flour
½ cup plain yellow cornmeal
¼ teaspoon cayenne pepper
Freshly ground black pepper, to taste

1. Whisk together the almond milk, onion powder, and garlic powder in a large bowl until smooth.
2. Add the flounder, coating well on both sides, and let marinate for about 20 minutes.
3. Meanwhile, combine the chickpea flour, cornmeal, cayenne, and pepper in a shallow dish.
4. Dredge each piece of flounder fillets in the flour mixture until completely coated.
5. Preheat the air fryer to 380ºF (193ºC).
6. Arrange the coated flounder fillets in the basket and cook for 12 minutes, flipping them halfway through.
7. Remove from the basket and serve on a plate.

Tip: If an air fryer isn't available, you can place the flounder fillets on a rimmed baking sheet and broil for 12 minutes, flipping once halfway through.

Per Serving
calories: 228 | fat: 5.7g | protein: 28.2g
carbs: 15.5g | fiber: 2.0g | sodium: 240mg

Glazed Broiled Salmon

Prep time: 5 minutes | Cook time: 5 to 10 minutes | Serves 4

4 (4-ounce / 113-g) salmon fillets
3 tablespoons miso paste
2 tablespoons raw
honey
1 teaspoon coconut aminos
1 teaspoon rice vinegar

1. Preheat the broiler to High. Line a baking dish with aluminum foil and add the salmon fillets.
2. Whisk together the miso paste, honey, coconut aminos, and vinegar in a small bowl. Pour the glaze over the fillets and spread it evenly with a brush.
3. Broil for about 5 minutes, or until the salmon is browned on top and opaque. Brush any remaining glaze over the salmon and broil for an additional 5 minutes if needed. The cooking time depends on the thickness of the salmon.
4. Let the salmon cool for 5 minutes before serving.

Tip: To add more flavors to this meal, serve the salmon with grilled asparagus or a green salad.

Per Serving
calories: 263 | fat: 8.9g | protein: 30.2g
carbs: 12.8g | fiber: 0.7g | sodium: 716mg

Simple Fried Cod Fillets

Prep time: 5 minutes | Cook time: 10 minutes | Serves 4

½ cup all-purpose flour
1 teaspoon garlic powder
1 teaspoon salt
4 (4- to 5-ounce / 113- to 142-g) cod fillets
1 tablespoon extra-virgin olive oil

1. Mix together the flour, garlic powder, and salt in a shallow dish.
2. Dredge each piece of fish in the seasoned flour until they are evenly coated.
3. Heat the olive oil in a medium skillet over medium-high heat.
4. Once hot, add the cod fillets and fry for 6 to 8 minutes, flipping the fish halfway through, or until the fish is opaque and flakes easily.
5. Remove from the heat and serve on plates.

Tip: You can use any variety of spices or herbs to season the flour, such as onion powder, paprika, black pepper, oregano, marjoram, or even tarragon.

Per Serving
calories: 333 | fat: 18.8g | protein: 21.2g
carbs: 20.0g | fiber: 5.7g | sodium: 870mg

10-Minute Cod with Parsley Pistou

Prep time: 15 minutes | Cook time: 10 minutes | Serves 4

1 cup packed roughly chopped fresh flat-leaf Italian parsley
Zest and juice of 1 lemon
1 to 2 small garlic cloves, minced
1 teaspoon salt
½ teaspoon freshly ground black pepper
1 cup extra-virgin olive oil, divided
1 pound (454 g) cod fillets, cut into 4 equal-sized pieces

1. Make the pistou: Place the parsley, lemon zest and juice, garlic, salt, and pepper in a food processor until finely chopped.
2. With the food processor running, slowly drizzle in ¾ cup of olive oil until a thick sauce forms. Set aside.
3. Heat the remaining ¼ cup of olive oil in a large skillet over medium-high heat.
4. Add the cod fillets, cover, and cook each side for 4 to 5 minutes, until browned and cooked through.
5. Remove the cod fillets from the heat to a plate and top each with generous spoonfuls of the prepared pistou. Serve immediately.

Tip: You can serve the pistou on steamed vegetables, toasted whole-wheat bread, salads, and other grilled meats or seafoods.

Per Serving
calories: 580 | fat: 54.6g | protein: 21.1g
carbs: 2.8g | fiber: 1.0g | sodium: 651mg

Mediterranean Braised Cod with Vegetables

Prep time: 10 minutes | Cook time: 18 minutes | Serves 2

1 tablespoon olive oil
½ medium onion, minced
2 garlic cloves, minced
1 teaspoon oregano
1 (15-ounce / 425-g) can artichoke hearts in water, drained and halved
1 (15-ounce / 425-g) can diced tomatoes with basil
¼ cup pitted Greek olives, drained
10 ounces (284 g) wild cod
Salt and freshly ground black pepper, to taste

1. In a skillet, heat the olive oil over medium-high heat.
2. Sauté the onion for about 5 minutes, stirring occasionally, or until tender.
3. Stir in the garlic and oregano and cook for 30 seconds more until fragrant.
4. Add the artichoke hearts, tomatoes, and olives and stir to combine. Top with the cod.
5. Cover and cook for 10 minutes, or until the fish flakes easily with a fork and juices run clean.
6. Sprinkle with the salt and pepper. Serve warm.

Tip: The cod can be substituted with other lean white fish such as bass, tilapia, haddock and halibut.

Per Serving
calories: 332 | fat: 10.5g | protein: 29.2g
carbs: 30.7g | fiber: 8.0g | sodium: 1906mg

Baked Salmon with Basil and Tomato

Prep time: 10 minutes | Cook time: 20 minutes | Serves 2

2 (6-ounce / 170-g) boneless salmon fillets
1 tablespoon dried basil
1 tomato, thinly sliced
1 tablespoon olive oil
2 tablespoons grated Parmesan cheese
Nonstick cooking spray

1. Preheat the oven to 375ºF (190ºC). Line a baking sheet with a piece of aluminum foil and mist with nonstick cooking spray.
2. Arrange the salmon fillets onto the aluminum foil and scatter with basil. Place the tomato slices on top and drizzle with olive oil. Top with the grated Parmesan cheese.
3. Bake for about 20 minutes, or until the flesh is opaque and it flakes apart easily.
4. Remove from the oven and serve on a plate.

Per Serving
calories: 403 | fat: 26.5g | protein: 36.3g
carbs: 3.8g | fiber: 0.1g | sodium: 179mg

Lemon-Parsley Swordfish

Prep time: 10 minutes | Cook time: 17 to 20 minutes | Serves 4

1 cup fresh Italian parsley	¼ cup fresh thyme
¼ cup lemon juice	2 cloves garlic
¼ cup extra-virgin olive oil	½ teaspoon salt
	4 swordfish steaks
	Olive oil spray

1. Preheat the oven to 450ºF (235ºC). Grease a large baking dish generously with olive oil spray.
2. Place the parsley, lemon juice, olive oil, thyme, garlic, and salt in a food processor and pulse until smoothly blended.
3. Arrange the swordfish steaks in the greased baking dish and spoon the parsley mixture over the top.
4. Bake in the preheated oven for 17 to 20 minutes until flaky.
5. Divide the fish among four plates and serve hot.

Tips: If you prefer a milder flavor, you can substitute the fresh cilantro or basil for parsley. To make this a complete meal, serve it with a cherry tomato salad.

Per Serving
calories: 396 | fat: 21.7g | protein: 44.2g carbs: 2.9g | fiber: 1.0g | sodium: 494mg

Baked Salmon with Tarragon Mustard Sauce

Prep time: 5 minutes | Cook time: 12 minutes | Serves 4

1¼ pounds (567 g) salmon fillet (skin on or removed), cut into 4 equal pieces	2 tablespoons chopped fresh tarragon
¼ cup Dijon mustard	½ teaspoon salt
¼ cup avocado oil mayonnaise	¼ teaspoon freshly ground black pepper
Zest and juice of ½ lemon	4 tablespoons extra-virgin olive oil, for serving

1. Preheat the oven to 425ºF (220ºC). Line a baking sheet with parchment paper.

2. Arrange the salmon pieces on the prepared baking sheet, skin-side down.
3. Stir together the mustard, avocado oil mayonnaise, lemon zest and juice, tarragon, salt, and pepper in a small bowl. Spoon the mustard mixture over the salmon.
4. Bake for 10 to 12 minutes, or until the top is golden and salmon is opaque in the center.
5. Divide the salmon among four plates and drizzle each top with 1 tablespoon of olive oil before serving.

Tip: You can use 1 to 2 teaspoons dried tarragon to replace the fresh tarragon.

Per Serving
calories: 386 | fat: 27.7g | protein: 29.3g carbs: 3.8g | fiber: 1.0g | sodium: 632mg

Peppercorn-Seared Tuna Steaks

Prep time: 5 minutes | Cook time: 10 minutes | Serves 2

2 (5-ounce / 142-g) ahi tuna steaks	pepper
1 teaspoon kosher salt	2 tablespoons olive oil
¼ teaspoon cayenne	1 teaspoon whole peppercorns

1. On a plate, Season the tuna steaks on both sides with salt and cayenne pepper.
2. In a skillet, heat the olive oil over medium-high heat until it shimmers.
3. Add the peppercorns and cook for about 5 minutes, or until they soften and pop.
4. Carefully put the tuna steaks in the skillet and sear for 1 to 2 minutes per side, depending on the thickness of the tuna steaks, or until the fish is cooked to the desired level of doneness.
5. Cool for 5 minutes before serving.

Tip: The seared tuna steaks pair perfectly with crispy green beans or roasted lemon potatoes.

Per Serving
calories: 260 | fat: 14.3g | protein: 33.4g carbs: 0.2g | fiber: 0.1g | sodium: 1033mg

Baked Lemon Salmon

Prep time: 5 minutes | Cook time: 20 minutes | Serves 4

¼ teaspoon dried thyme
Zest and juice of ½ lemon
¼ teaspoon salt
½ teaspoon freshly

ground black pepper
1 pound (454 g) salmon fillet
Nonstick cooking spray

1. Preheat the oven to 425ºF (220ºC). Coat a baking sheet with nonstick cooking spray.
2. Mix together the thyme, lemon zest and juice, salt, and pepper in a small bowl and stir to incorporate.
3. Arrange the salmon, skin-side down, on the coated baking sheet. Spoon the thyme mixture over the salmon and spread it all over.
4. Bake in the preheated oven for about 15 to 20 minutes, or until the fish flakes apart easily. Serve warm.

Tip: To make this a complete meal, you can toss the cut-up asparagus, cauliflower, and broccoli with 1 teaspoon olive oil in a large bowl until well coated and add them to the baking sheet.

Per Serving
calories: 162 | fat: 7.0g | protein: 23.1g
carbs: 1.0g | fiber: 0g | sodium: 166mg

Honey-Mustard Roasted Salmon

Prep time: 5 minutes | Cook time: 15 to 20 minutes | Serves 4

2 tablespoons whole-grain mustard
2 garlic cloves, minced
1 tablespoon honey
¼ teaspoon salt

¼ teaspoon freshly ground black pepper
1 pound (454 g) salmon fillet
Nonstick cooking spray

1. Preheat the oven to 425ºF (220ºC). Coat a baking sheet with nonstick cooking spray.
2. Stir together the mustard, garlic, honey, salt, and pepper in a small bowl.
3. Arrange the salmon fillet, skin-side down,

on the coated baking sheet. Spread the mustard mixture evenly over the salmon fillet.
4. Roast in the preheated oven for 15 to 20 minutes, or until it flakes apart easily and reaches an internal temperature of 145ºF (63ºC).
5. Serve hot.

Tip: If the whole-grain mustard isn't available, the Dijon mustard will work, too.

Per Serving
calories: 185 | fat: 7.0g | protein: 23.2g
carbs: 5.8g | fiber: 0g | sodium: 311mg

Salmon and Mushroom Hash with Pesto

Prep time: 15 minutes | Cook time: 20 minutes | Serves 6

Pesto:

¼ cup extra-virgin olive oil
1 bunch fresh basil
Juice and zest of 1

lemon
$1/_3$ cup water
¼ teaspoon salt, plus additional as needed

Hash:

2 tablespoons extra-virgin olive oil
6 cups mixed mushrooms (brown, white, shiitake,

cremini, portobello, etc.), sliced
1 pound (454 g) wild salmon, cubed

1. Make the pesto: Pulse the olive oil, basil, juice and zest, water, and salt in a blender or food processor until smoothly blended. Set aside.
2. Heat the olive oil in a large skillet over medium heat.
3. Stir-fry the mushrooms for 6 to 8 minutes, or until they begin to exude their juices.
4. Add the salmon and cook each side for 5 to 6 minutes until cooked through.
5. Fold in the prepared pesto and stir well. Taste and add additional salt as needed. Serve warm.

Tip: You can use the coconut oil to replace the extra-virgin olive oil.

Per Serving
calories: 264 | fat: 14.7g | protein: 7.0g
carbs: 30.9g | fiber: 4.0g | sodium: 480mg

Spiced Citrus Sole

Prep time: 10 minutes | Cook time: 10 minutes | Serves 4

1 teaspoon garlic powder
1 teaspoon chili powder
½ teaspoon lemon zest
½ teaspoon lime zest
¼ teaspoon smoked paprika

¼ teaspoon freshly ground black pepper
Pinch sea salt
4 (6-ounce / 170-g) sole fillets, patted dry
1 tablespoon extra-virgin olive oil
2 teaspoons freshly squeezed lime juice

1. Preheat the oven to 450ºF (235ºC). Line a baking sheet with aluminum foil and set aside.
2. Mix together the garlic powder, chili powder, lemon zest, lime zest, paprika, pepper, and salt in a small bowl until well combined.
3. Arrange the sole fillets on the prepared baking sheet and rub the spice mixture all over the fillets until well coated. Drizzle the olive oil and lime juice over the fillets.
4. Bake in the preheated oven for about 8 minutes until flaky.
5. Remove from the heat to a plate and serve.

Tip: You can store the spice mixture in an airtight container for up to 2 weeks.

Per Serving
calories: 183 | fat: 5.0g | protein: 32.1g
carbs: 0g | fiber: 0g | sodium: 136mg

Asian-Inspired Tuna Lettuce Wraps

Prep time: 10 minutes | Cook time: 0 minutes | Serves 2

⅓ cup almond butter
1 tablespoon freshly squeezed lemon juice
1 teaspoon low-sodium soy sauce
1 teaspoon curry powder
½ teaspoon sriracha, or to taste

½ cup canned water chestnuts, drained and chopped
2 (2.6-ounce / 74-g) package tuna packed in water, drained
2 large butter lettuce leaves

1. Stir together the almond butter, lemon juice, soy sauce, curry powder, sriracha in a medium bowl until well mixed. Add the water chestnuts and tuna and stir until well incorporated.
2. Place 2 butter lettuce leaves on a flat work surface, spoon half of the tuna mixture onto each leaf and roll up into a wrap. Serve immediately.

Tips: To make this a complete meal, you can serve it with any whole-wheat bread or crackers. You also can spoon the tuna mixture into avocado halves.

Per Serving
calories: 270 | fat: 13.9g | protein: 19.1g
carbs: 18.5g | fiber: 3.0g | sodium: 626mg

Canned Sardine Donburi (Rice Bowl)

Prep time: 10 minutes | Cook time: 40 to 50 minutes | Serves 4 to 6

4 cups water
2 cups brown rice, rinsed well
½ teaspoon salt
3 (4-ounce / 113-g) cans sardines packed in water, drained

3 scallions, sliced thin
1-inch piece fresh ginger, grated
4 tablespoons sesame oil

1. Place the water, brown rice, and salt to a large saucepan and stir to combine. Allow the mixture to boil over high heat.
2. Once boiling, reduce the heat to low, and cook covered for 45 to 50 minutes, or until the rice is tender.
3. Meanwhile, roughly mash the sardines with a fork in a medium bowl.
4. When the rice is done, stir in the mashed sardines, scallions, and ginger.
5. Divide the mixture into four bowls. Top each bowl with a drizzle of sesame oil. Serve warm.

Tips: If you want to save time, you can substitute the quinoa or buckwheat for the brown rice. And the sesame oil can be replaced with extra-virgin olive oil, if desired.

Per Serving
calories: 603 | fat: 23.6g | protein: 25.2g
carbs: 73.8g | fiber: 4.0g | sodium: 498mg

Orange Flavored Scallops

Prep time: 10 minutes | Cook time: 10 minutes | Serves 4

2 pounds (907 g) sea scallops, patted dry
Sea salt and freshly ground black pepper, to taste
2 tablespoons extra-virgin olive oil
1 tablespoon minced garlic
¼ cup freshly squeezed orange juice
1 teaspoon orange zest
2 teaspoons chopped fresh thyme, for garnish

1. In a bowl, lightly season the scallops with salt and pepper. Set aside.
2. Heat the olive oil in a large skillet over medium-high heat until it shimmers.
3. Add the garlic and sauté for about 3 minutes, or until fragrant.
4. Stir in the seasoned scallops and sear each side for about 4 minutes, or until the scallops are browned.
5. Remove the scallops from the heat to a plate and set aside.
6. Add the orange juice and zest to the skillet, scraping up brown bits from bottom of skillet.
7. Drizzle the sauce over the scallops and garnish with the thyme before serving.

Tip: To make this a complete meal, you can serve it with cooked rice or quinoa.

Per Serving
calories: 266 | fat: 7.6g | protein: 38.1g
carbs: 7.9g | fiber: 0g | sodium: 360mg

Instant Pot Poached Salmon

Prep time: 10 minutes | Cook time: 3 minutes | Serves 4

1 lemon, sliced ¼ inch thick
4 (6-ounce / 170-g) skinless salmon fillets, 1½ inches
thick
½ teaspoon salt
¼ teaspoon pepper
½ cup water

1. Layer the lemon slices in the bottom of the Instant Pot.
2. Season the salmon with salt and pepper,

then arrange the salmon (skin- side down) on top of the lemon slices. Pour in the water.
3. Secure the lid. Select the Manual mode and set the cooking time for 3 minutes at High Pressure.
4. Once cooking is complete, do a quick pressure release. Carefully open the lid.
5. Serve warm.

Per Serving
calories: 350 | fat: 23.0g | protein: 35.0g
carbs: 0g | fiber: 0g | sodium: 390mg

Spicy Grilled Shrimp with Lemon Wedges

Prep time: 15 minutes | Cook time: 6 minutes | Serves 6

1 large clove garlic, crushed
1 teaspoon coarse salt
1 teaspoon paprika
½ teaspoon cayenne pepper
2 teaspoons lemon juice
2 tablespoons plus 1 teaspoon olive oil, divided
2 pounds (907 g) large shrimp, peeled and deveined
8 wedges lemon, for garnish

1. Preheat the grill to medium heat.
2. Stir together the garlic, salt, paprika, cayenne pepper, lemon juice, and 2 tablespoons of olive oil in a small bowl until a paste forms. Add the shrimp and toss until well coated.
3. Grease the grill grates lightly with remaining 1 teaspoon of olive oil.
4. Grill the shrimp for 4 to 6 minutes, flipping the shrimp halfway through, or until the shrimp is totally pink and opaque.
5. Garnish the shrimp with lemon wedges and serve hot.

Tip: To make this a complete meal, you can serve it with zucchini noodle salad.

Per Serving
calories: 163 | fat: 5.8g | protein: 25.2g
carbs: 2.8g | fiber: 0.4g | sodium: 585mg

Crispy Tilapia with Mango Salsa

Prep time: 5 minutes | Cook time: 10 minutes | Serves 2

Salsa:

1 cup chopped mango
2 tablespoons chopped fresh cilantro
2 tablespoons chopped red onion
2 tablespoons freshly squeezed lime juice
½ jalapeño pepper, seeded and minced
Pinch salt

Tilapia:

1 tablespoon paprika
1 teaspoon onion powder
½ teaspoon dried thyme
½ teaspoon freshly ground black pepper
¼ teaspoon cayenne pepper
½ teaspoon garlic powder
¼ teaspoon salt
½ pound (227 g) boneless tilapia fillets
2 teaspoons extra-virgin olive oil
1 lime, cut into wedges, for serving

1. Make the salsa: Place the mango, cilantro, onion, lime juice, jalapeño, and salt in a medium bowl and toss to combine. Set aside.
2. Make the tilapia: Stir together the paprika, onion powder, thyme, black pepper, cayenne pepper, garlic powder, and salt in a small bowl until well mixed. Rub both sides of fillets generously with the mixture.
3. Heat the olive oil in a large skillet over medium heat.
4. Add the fish fillets and cook each side for 3 to 5 minutes until golden brown and cooked through.
5. Divide the fillets among two plates and spoon half of the prepared salsa onto each fillet. Serve the fish alongside the lime wedges.

Tip: You can serve the fillets with the pineapple salsa on top. Simple use the same amount of fresh or canned pineapple to replace the mango.

Per Serving

calories: 239 | fat: 7.8g | protein: 25.0g carbs: 21.9g | fiber: 4.0g | sodium: 416mg

Lemon Rosemary Roasted Branzino

Prep time: 15 minutes | Cook time: 30 minutes | Serves 2

4 tablespoons extra-virgin olive oil, divided
2 (8-ounce / 227-g) branzino fillets, preferably at least 1 inch thick
1 garlic clove, minced
1 bunch scallions (white part only), thinly sliced
10 to 12 small cherry tomatoes, halved
1 large carrot, cut into ¼-inch rounds
½ cup dry white wine
2 tablespoons paprika
2 teaspoons kosher salt
½ tablespoon ground chili pepper
2 rosemary sprigs or 1 tablespoon dried rosemary
1 small lemon, thinly sliced
½ cup sliced pitted kalamata olives

1. Heat a large ovenproof skillet over high heat until hot, about 2 minutes. Add 1 tablespoon of olive oil and heat for 10 to 15 seconds until it shimmers.
2. Add the branzino fillets, skin-side up, and sear for 2 minutes. Flip the fillets and cook for an additional 2 minutes. Set aside.
3. Swirl 2 tablespoons of olive oil around the skillet to coat evenly.
4. Add the garlic, scallions, tomatoes, and carrot, and sauté for 5 minutes, or until softened.
5. Add the wine, stirring until all ingredients are well combined. Carefully place the fish over the sauce.
6. Preheat the oven to 450ºF (235ºC).
7. Brush the fillets with the remaining 1 tablespoon of olive oil and season with paprika, salt, and chili pepper. Top each fillet with a rosemary sprig and lemon slices. Scatter the olives over fish and around the skillet.
8. Roast for about 10 minutes until the lemon slices are browned. Serve hot.

Per Serving

calories: 724 | fat: 43.0g | protein: 57.7g carbs: 25.0g | fiber: 10.0g | sodium: 2950mg

Braised Branzino with Wine Sauce

Prep time: 15 minutes | Cook time: 15 minutes | Serves 2 to 3

Sauce:

¾ cup dry white wine
2 tablespoons white wine vinegar
2 tablespoons cornstarch
1 tablespoon honey

Fish:

1 large branzino, butterflied and patted dry
2 tablespoons onion powder
2 tablespoons paprika
½ tablespoon salt
6 tablespoons extra-virgin olive oil,
divided
4 garlic cloves, thinly sliced
4 scallions, both green and white parts, thinly sliced
1 large tomato, cut into ¼-inch cubes
4 kalamata olives, pitted and chopped

1. Make the sauce: Mix together the white wine, vinegar, cornstarch, and honey in a bowl and keep stirring until the honey has dissolved. Set aside.
2. Make the fish: Place the fish on a clean work surface, skin-side down. Sprinkle the onion powder, paprika, and salt to season. Drizzle 2 tablespoons of olive oil all over the fish.
3. Heat 2 tablespoons of olive oil in a large skillet over high heat until it shimmers.
4. Add the fish, skin-side up, to the skillet and brown for about 2 minutes. Carefully flip the fish and cook for another 3 minutes. Remove from the heat to a plate and set aside.
5. Add the remaining 2 tablespoons olive oil to the skillet and swirl to coat. Stir in the garlic cloves, scallions, tomato, and kalamata olives and sauté for 5 minutes. Pour in the prepared sauce and stir to combine.
6. Return the fish (skin-side down) to the skillet, flipping to coat in the sauce. Reduce the heat to medium-low, and cook for an additional 5 minutes until cooked through.
7. Using a slotted spoon, transfer the fish to a plate and serve warm.

Tip: If you have any leftovers, you can serve with steamed brown rice or roasted potatoes.

Per Serving
calories: 1059 | fat: 71.9g | protein: 46.2g
carbs: 55.8g | fiber: 5.1g | sodium: 2807mg

Cioppino (Seafood Tomato Stew)

Prep time: 10 minutes | Cook time: 20 minutes | Serves 2

2 tablespoons olive oil
½ small onion, diced
½ green pepper, diced
2 teaspoons dried basil
2 teaspoons dried oregano
½ cup dry white wine
1 (14.5-ounce / 411-g) can diced tomatoes with basil
1 (8-ounce / 227-g) can no-salt-added
tomato sauce
1 (6.5-ounce / 184-g) can minced clams with their juice
8 ounces (227 g) peeled, deveined raw shrimp
4 ounces (113 g) any white fish (a thick piece works best)
3 tablespoons fresh parsley
Salt and freshly ground black pepper, to taste

1. In a Dutch oven, heat the olive oil over medium heat.
2. Sauté the onion and green pepper for 5 minutes, or until tender.
3. Stir in the basil, oregano, wine, diced tomatoes, and tomato sauce and bring to a boil.
4. Once boiling, reduce the heat to low and bring to a simmer for 5 minutes.
5. Add the clams, shrimp, and fish and cook for about 10 minutes, or until the shrimp are pink and cooked through.
6. Scatter with the parsley and add the salt and black pepper to taste.
7. Remove from the heat and serve warm.

Tip: You can prepare the base of this stew in advance, but do not stir in the fish until just before serving.

Per Serving
calories: 221 | fat: 7.7g | protein: 23.1g
carbs: 10.9g | fiber: 4.2g | sodium: 720mg

Lemon Grilled Shrimp

Prep time: 20 minutes | Cook time: 4 to 6 minutes | Serves 4

2 tablespoons garlic, minced
3 tablespoons fresh Italian parsley, finely chopped
¼ cup extra-virgin olive oil
½ cup lemon juice
1 teaspoon salt
2 pounds (907 g) jumbo shrimp (21 to 25), peeled and deveined

Special Equipment:
4 skewers, soaked in water for at least 30 minutes

1. Whisk together the garlic, parsley, olive oil, lemon juice, and salt in a large bowl.
2. Add the shrimp to the bowl and toss well, making sure the shrimp are coated in the marinade. Set aside to sit for 15 minutes.
3. When ready, skewer the shrimps by piercing through the center. You can place about 5 to 6 shrimps on each skewer.
4. Preheat the grill to high heat.
5. Grill the shrimp for 4 to 6 minutes, flipping the shrimp halfway through, or until the shrimp are pink on the outside and opaque in the center.
6. Serve hot.

Tip: You can try adding 1 teaspoon paprika to the marinade for added color and flavor. To save time, you can marinate the shrimp ahead of time.

Per Serving
calories: 401 | fat: 17.8g | protein: 56.9g
carbs: 3.9g | fiber: 0g | sodium: 1223mg

Baked Halibut Steaks with Vegetables

Prep time: 15 minutes | Cook time: 20 minutes | Serves 4

2 teaspoon olive oil, divided
1 clove garlic, peeled and minced
½ cup minced onion
1 cup diced zucchini
2 cups diced fresh tomatoes
2 tablespoons
chopped fresh basil
¼ teaspoon salt
¼ teaspoon ground black pepper
4 (6-ounce / 170-g) halibut steaks
⅓ cup crumbled feta cheese

1. Preheat oven to 450°F (235°C). Coat a shallow baking dish lightly with 1 teaspoon of olive oil.
2. In a medium saucepan, heat the remaining 1 teaspoon of olive oil.
3. Add the garlic, onion, and zucchini and mix well. Cook for 5 minutes, stirring occasionally, or until the zucchini is softened.
4. Remove the saucepan from the heat and stir in the tomatoes, basil, salt, and pepper.
5. Place the halibut steaks in the coated baking dish in a single layer. Spread the zucchini mixture evenly over the steaks. Scatter the top with feta cheese.
6. Bake in the preheated oven for about 15 minutes, or until the fish flakes when pressed lightly with a fork. Serve hot.

Tip: To make this a complete meal, serve it with roasted potatoes, sautéed asparagus, roasted vegetables, or even a green salad.

Per Serving
calories: 258 | fat: 7.6g | protein: 38.6g
carbs: 6.5g | fiber: 1.2g | sodium: 384mg

Spicy Haddock Stew

Prep time: 15 minutes | Cook time: 35 minutes | Serves 6

¼ cup coconut oil
1 tablespoon minced garlic
1 onion, chopped
2 celery stalks, chopped
½ fennel bulb, thinly sliced
1 carrot, diced
1 sweet potato, diced
1 (15-ounce / 425-g) can low-sodium diced tomatoes
1 cup coconut milk
1 cup low-sodium chicken broth
¼ teaspoon red pepper flakes
12 ounces (340 g) haddock, cut into 1-inch chunks
2 tablespoons chopped fresh cilantro, for garnish

1. In a large saucepan, heat the coconut oil over medium-high heat.
2. Add the garlic, onion, and celery and sauté for about 4 minutes, stirring occasionally, or until they are tender.
3. Stir in the fennel bulb, carrot, and sweet potato and sauté for 4 minutes more.
4. Add the diced tomatoes, coconut milk, chicken broth, and red pepper flakes and stir to incorporate, then bring the mixture to a boil.
5. Once it starts to boil, reduce the heat to low, and bring to a simmer for about 15 minutes, or until the vegetables are fork-tender.
6. Add the haddock chunks and continue simmering for about 10 minutes, or until the fish is cooked through.
7. Sprinkle the cilantro on top for garnish before serving.

Tip: If you prefer a bit of heat, you could add a bit of chiles.

Per Serving
calories: 276 | fat: 20.9g | protein: 14.2g
carbs: 6.8g | fiber: 3.0g | sodium: 226mg

Garlic Shrimp with Mushrooms

Prep time: 10 minutes | Cook time: 15 minutes | Serves 4

1 pound (454 g) fresh shrimp, peeled, deveined, and patted dry
1 teaspoon salt
1 cup extra-virgin olive oil
8 large garlic cloves, thinly sliced
4 ounces (113 g) sliced mushrooms (shiitake, baby bella, or button)
½ teaspoon red pepper flakes
¼ cup chopped fresh flat-leaf Italian parsley

1. In a bowl, season the shrimp with salt. Set aside.
2. Heat the olive oil in a large skillet over medium-low heat.
3. Add the garlic and cook for 3 to 4 minutes until fragrant, stirring occasionally.
4. Sauté the mushrooms for 5 minutes, or until they start to exude their juices.
5. Stir in the shrimp and sprinkle with red pepper flakes and sauté for 3 to 4 minutes more, or until the shrimp start to turn pink.
6. Remove the skillet from the heat and add the parsley. Stir to combine and serve warm.

Tips: If you have any leftovers, you can serve with mixed greens. If you want to make an easy vinaigrette, you can pour 1 to 2 tablespoons lemon juice or red wine vinegar into the garlic oil.

Per Serving
calories: 619 | fat: 55.5g | protein: 24.1g
carbs: 3.7g | fiber: 0g | sodium: 735mg

Lemony Shrimp with Orzo Salad

Prep time: 10 minutes | Cook time: 22 minutes | Serves 4

1 cup orzo
1 hothouse cucumber, deseeded and chopped
½ cup finely diced red onion
2 tablespoons extra-virgin olive oil
2 pounds (907 g) shrimp, peeled and deveined
3 lemons, juiced
Salt and freshly ground black pepper, to taste
¾ cup crumbled feta cheese
2 tablespoons dried dill
1 cup chopped fresh flat-leaf parsley

1. Bring a large pot of water to a boil. Add the orzo and cook covered for 15 to 18 minutes, or until the orzo is tender. Transfer to a colander to drain and set aside to cool.
2. Mix the cucumber and red onion in a bowl. Set aside.
3. Heat the olive oil in a medium skillet over medium heat until it shimmers.
4. Reduce the heat, add the shrimp, and cook each side for 2 minutes until cooked through.
5. Add the cooked shrimp to the bowl of cucumber and red onion. Mix in the cooked orzo and lemon juice and toss to combine. Sprinkle with salt and pepper. Scatter the top with the feta cheese and dill. Garnish with the parsley and serve immediately.

Tips: To add more flavors to this meal, try adding halved cherry tomatoes to the salad. And you can serve the shrimp with grilled vegetables or over a bed of lettuce.

Per Serving
calories: 565 | fat: 17.8g | protein: 63.3g
carbs: 43.9g | fiber: 4.1g | sodium: 2225mg

Avocado Shrimp Ceviche

Prep time: 15 minutes | Cook time: 0 minutes | Serves 4

1 pound (454 g) fresh shrimp, peeled, deveined, and cut in half lengthwise
1 small red or yellow bell pepper, cut into ½-inch chunks
½ small red onion, cut into thin slivers
½ English cucumber, peeled and cut into ½-inch chunks
¼ cup chopped fresh cilantro
½ cup extra-virgin olive oil
⅓ cup freshly squeezed lime juice
2 tablespoons freshly squeezed clementine juice
2 tablespoons freshly squeezed lemon juice
1 teaspoon salt
½ teaspoon freshly ground black pepper
2 ripe avocados, peeled, pitted, and cut into ½-inch chunks

1. Place the shrimp, bell pepper, red onion, cucumber, and cilantro in a large bowl and toss to combine.
2. In a separate bowl, stir together the olive oil, lime, clementine, and lemon juice, salt, and black pepper until smooth. Pour the mixture into the bowl of shrimp and vegetable mixture and toss until they are completely coated.
3. Cover the bowl with plastic wrap and transfer to the refrigerator to marinate for at least 2 hours, or up to 8 hours.
4. When ready, stir in the avocado chunks and toss to incorporate. Serve immediately.

Tip: If the clementine juice isn't available, the orange juice will work, too. And you can add the parsley to the marinade for added flavor.

Per Serving
calories: 496 | fat: 39.5g | protein: 25.3g
carbs: 13.8g | fiber: 6.0g | sodium: 755mg

Garlic Skillet Salmon

Prep time: 5 minutes | Cook time: 14 to 16 minutes | Serves 4

1 tablespoon extra-virgin olive oil
2 garlic cloves, minced
1 teaspoon smoked paprika
1½ cups grape or cherry tomatoes, quartered
1 (12-ounce / 340-g) jar roasted red peppers, drained and chopped
1 tablespoon water
¼ teaspoon freshly ground black pepper
¼ teaspoon kosher or sea salt
1 pound (454 g) salmon fillets, skin removed and cut into 8 pieces
1 tablespoon freshly squeezed lemon juice

1. In a large skillet over medium heat, heat the oil. Add the garlic and smoked paprika and cook for 1 minute, stirring often. Add the tomatoes, roasted peppers, water, black pepper, and salt. Turn up the heat to medium-high, bring to a simmer, and cook for 3 minutes, stirring occasionally and smashing the tomatoes with a wooden spoon toward the end of the cooking time.
2. Add the salmon to the skillet, and spoon some of the sauce over the top. Cover and cook for 10 to 12 minutes, or until the salmon is cooked through and just starts to flake.
3. Remove the skillet from the heat, and drizzle lemon juice over the top of the fish. Stir the sauce, then break up the salmon into chunks with a fork. Serve hot.

Per Serving
calories: 255 | fat: 11.7g | protein: 24.2g
carbs: 5.9g | fiber: 1.2g | sodium: 809mg

Salmon Baked in Foil

Prep time: 5 minutes | Cook time: 25 minutes | Serves 4

2 cups cherry tomatoes
3 tablespoons extra-virgin olive oil
3 tablespoons lemon juice
3 tablespoons almond butter
1 teaspoon oregano
½ teaspoon salt
4 (5-ounce / 142-g) salmon fillets

1. Preheat the oven to 400ºF (205ºC).
2. Cut the tomatoes in half and put them in a bowl.
3. Add the olive oil, lemon juice, butter, oregano, and salt to the tomatoes and gently toss to combine.
4. Cut 4 pieces of foil, about 12-by-12 inches each.
5. Place the salmon fillets in the middle of each piece of foil.
6. Divide the tomato mixture evenly over the 4 pieces of salmon. Bring the ends of the foil together and seal to form a closed pocket.
7. Place the 4 pockets on a baking sheet. Bake in the preheated oven for 25 minutes.
8. Remove from the oven and serve on a plate.

Per Serving
calories: 410 | fat: 32.0g | protein: 30.0g
carbs: 4.0g | fiber: 1.0g | sodium: 370mg

Balsamic-Honey Glazed Salmon

Prep time: 2 minutes | Cook time: 8 minutes | Serves 4

½ cup balsamic vinegar
1 tablespoon honey
4 (8-ounce / 227-g) salmon fillets
Sea salt and freshly ground pepper, to taste
1 tablespoon olive oil

1. Heat a skillet over medium-high heat. Combine the vinegar and honey in a small bowl.
2. Season the salmon fillets with the sea salt and freshly ground pepper; brush with the honey-balsamic glaze.
3. Add olive oil to the skillet, and sear the salmon fillets, cooking for 3 to 4 minutes on each side until lightly browned and medium rare in the center.
4. Let sit for 5 minutes before serving.

Per Serving
calories: 454 | fat: 17.3g | protein: 65.3g
carbs: 9.7g | fiber: 0g | sodium: 246mg

Seared Salmon with Lemon Cream Sauce

Prep time: 10 minutes | Cook time: 20 minutes | Serves 4

4 (5-ounce / 142-g) salmon fillets
Sea salt and freshly ground black pepper, to taste
1 tablespoon extra-virgin olive oil
½ cup low-sodium vegetable broth

Juice and zest of 1 lemon
1 teaspoon chopped fresh thyme
½ cup fat-free sour cream
1 teaspoon honey
1 tablespoon chopped fresh chives

1. Preheat the oven to 400ºF (205ºC).
2. Season the salmon lightly on both sides with salt and pepper.
3. Place a large ovenproof skillet over medium-high heat and add the olive oil.
4. Sear the salmon fillets on both sides until golden, about 3 minutes per side.
5. Transfer the salmon to a baking dish and bake in the preheated oven until just cooked through, about 10 minutes.
6. Meanwhile, whisk together the vegetable broth, lemon juice and zest, and thyme in a small saucepan over medium-high heat until the liquid reduces by about one-quarter, about 5 minutes.
7. Whisk in the sour cream and honey.
8. Stir in the chives and serve the sauce over the salmon.

Per Serving
calories: 310 | fat: 18.0g | protein: 29.0g
carbs: 6.0g | fiber: 0g | sodium: 129mg

Slow Cooker Salmon in Foil

Prep time: 5 minutes | Cook time: 2 hours | Serves 2

2 (6-ounce / 170-g) salmon fillets
1 tablespoon olive oil
2 cloves garlic, minced
½ tablespoon lime

juice
1 teaspoon finely chopped fresh parsley
¼ teaspoon black pepper

1. Spread a length of foil onto a work surface and place the salmon fillets in the middle.

2. Mix together the olive oil, garlic, lime juice, parsley, and black pepper in a small bowl. Brush the mixture over the fillets. Fold the foil over and crimp the sides to make a packet.
3. Place the packet into the slow cooker, cover, and cook on High for 2 hours, or until the fish flakes easily with a fork.
4. Serve hot.

Per Serving
calories: 446 | fat: 20.7g | protein: 65.4g
carbs: 1.5g | fiber: 0.2g | sodium: 240mg

Baked Fish with Pistachio Crust

Prep time: 10 minutes | Cook time: 15 to 20 minutes | Serves 4

½ cup extra-virgin olive oil, divided
1 pound (454 g) flaky white fish (such as cod, haddock, or halibut), skin removed
½ cup shelled finely chopped pistachios
½ cup ground

flaxseed
Zest and juice of 1 lemon, divided
1 teaspoon ground cumin
1 teaspoon ground allspice
½ teaspoon salt
¼ teaspoon freshly ground black pepper

1. Preheat the oven to 400ºF (205ºC).
2. Line a baking sheet with parchment paper or aluminum foil and drizzle 2 tablespoons of olive oil over the sheet, spreading to evenly coat the bottom.
3. Cut the fish into 4 equal pieces and place on the prepared baking sheet.
4. In a small bowl, combine the pistachios, flaxseed, lemon zest, cumin, allspice, salt, and pepper. Drizzle in ¼ cup of olive oil and stir well.
5. Divide the nut mixture evenly on top of the fish pieces. Drizzle the lemon juice and remaining 2 tablespoons of olive oil over the fish and bake until cooked through, 15 to 20 minutes, depending on the thickness of the fish.
6. Cool for 5 minutes before serving.

Per Serving
calories: 509 | fat: 41.0g | protein: 26.0g
carbs: 9.0g | fiber: 6.0g | sodium: 331mg

Mackerel and Green Bean Salad

Prep time: 10 minutes | Cook time: 10 minutes | Serves 2

2 cups green beans
1 tablespoon avocado oil
2 mackerel fillets
4 cups mixed salad greens
2 hard-boiled eggs, sliced
1 avocado, sliced
2 tablespoons lemon juice
2 tablespoons olive oil
1 teaspoon Dijon mustard
Salt and black pepper, to taste

1. Cook the green beans in a medium saucepan of boiling water for about 3 minutes until crisp-tender. Drain and set aside.
2. Melt the avocado oil in a pan over medium heat. Add the mackerel fillets and cook each side for 4 minutes.
3. Divide the greens between two salad bowls. Top with the mackerel, sliced egg, and avocado slices.
4. In another bowl, whisk together the lemon juice, olive oil, mustard, salt, and pepper, and drizzle over the salad. Add the cooked green beans and toss to combine, then serve.

Per Serving
calories: 737 | fat: 57.3g | protein: 34.2g
carbs: 22.1g | fiber: 13.4g | sodium: 398mg

Fennel Poached Cod with Tomatoes

Prep time: 10 minutes | Cook time: 20 minutes | Serves 4

1 tablespoon olive oil
1 cup thinly sliced fennel
½ cup thinly sliced onion
1 tablespoon minced garlic
1 (15-ounce / 425-g) can diced tomatoes
2 cups chicken broth
½ cup white wine
Juice and zest of 1 orange
1 pinch red pepper flakes
1 bay leaf
1 pound (454 g) cod

1. Heat the olive oil in a large skillet. Add the onion and fennel and cook for 6 minutes, stirring occasionally, or until translucent. Add the garlic and cook for 1 minute more.
2. Add the tomatoes, chicken broth, wine, orange juice and zest, red pepper flakes, and bay leaf, and simmer for 5 minutes to meld the flavors.
3. Carefully add the cod in a single layer, cover, and simmer for 6 to 7 minutes.
4. Transfer fish to a serving dish, ladle the remaining sauce over the fish, and serve.

Per Serving
calories: 336 | fat: 12.5g | protein: 45.1g
carbs:11.0g | fiber: 3.3g | sodium: 982mg

Sole Piccata with Capers

Prep time: 10 minutes | Cook time: 17 minutes | Serves 4

1 teaspoon extra-virgin olive oil
4 (5-ounce / 142-g) sole fillets, patted dry
3 tablespoons almond butter
2 teaspoons minced garlic
2 tablespoons all-purpose flour
2 cups low-sodium chicken broth
Juice and zest of ½ lemon
2 tablespoons capers

1. Place a large skillet over medium-high heat and add the olive oil.
2. Sear the sole fillets until the fish flakes easily when tested with a fork, about 4 minutes on each side. Transfer the fish to a plate and set aside.
3. Return the skillet to the stove and add the butter.
4. Sauté the garlic until translucent, about 3 minutes.
5. Whisk in the flour to make a thick paste and cook, stirring constantly, until the mixture is golden brown, about 2 minutes.
6. Whisk in the chicken broth, lemon juice and zest.
7. Cook for about 4 minutes until the sauce is thickened.
8. Stir in the capers and serve the sauce over the fish.

Per Serving
calories: 271 | fat:13.0g | protein: 30.0g
carbs: 7.0g | fiber: 0g | sodium: 413mg

Dill Baked Sea Bass

Prep time: 10 minutes | Cook time: 10 to 15 minutes | Serves 6

¼ cup olive oil
2 pounds (907 g) sea bass
Sea salt and freshly ground pepper, to taste

1 garlic clove, minced
¼ cup dry white wine
3 teaspoons fresh dill
2 teaspoons fresh thyme

1. Preheat the oven to 425ºF (220ºC).
2. Brush the bottom of a roasting pan with the olive oil. Place the fish in the pan and brush the fish with oil.
3. Season the fish with sea salt and freshly ground pepper. Combine the remaining ingredients and pour over the fish.
4. Bake in the preheated oven for 10 to 15 minutes, depending on the size of the fish.
5. Serve hot.

Per Serving
calories: 224 | fat: 12.1g | protein: 28.1g
carbs: 0.9g | fiber: 0.3g | sodium: 104mg

Tuna and Zucchini Patties

Prep time: 10 minutes | Cook time: 12 minutes | Serves 4

3 slices whole-wheat sandwich bread, toasted
2 (5-ounce / 142-g) cans tuna in olive oil, drained
1 cup shredded zucchini
1 large egg, lightly beaten
¼ cup diced red bell pepper
1 tablespoon dried

oregano
1 teaspoon lemon zest
¼ teaspoon freshly ground black pepper
¼ teaspoon kosher or sea salt
1 tablespoon extra-virgin olive oil
Salad greens or 4 whole-wheat rolls, for serving (optional)

1. Crumble the toast into bread crumbs with your fingers (or use a knife to cut into ¼-inch cubes) until you have 1 cup of loosely packed crumbs. Pour the crumbs into a large bowl. Add the tuna, zucchini, beaten egg, bell pepper, oregano, lemon zest, black pepper, and salt. Mix well with a fork. With your hands, form the mixture into four (½-cup-size) patties.

Place them on a plate, and press each patty flat to about ¾-inch thick.
2. In a large skillet over medium-high heat, heat the oil until it's very hot, about 2 minutes.
3. Add the patties to the hot oil, then reduce the heat down to medium. Cook the patties for 5 minutes, flip with a spatula, and cook for an additional 5 minutes. Serve the patties on salad greens or whole-wheat rolls, if desired.

Per Serving
calories: 757 | fat: 72.0g | protein: 5.0g
carbs: 26.0g | fiber: 4.0g | sodium: 418mg

Mediterranean Cod Stew

Prep time: 10 minutes | Cook time: 20 minutes | Serves 6

2 tablespoons extra-virgin olive oil
2 cups chopped onion
2 garlic cloves, minced
¾ teaspoon smoked paprika
1 (14.5-ounce / 411-g) can diced tomatoes, undrained
1 (12-ounce / 340-g) jar roasted red peppers, drained and

chopped
1 cup sliced olives, green or black
⅓ cup dry red wine
¼ teaspoon kosher or sea salt
¼ teaspoon freshly ground black pepper
1½ pounds (680 g) cod fillets, cut into 1-inch pieces
3 cups sliced mushrooms

1. In a large stockpot over medium heat, heat the oil. Add the onion and cook for 4 minutes, stirring occasionally. Add the garlic and smoked paprika and cook for 1 minute, stirring often.
2. Mix in the tomatoes with their juices, roasted peppers, olives, wine, pepper, and salt, and turn the heat to medium-high. Bring the mixture to a boil. Add the cod fillets and mushrooms, and reduce the heat to medium.
3. Cover and cook for about 10 minutes, stirring a few times, until the cod is cooked through and flakes easily, and serve.

Per Serving
calories: 167 | fat: 5.0g | protein: 19.0g
carbs: 11.0g | fiber: 5.0g | sodium: 846mg

Haddock with Cucumber Sauce

Prep time: 10 minutes | Cook time: 10 minutes | Serves 4

¼ cup plain Greek yogurt
½ scallion, white and green parts, finely chopped
½ English cucumber, grated, liquid squeezed out
2 teaspoons chopped fresh mint
1 teaspoon honey
Sea salt and freshly ground black pepper, to taste
4 (5-ounce / 142-g) haddock fillets, patted dry
Nonstick cooking spray

1. In a small bowl, stir together the yogurt, cucumber, scallion, mint, honey, and a pinch of salt. Set aside.
2. Season the fillets lightly with salt and pepper.
3. Place a large skillet over medium-high heat and spray lightly with cooking spray.
4. Cook the haddock, turning once, until it is just cooked through, about 5 minutes per side.
5. Remove the fish from the heat and transfer to plates.
6. Serve topped with the cucumber sauce.

Per Serving
calories: 164 | fat: 2.0g | protein: 27.0g
carbs: 4.0g | fiber: 0g | sodium: 104mg

Crispy Herb Crusted Halibut

Prep time: 10 minutes | Cook time: 20 minutes | Serves 4

4 (5-ounce / 142-g) halibut fillets, patted dry
Extra-virgin olive oil, for brushing
½ cup coarsely ground unsalted pistachios
1 tablespoon chopped
fresh parsley
1 teaspoon chopped fresh basil
1 teaspoon chopped fresh thyme
Pinch sea salt
Pinch freshly ground black pepper

1. Preheat the oven to 350ºF (180ºC). Line a baking sheet with parchment paper.
2. Place the fillets on the baking sheet and brush them generously with olive oil.

3. In a small bowl, stir together the pistachios, parsley, basil, thyme, salt, and pepper.
4. Spoon the nut mixture evenly on the fish, spreading it out so the tops of the fillets are covered.
5. Bake in the preheated oven until it flakes when pressed with a fork, about 20 minutes.
6. Serve immediately.

Per Serving
calories: 262 | fat: 11.0g | protein: 32.0g
carbs: 4.0g | fiber: 2.0g | sodium: 77mg

Roasted Trout Stuffed with Veggies

Prep time: 10 minutes | Cook time: 25 minutes | Serves 2

2 (8-ounce / 227-g) whole trout fillets, dressed (cleaned but with bones and skin intact)
1 tablespoon extra-virgin olive oil
¼ teaspoon salt
⅛ teaspoon freshly ground black pepper
1 small onion, thinly sliced
½ red bell pepper, seeded and thinly sliced
1 poblano pepper, seeded and thinly sliced
2 or 3 shiitake mushrooms, sliced
1 lemon, sliced
Nonstick cooking spray

1. Preheat the oven to 425ºF (220ºC). Spray a baking sheet with nonstick cooking spray.
2. Rub both trout fillets, inside and out, with the olive oil. Season with salt and pepper.
3. Mix together the onion, bell pepper, poblano pepper, and mushrooms in a large bowl. Stuff half of this mixture into the cavity of each fillet. Top the mixture with 2 or 3 lemon slices inside each fillet.
4. Place the fish on the prepared baking sheet side by side. Roast in the preheated oven for 25 minutes, or until the fish is cooked through and the vegetables are tender.
5. Remove from the oven and serve on a plate.

Per Serving
calories: 453 | fat: 22.1g | protein: 49.0g
carbs: 13.8g | fiber: 3.0g | sodium: 356mg

Garlic-Butter Parmesan Salmon and Asparagus

Prep time: 10 minutes | Cook time: 15 minutes | Serves 2

2 (6-ounce / 170-g) salmon fillets, skin on and patted dry
Pink Himalayan salt
Freshly ground black pepper, to taste
1 pound (454 g) fresh asparagus,
ends snapped off
3 tablespoons almond butter
2 garlic cloves, minced
¼ cup grated Parmesan cheese

1. Preheat the oven to 400ºF (205ºC). Line a baking sheet with aluminum foil.
2. Season both sides of the salmon fillets with salt and pepper.
3. Put the salmon in the middle of the baking sheet and arrange the asparagus around the salmon.
4. Heat the almond butter in a small saucepan over medium heat.
5. Add the minced garlic and cook for about 3 minutes, or until the garlic just begins to brown.
6. Drizzle the garlic-butter sauce over the salmon and asparagus and scatter the Parmesan cheese on top.
7. Bake in the preheated oven for about 12 minutes, or until the salmon is cooked through and the asparagus is crisp-tender. You can switch the oven to broil at the end of cooking time for about 3 minutes to get a nice char on the asparagus.
8. Let cool for 5 minutes before serving.

Per Serving
calories: 435 | fat: 26.1g | protein: 42.3g carbs: 10.0g | fiber: 5.0g | sodium: 503mg

Easy Breaded Shrimp

Prep time: 10 minutes | Cook time: 4 to 6 minutes | Serves 4

2 large eggs
1 tablespoon water
2 cups seasoned Italian bread crumbs
1 teaspoon salt
1 cup flour
1 pound (454 g) large shrimp (21 to 25), peeled and deveined
Extra-virgin olive oil, as needed

1. In a small bowl, beat the eggs with the water, then transfer to a shallow dish.
2. Add the bread crumbs and salt to a separate shallow dish, then mix well.
3. Place the flour into a third shallow dish.
4. Coat the shrimp in the flour, then the beaten egg, and finally the bread crumbs. Place on a plate and repeat with all of the shrimp.
5. Heat a skillet over high heat. Pour in enough olive oil to coat the bottom of the skillet. Cook the shrimp in the hot skillet for 2 to 3 minutes on each side. Remove and drain on a paper towel. Serve warm.

Per Serving
calories: 714 | fat: 34.0g | protein: 37.0g carbs: 63.0g | fiber: 3.0g | sodium: 1727mg

Pesto Shrimp over Zoodles

Prep time: 15 minutes | Cook time: 10 minutes | Serves 4

1 pound (454 g) fresh shrimp, peeled and deveined
Salt and freshly ground black pepper, to taste
2 tablespoons extra-virgin olive oil
½ small onion, slivered
8 ounces (227 g)
store-bought jarred pesto
¾ cup crumbled goat or feta cheese, plus additional for serving
2 large zucchini, spiralized, for serving
¼ cup chopped flat-leaf Italian parsley, for garnish

1. In a bowl, season the shrimp with salt and pepper. Set aside.
2. In a large skillet, heat the olive oil over medium-high heat. Sauté the onion until just golden, 5 to 6 minutes.
3. Reduce the heat to low and add the pesto and cheese, whisking to combine and melt the cheese. Bring to a low simmer and add the shrimp. Reduce the heat back to low and cover. Cook until the shrimp is cooked through and pink, about 3 to 4 minutes.
4. Serve the shrimp warm over zoodles, garnishing with chopped parsley and additional crumbled cheese.

Per Serving
calories: 491 | fat: 35.0g | protein: 29.0g carbs: 15.0g | fiber: 4.0g | sodium: 870mg

Salt and Pepper Calamari and Scallops

Prep time: 5 minutes | Cook time: 10 minutes | Serves 4

8 ounces (227 g) calamari steaks, cut into ½-inch-thick rings
8 ounces (227 g) sea scallops
1½ teaspoons salt, divided

1 teaspoon garlic powder
1 teaspoon freshly ground black pepper
⅓ cup extra-virgin olive oil
2 tablespoons almond butter

1. Place the calamari and scallops on several layers of paper towels and pat dry. Sprinkle with 1 teaspoon of salt and allow to sit for 15 minutes at room temperature. Pat dry with additional paper towels. Sprinkle with pepper and garlic powder.
2. In a deep medium skillet, heat the olive oil and butter over medium-high heat. When the oil is hot but not smoking, add the scallops and calamari in a single layer to the skillet and sprinkle with the remaining ½ teaspoon of salt. Cook for 2 to 4 minutes on each side, depending on the size of the scallops, until just golden but still slightly opaque in center.
3. Using a slotted spoon, remove from the skillet and transfer to a serving platter. Allow the cooking oil to cool slightly and drizzle over the seafood before serving.

Per Serving
calories: 309 | fat: 25.0g | protein: 18.0g
carbs: 3.0g | fiber: 0g | sodium: 928mg

Easy Tomato Tuna Melts

Prep time: 5 minutes | Cook time: 3 to 4 minutes | Serves 2

1 (5-ounce / 142-g) can chunk light tuna packed in water, drained
2 tablespoons plain Greek yogurt
2 tablespoons finely chopped celery
1 tablespoon finely

chopped red onion
2 teaspoons freshly squeezed lemon juice
Pinch cayenne pepper
1 large tomato, cut into ¾-inch-thick rounds
½ cup shredded Cheddar cheese

1. Preheat the broiler to High.
2. Stir together the tuna, yogurt, celery, red onion, lemon juice, and cayenne pepper in a medium bowl.
3. Place the tomato rounds on a baking sheet. Top each with some tuna salad and Cheddar cheese.
4. Broil for 3 to 4 minutes until the cheese is melted and bubbly. Cool for 5 minutes before serving.

Per Serving
calories: 244 | fat: 10.0g | protein: 30.1g
carbs: 6.9g | fiber: 1.0g | sodium: 445mg

Steamed Trout with Lemon Herb Crust

Prep time: 10 minutes | Cook time: 15 minutes | Serves 2

3 tablespoons olive oil
3 garlic cloves, chopped
2 tablespoons fresh lemon juice
1 tablespoon chopped fresh mint

1 tablespoon chopped fresh parsley
¼ teaspoon dried ground thyme
1 teaspoon sea salt
1 pound (454 g) fresh trout (2 pieces)
2 cups fish stock

1. Stir together the olive oil, garlic, lemon juice, mint, parsley, thyme, and salt in a small bowl. Brush the marinade onto the fish.
2. Insert a trivet in the Instant Pot. Pour in the fish stock and place the fish on the trivet.
3. Secure the lid. Select the Steam mode and set the cooking time for 15 minutes at High Pressure.
4. Once cooking is complete, do a quick pressure release. Carefully open the lid. Serve warm.

Per Serving
calories: 477 | fat: 29.6g | protein: 51.7g
carbs: 3.6g | fiber: 0.2g | sodium: 2011mg

Hazelnut Crusted Sea Bass

Prep time: 10 minutes | Cook time: 15 minutes | Serves 2

2 tablespoons almond butter
2 sea bass fillets
⅓ cup roasted hazelnuts
A pinch of cayenne pepper

1. Preheat the oven to 425ºF (220ºC). Line a baking dish with waxed paper.
2. Brush the almond butter over the fillets.
3. Pulse the hazelnuts and cayenne in a food processor. Coat the sea bass with the hazelnut mixture, then transfer to the baking dish.
4. Bake in the preheated oven for about 15 minutes. Cool for 5 minutes before serving.

Per Serving
calories: 468 | fat: 30.8g | protein: 40.0g
carbs: 8.8g | fiber: 4.1g | sodium: 90mg

Lemony Trout with Caramelized Shallots

Prep time: 10 minutes | Cook time: 20 minutes | Serves 2

Shallots:
1 teaspoon almond butter
2 shallots, thinly sliced
Dash salt

Trout:
1 tablespoon plus 1 teaspoon almond butter, divided
2 (4-ounce / 113-g) trout fillets
3 tablespoons capers
¼ cup freshly squeezed lemon juice
¼ teaspoon salt
Dash freshly ground black pepper
1 lemon, thinly sliced

Make the Shallots
1. In a large skillet over medium heat, cook the butter, shallots, and salt for 20 minutes, stirring every 5 minutes, or until the shallots are wilted and caramelized.

Make the Trout
1. Meanwhile, in another large skillet over medium heat, heat 1 teaspoon of almond butter.

2. Add the trout fillets and cook each side for 3 minutes, or until flaky. Transfer to a plate and set aside.
3. In the skillet used for the trout, stir in the capers, lemon juice, salt, and pepper, then bring to a simmer. Whisk in the remaining 1 tablespoon of almond butter. Spoon the sauce over the fish.
4. Garnish the fish with the lemon slices and caramelized shallots before serving.

Per Serving
calories: 344 | fat: 18.4g | protein: 21.1g
carbs: 14.7g | fiber: 5.0g | sodium: 1090mg

Garlic Shrimp with Arugula Pesto

Prep time: 20 minutes | Cook time: 5 minutes | Serves 2

3 cups lightly packed arugula
½ cup lightly packed basil leaves
¼ cup walnuts
3 tablespoons olive oil
3 medium garlic cloves
2 tablespoons grated Parmesan cheese
1 tablespoon freshly squeezed lemon juice
Salt and freshly ground black pepper, to taste
1 (10-ounce / 283-g) package zucchini noodles
8 ounces (227 g) cooked, shelled shrimp
2 Roma tomatoes, diced

1. Process the arugula, basil, walnuts, olive oil, garlic, Parmesan cheese, and lemon juice in a food processor until smooth, scraping down the sides as needed. Season with salt and pepper to taste.
2. Heat a skillet over medium heat. Add the pesto, zucchini noodles, and cooked shrimp. Toss to combine the sauce over the noodles and shrimp, and cook until heated through.
3. Taste and season with more salt and pepper as needed. Serve topped with the diced tomatoes.

Per Serving
calories: 435 | fat: 30.2g | protein: 33.0g
carbs: 15.1g | fiber: 5.0g | sodium: 413mg

Baked Cod with Vegetables

Prep time: 15 minutes | Cook time: 25 minutes | Serves 2

1 pound (454 g) thick cod fillet, cut into 4 even portions
¼ teaspoon onion powder (optional)
¼ teaspoon paprika
3 tablespoons extra-virgin olive oil
4 medium scallions
½ cup fresh chopped basil, divided
3 tablespoons minced garlic (optional)
2 teaspoons salt
2 teaspoons freshly ground black pepper
¼ teaspoon dry marjoram (optional)
6 sun-dried tomato slices
½ cup dry white wine
½ cup crumbled feta cheese
1 (15-ounce / 425-g) can oil-packed artichoke hearts, drained
1 lemon, sliced
1 cup pitted kalamata olives
1 teaspoon capers (optional)
4 small red potatoes, quartered

1. Preheat the oven to 375ºF (190ºC).
2. Season the fish with paprika and onion powder (if desired).
3. Heat an ovenproof skillet over medium heat and sear the top side of the cod for about 1 minute until golden. Set aside.
4. Heat the olive oil in the same skillet over medium heat. Add the scallions, ¼ cup of basil, garlic (if desired), salt, pepper, marjoram (if desired), tomato slices, and white wine and stir to combine. Bring to a boil and remove from heat.
5. Evenly spread the sauce on the bottom of skillet. Place the cod on top of the tomato basil sauce and scatter with feta cheese. Place the artichokes in the skillet and top with the lemon slices.
6. Scatter with the olives, capers (if desired), and the remaining ¼ cup of basil. Remove from the heat and transfer to the preheated oven. Bake for 15 to 20 minutes, or until it flakes easily with a fork.
7. Meanwhile, place the quartered potatoes on a baking sheet or wrapped in aluminum foil. Bake in the oven for 15 minutes until fork-tender.
8. Cool for 5 minutes before serving.

Per Serving
calories: 1168 | fat: 60.0g | protein: 63.8g
carbs: 94.0g | fiber: 13.0g | sodium: 4620mg

Baked Oysters with Vegetables

Prep time: 30 minutes | Cook time: 15 to 17 minutes | Serves 2

2 cups coarse salt, for holding the oysters
1 dozen fresh oysters, scrubbed
1 tablespoon almond butter
¼ cup finely chopped scallions, both white and green parts
½ cup finely chopped artichoke hearts
¼ cup finely chopped red bell pepper
1 garlic clove, minced
1 tablespoon finely chopped fresh parsley
Zest and juice of ½ lemon
Pinch salt
Freshly ground black pepper, to taste

1. Pour the salt into a baking dish and spread to evenly fill the bottom of the dish.
2. Prepare a clean work surface to shuck the oysters. Using a shucking knife, insert the blade at the joint of the shell, where it hinges open and shut. Firmly apply pressure to pop the blade in, and work the knife around the shell to open. Discard the empty half of the shell. Using the knife, gently loosen the oyster, and remove any shell particles. Set the oysters in their shells on the salt, being careful not to spill the juices.
3. Preheat the oven to 425ºF (220ºC).
4. Heat the almond butter in a large skillet over medium heat. Add the scallions, artichoke hearts, and bell pepper, and cook for 5 to 7 minutes. Add the garlic and cook for 1 minute more.
5. Remove from the heat and stir in the parsley, lemon zest and juice, and season to taste with salt and pepper.
6. Divide the vegetable mixture evenly among the oysters. Bake in the preheated oven for 10 to 12 minutes, or until the vegetables are lightly browned. Serve warm.

Per Serving
calories: 135 | fat: 7.2g | protein: 6.0g
carbs: 10.7g | fiber: 2.0g | sodium: 280mg

Dill Chutney Salmon

Prep time: 5 minutes | Cook time: 3 minutes | Serves 2

Chutney:

¼ cup fresh dill
¼ cup extra virgin olive oil
Juice from ½ lemon
Sea salt, to taste

Fish:

2 cups water
2 salmon fillets
Juice from ½ lemon
¼ teaspoon paprika
Salt and freshly ground pepper to taste

1. Pulse all the chutney ingredients in a food processor until creamy. Set aside.
2. Add the water and steamer basket to the Instant Pot. Place salmon fillets, skin-side down, on the steamer basket. Drizzle the lemon juice over salmon and sprinkle with the paprika.
3. Secure the lid. Select the Manual mode and set the cooking time for 3 minutes at High Pressure.
4. Once cooking is complete, do a quick pressure release. Carefully open the lid.
5. Season the fillets with pepper and salt to taste. Serve topped with the dill chutney.

Per Serving
calories: 636 | fat: 41.1g | protein: 65.3g
carbs: 1.9g | fiber: 0.2g | sodium: 477mg

Shrimp and Pea Paella

Prep time: 20 minutes | Cook time: 60 minutes | Serves 2

2 tablespoons olive oil
1 garlic clove, minced
½ large onion, minced
1 cup diced tomato
½ cup short-grain rice
½ teaspoon sweet paprika
½ cup dry white wine
1¼ cups low-sodium chicken stock
8 ounces (227 g) large raw shrimp
1 cup frozen peas
¼ cup jarred roasted red peppers, cut into strips
Salt, to taste

1. Heat the olive oil in a large skillet over medium-high heat.
2. Add the garlic and onion and sauté for 3 minutes, or until the onion is softened.
3. Add the tomato, rice, and paprika and stir for 3 minutes to toast the rice.
4. Add the wine and chicken stock and stir to combine. Bring the mixture to a boil.
5. Cover and reduce the heat to medium-low, and simmer for 45 minutes, or until the rice is just about tender and most of the liquid has been absorbed.
6. Add the shrimp, peas, and roasted red peppers. Cover and cook for an additional 5 minutes. Season with salt to taste and serve.

Per Serving
calories: 646 | fat: 27.1g | protein: 42.0g
carbs: 59.7g | fiber: 7.0g | sodium: 687mg

Grilled Lemon Pesto Salmon

Prep time: 5 minutes | Cook time: 6 to 10 minutes | Serves 2

10 ounces (283 g) salmon fillet (1 large piece or 2 smaller ones)
Salt and freshly ground black pepper,
to taste
2 tablespoons prepared pesto sauce
1 large fresh lemon, sliced
Cooking spray

1. Preheat the grill to medium-high heat. Spray the grill grates with cooking spray.
2. Season the salmon with salt and black pepper. Spread the pesto sauce on top.
3. Make a bed of fresh lemon slices about the same size as the salmon fillet on the hot grill, and place the salmon on top of the lemon slices. Put any additional lemon slices on top of the salmon.
4. Grill the salmon for 6 to 10 minutes, or until the fish is opaque and flakes apart easily.
5. Serve hot.

Per Serving
calories: 316 | fat: 21.1g | protein: 29.0g
carbs: 1.0g | fiber: 0g | sodium: 175mg

Chapter 9 Fruits and Desserts

Apple and Berries Ambrosia

Prep time: 15 minutes | Cook time: 0 minutes | Serves 4

2 cups unsweetened coconut milk, chilled
2 tablespoons raw honey
1 apple, peeled, cored, and chopped
2 cups fresh raspberries
2 cups fresh blueberries

1. Spoon the chilled milk in a large bowl, then mix in the honey. Stir to mix well.
2. Then mix in the remaining ingredients. Stir to coat the fruits well and serve immediately.

Tip: You can also try this recipe out with any kinds of fruit chunks, such as pears, peaches, bananas, nectarines, or melons.

Per Serving
calories: 386 | fat: 21.1g | protein: 4.2g
carbs: 45.9g | fiber: 11.0g | sodium: 16mg

Easy Blueberry and Oat Crisp

Prep time: 15 minutes | Cook time: 20 minutes | Serves 4

2 tablespoons coconut oil, melted, plus additional for greasing
4 cups fresh blueberries
Juice of ½ lemon
2 teaspoons lemon zest
¼ cup maple syrup
1 cup gluten-free rolled oats
½ cup chopped pecans
½ teaspoon ground cinnamon
Sea salt, to taste

1. Preheat the oven to 350ºF (180ºC). Grease a baking sheet with coconut oil.
2. Combine the blueberries, lemon juice and zest, and maple syrup in a bowl. Stir to mix well, then spread the mixture on the baking sheet.

3. Combine the remaining ingredients in a small bowl. Stir to mix well. Pour the mixture over the blueberries mixture.
4. Bake in the preheated oven for 20 minutes or until the oats are golden brown.
5. Serve immediately with spoons.

Tip: You can use quinoa to replace the rolled oats, if needed.

Per Serving
calories: 496 | fat: 32.9g | protein: 5.1g
carbs: 50.8g | fiber: 7.0g | sodium: 41mg

Banana, Cranberry, and Oat Bars

Prep time: 15 minutes | Cook time: 40 minutes | Makes 16 bars

2 tablespoon extra-virgin olive oil
2 medium ripe bananas, mashed
½ cup almond butter
½ cup maple syrup
⅓ cup dried cranberries
1½ cups old-fashioned rolled oats
¼ cup oat flour
¼ cup ground flaxseed
¼ teaspoon ground cloves
½ cup shredded coconut
½ teaspoon ground cinnamon
1 teaspoon vanilla extract

1. Preheat the oven to 400ºF (205ºC). Line a 8-inch square pan with parchment paper, then grease with olive oil.
2. Combine the mashed bananas, almond butter, and maple syrup in a bowl. Stir to mix well.
3. Mix in the remaining ingredients and stir to mix well until thick and sticky.
4. Spread the mixture evenly on the square pan with a spatula, then bake in the preheated oven for 40 minutes or until a toothpick inserted in the center comes out clean.
5. Remove them from the oven and slice into 16 bars to serve.

Tip: Instead of oat flour, you can also use almond flour or coconut flour.

Per Serving
calories: 145 | fat: 7.2g | protein: 3.1g
carbs: 18.9g | fiber: 2.0g | sodium: 3mg

Lemony Tea and Chia Pudding

Prep time: 30 minutes | Cook time: 0 minutes | Serves 3 to 4

2 teaspoons matcha green tea powder (optional)
2 tablespoons ground chia seeds

1 to 2 dates
2 cups unsweetened coconut milk
Zest and juice of 1 lime

1. Put all the ingredients in a food processor and pulse until creamy and smooth.
2. Pour the mixture in a bowl, then wrap in plastic. Store in the refrigerator for at least 20 minutes, then serve chilled.

Tip: Dates are used as sugar, so you can replace them with 1 tablespoon of coconut sugar / maple syrup, or 15 drops liquid stevia.

Per Serving
calories: 225 | fat: 20.1g | protein: 3.2g
carbs: 5.9g | fiber: 5.0g | sodium: 314mg

Berry and Rhubarb Cobbler

Prep time: 15 minutes | Cook time: 35 minutes | Serves 8

Cobbler:
1 cup fresh raspberries
2 cups fresh blueberries
1 cup sliced (½-inch) rhubarb pieces
1 tablespoon

arrowroot powder
¼ cup unsweetened apple juice
2 tablespoons melted coconut oil
¼ cup raw honey

Topping:
1 cup almond flour
1 tablespoon arrowroot powder
½ cup shredded

coconut
¼ cup raw honey
½ cup coconut oil

Make the Cobbler
1. Preheat the oven to 350ºF (180ºC). Grease a baking dish with melted coconut oil.
2. Combine the ingredients for the cobbler in a large bowl. Stir to mix well.
3. Spread the mixture in the single layer on the baking dish. Set aside.

Make the Topping
1. Combine the almond flour, arrowroot powder, and coconut in a bowl. Stir to mix well.
2. Fold in the honey and coconut oil. Stir with a fork until the mixture crumbled.
3. Spread the topping over the cobbler, then bake in the preheated oven for 35 minutes or until frothy and golden brown.
4. Serve immediately.

Tip: For more variation, you can replace the berries and rhubarb with plums, pears, or pumpkin, cherry, and sweet potato.

Per Serving
calories: 305 | fat: 22.1g | protein: 3.2g
carbs: 29.8g | fiber: 4.0g | sodium: 3mg

Sweet Spiced Pumpkin Pudding

Prep time: 2 hours 10 minutes | Cook time: 0 minutes | Serves 6

1 cup pure pumpkin purée
2 cups unsweetened coconut milk
1 teaspoon ground cinnamon
¼ teaspoon ground nutmeg

½ teaspoon ground ginger
Pinch cloves
¼ cup pure maple syrup
2 tablespoons chopped pecans, for garnish

1. Combine all the ingredients, except for the chopped pecans, in a large bowl. Stir to mix well.
2. Wrap the bowl in plastic and refrigerate for at least 2 hours.
3. Remove the bowl from the refrigerator and discard the plastic. Spread the pudding with pecans and serve chilled.

Tip: Instead of pumpkin purée, you can use the same amount of puréed butternut squash or sweet potato to replace it.

Per Serving
calories: 249 | fat: 21.1g | protein: 2.8g
carbs: 17.2g | fiber: 3.0g | sodium: 46mg

Coconut Blueberries with Brown Rice

Prep time: 55 minutes | Cook time: 10 minutes | Serves 4

1 cup fresh blueberries
2 cups unsweetened coconut milk
1 teaspoon ground ginger
¼ cup maple syrup
Sea salt, to taste
2 cups cooked brown rice

1. Put all the ingredients, except for the brown rice, in a pot. Stir to combine well.
2. Cook over medium-high heat for 7 minutes or until the blueberries are tender.
3. Pour in the brown rice and cook for 3 more minute or until the rice is soft. Stir constantly.
4. Serve immediately.

Tip: How to cook the brown rice: Pour the rinsed brown rice in a pot, then pour in enough water to cover the rice about 1-inch. Sprinkle with salt, if desired. Bring to a boil. Reduce the heat to low and simmer for 45 minutes or until the rice is tender. Drain the cooked rice and fluff with a fork. Allow to cool before using.

Per Serving
calories: 470 | fat: 24.8g | protein: 6.2g
carbs: 60.1g | fiber: 5.0g | sodium: 75mg

Citrus Cranberry and Quinoa Energy Bites

Prep time: 25 minutes | Cook time: 0 minutes | Makes 12 bites

2 tablespoons almond butter
2 tablespoons maple syrup
¾ cup cooked quinoa
1 tablespoon dried cranberries
1 tablespoon chia seeds
¼ cup ground almonds
¼ cup sesame seeds, toasted
Zest of 1 orange
½ teaspoon vanilla extract

1. Line a baking sheet with parchment paper.
2. Combine the butter and maple syrup in a bowl. Stir to mix well.
3. Fold in the remaining ingredients and stir until the mixture holds together and smooth.
4. Divide the mixture into 12 equal parts, then shape each part into a ball.
5. Arrange the balls on the baking sheet, then refrigerate for at least 15 minutes.
6. Serve chilled.

Tip: How to cook quinoa: Pour the quinoa in a pot, then pour in enough water to cover. Sprinkle with a dash of salt, if needed. Bring to a boil. Reduce the heat to low and simmer for 15 minutes or until the quinoa is tender and the liquid is almost absorbed. Fluffy with a fork and allow to cool before using.

Per Serving (1 bite)
calories: 110 | fat: 10.8g | protein: 3.1g
carbs: 4.9g | fiber: 3.0g | sodium: 211mg

Chocolate, Almond, and Cherry Clusters

Prep time: 15 minutes | Cook time: 3 minutes | Makes 10 clusters

1 cup dark chocolate (60% cocoa or higher), chopped
1 tablespoon coconut oil
½ cup dried cherries
1 cup roasted salted almonds

1. Line a baking sheet with parchment paper.
2. Melt the chocolate and coconut oil in a saucepan for 3 minutes. Stir constantly.
3. Turn off the heat and mix in the cherries and almonds.
4. Drop the mixture on the baking sheet with a spoon. Place the sheet in the refrigerator and chill for at least 1 hour or until firm.
5. Serve chilled.

Tip: You can also melt the chocolate and coconut oil in the microwave for 1 minute.

Per Serving
calories: 197 | fat: 13.2g | protein: 4.1g
carbs: 17.8g | fiber: 4.0g | sodium: 57mg

Chocolate and Avocado Mousse

Prep time: 40 minutes | Cook time: 5 minutes | Serves 4 to 6

8 ounces (227 g) dark chocolate (60% cocoa or higher), chopped
¼ cup unsweetened coconut milk

2 tablespoons coconut oil
2 ripe avocados, deseeded
¼ cup raw honey
Sea salt, to taste

1. Put the chocolate in a saucepan. Pour in the coconut milk and add the coconut oil.
2. Cook for 3 minutes or until the chocolate and coconut oil melt. Stir constantly.
3. Put the avocado in a food processor, then drizzle with honey and melted chocolate. Pulse to combine until smooth.
4. Pour the mixture in a serving bowl, then sprinkle with salt. Refrigerate to chill for 30 minutes and serve.

Tip: You can chopped the avocado in chunks or slices before pulsing in the food processor to make the purée process easier.

Per Serving
calories: 654 | fat: 46.8g | protein: 7.2g
carbs: 55.9g | fiber: 9.0g | sodium: 112mg

Glazed Pears with Hazelnuts

Prep time: 10 minutes | Cook time: 20 minutes | Serves 4

4 pears, peeled, cored, and quartered lengthwise
1 cup apple juice
1 tablespoon grated

fresh ginger
½ cup pure maple syrup
¼ cup chopped hazelnuts

1. Put the pears in a pot, then pour in the apple juice. Bring to a boil over medium-high heat, then reduce the heat to medium-low. Stir constantly.
2. Cover and simmer for an additional 15 minutes or until the pears are tender.
3. Meanwhile, combine the ginger and maple syrup in a saucepan. Bring to a boil over medium-high heat. Stir frequently. Turn off the heat and transfer the syrup to a small bowl and let sit until ready to use.
4. Transfer the pears in a large serving bowl with a slotted spoon, then top the pears with syrup.
5. Spread the hazelnuts over the pears and serve immediately.

Tip: If you want to add a milky flavor for the pears, you can pour in 1 cup of unsweetened almond milk in the pot and boil with peas and apple juice.

Per Serving
calories: 287 | fat: 3.1g | protein: 2.2g
carbs: 66.9g | fiber: 7.0g | sodium: 8mg

Lemony Blackberry Granita

Prep time: 10 minutes | Cook time: 0 minutes | Serves 4

1 pound (454 g) fresh blackberries
1 teaspoon chopped fresh thyme

¼ cup freshly squeezed lemon juice
½ cup raw honey
½ cup water

1. Put all the ingredients in a food processor, then pulse to purée.
2. Pour the mixture through a sieve into a baking dish. Discard the seeds remain in the sieve.
3. Put the baking dish in the freezer for 2 hours. Remove the dish from the refrigerator and stir to break any frozen parts.
4. Return the dish back to the freezer for an hour, then stir to break any frozen parts again.
5. Return the dish to the freezer for 4 hours until the granita is completely frozen.
6. Remove it from the freezer and mash to serve.

Tip: You can mix other kinds of the berries, such as blueberries or strawberries, with blackberries for a magic mixed flavor.

Per Serving
calories: 183 | fat: 1.1g | protein: 2.2g
carbs: 45.9g | fiber: 6.0g | sodium: 6mg

Mango and Coconut Frozen Pie

Prep time: 1 hour 10 minutes | Cook time: 0 minutes | Serves 8

Crust:

1 cup cashews
½ cup rolled oats
1 cup soft pitted dates

Filling:

2 large mangoes, peeled and chopped
½ cup unsweetened shredded coconut
1 cup unsweetened coconut milk
½ cup water

1. Combine the ingredients for the crust in a food processor. Pulse to combine well.
2. Pour the mixture in an 8-inch springform pan, then press to coat the bottom. Set aside.
3. Combine the ingredients for the filling in the food processor, then pulse to purée until smooth.
4. Pour the filling over the crust, then use a spatula to spread the filling evenly. Put the pan in the freeze for 30 minutes.
5. Remove the pan from the freezer and allow to sit for 15 minutes under room temperature before serving.

Tip: If you have mango allergy, then you can replace the mangoes with peach chunks or sliced apples.

Per Serving (1 slice)
calories: 426 | fat: 28.2g | protein: 8.1g
carbs: 14.9g | fiber: 6.0g | sodium: 174mg

Mini Nuts and Fruits Crumble

Prep time: 15 minutes | Cook time: 15 minutes | Serves 6

Topping:

¼ cup coarsely chopped hazelnuts
1 cup coarsely chopped walnuts
1 teaspoon ground
cinnamon
Sea salt, to taste
1 tablespoon melted coconut oil

Filling:

6 fresh figs, quartered
2 nectarines, pitted and sliced
1 cup fresh blueberries
2 teaspoons lemon zest
½ cup raw honey
1 teaspoon vanilla extract

Make the Topping:
1. Combine the ingredients for the topping in a bowl. Stir to mix well. Set aside until ready to use.

Make the Filling:
1. Preheat the oven to 375ºF (190ºC).
2. Combine the ingredients for the fillings in a bowl. Stir to mix well.
3. Divide the filling in six ramekins, then divide and top with nut topping.
4. Bake in the preheated oven for 15 minutes or until the topping is lightly browned and the filling is frothy.
5. Serve immediately.

Tip: You can use coconut sugar, pure date sugar, maple sugar, or liquid stevia to replace the raw honey, if needed.

Per Serving
calories: 336 | fat: 18.8g | protein: 6.3g
carbs: 41.9g | fiber: 6.0g | sodium: 31mg

Mint Banana Chocolate Sorbet

Prep time: 4 hours 5 minutes | Cook time: 0 minutes | Serves 1

1 frozen banana
1 tablespoon almond butter
2 tablespoons minced fresh mint
2 to 3 tablespoons
dark chocolate chips (60% cocoa or higher)
2 to 3 tablespoons goji (optional)

1. Put the banana, butter, and mint in a food processor. Pulse to purée until creamy and smooth.
2. Add the chocolate and goji, then pulse for several more times to combine well.
3. Pour the mixture in a bowl or a ramekin, then freeze for at least 4 hours before serving chilled.

Tip: You can pour ¼ cup of almond milk when purée the banana, butter, and mint to help them to purée.

Per Serving
calories: 213 | fat: 9.8g | protein: 3.1g
carbs: 2.9g | fiber: 4.0g | sodium: 155mg

Pecan and Carrot Cake

Prep time: 15 minutes | Cook time: 45 minutes | Serves 12

½ cup coconut oil, at room temperature, plus more for greasing the baking dish
2 teaspoons pure vanilla extract
¼ cup pure maple syrup
6 eggs
½ cup coconut flour
1 teaspoon baking powder
1 teaspoon baking soda
½ teaspoon ground nutmeg
1 teaspoon ground cinnamon
⅛ teaspoon sea salt
½ cup chopped pecans
3 cups finely grated carrots

1. Preheat the oven to 350ºF (180ºC). Grease a 13-by-9-inch baking dish with coconut oil.
2. Combine the vanilla extract, maple syrup, and ½ cup of coconut oil in a large bowl. Stir to mix well.
3. Break the eggs in the bowl and whisk to combine well. Set aside.
4. Combine the coconut flour, baking powder, baking soda, nutmeg, cinnamon, and salt in a separate bowl. Stir to mix well.
5. Make a well in the center of the flour mixture, then pour the egg mixture into the well. Stir to combine well.
6. Add the pecans and carrots to the bowl and toss to mix well. Pour the mixture in the single layer on the baking dish.
7. Bake in the preheated oven for 45 minutes or until puffed and the cake spring back when lightly press with your fingers.
8. Remove the cake from the oven. Allow to cool for at least 15 minutes, then serve.

Tip: If you have nut allergies, just omit the pecans, or you can replace it with goji or cherries.

Per Serving
calories: 255 | fat: 21.2g | protein: 5.1g
carbs: 12.8g | fiber: 2.0g | sodium: 202mg

Raspberry Yogurt Basted Cantaloupe

Prep time: 15 minutes | Cook time: 0 minutes | Serves 6

2 cups fresh raspberries, mashed
1 cup plain coconut yogurt
½ teaspoon vanilla extract
1 cantaloupe, peeled and sliced
½ cup toasted coconut flakes

1. Combine the mashed raspberries with yogurt and vanilla extract in a small bowl. Stir to mix well.
2. Place the cantaloupe slices on a platter, then top with raspberry mixture and spread with toasted coconut.
3. Serve immediately.

Tip: How to toast the coconut: Preheat the oven to 325ºF (163ºC), then put the coconut flakes on a baking sheet directly. Bake in the preheated oven for 5 minutes or until lightly browned.

Per Serving
calories: 75 | fat: 4.1g | protein: 1.2g
carbs: 10.9g | fiber: 6.0g | sodium: 36mg

Simple Apple Compote

Prep time: 15 minutes | Cook time: 10 minutes | Serves 4

6 apples, peeled, cored, and chopped
¼ cup raw honey
1 teaspoon ground
cinnamon
¼ cup apple juice
Sea salt, to taste

1. Put all the ingredients in a stockpot. Stir to mix well, then cook over medium-high heat for 10 minutes or until the apples are glazed by honey and lightly saucy. Stir constantly.
2. Serve immediately.

Tip: You can try this recipe with different fruits, such as pears or peaches.

Per Serving
calories: 246 | fat: 0.9g | protein: 1.2g
carbs: 66.3g | fiber: 9.0g | sodium: 62mg

Simple Peanut Butter and Chocolate Balls

Prep time: 45 minutes | Cook time: 0 minutes | Serves 15 balls

¾ cup creamy peanut butter
¼ cup unsweetened cocoa powder
2 tablespoons

softened almond butter
½ teaspoon vanilla extract
1¾ cups maple sugar

1. Line a baking sheet with parchment paper.
2. Combine all the ingredients in a bowl. Stir to mix well.
3. Divide the mixture into 15 parts and shape each part into a 1-inch ball.
4. Arrange the balls on the baking sheet and refrigerate for at least 30 minutes, then serve chilled.

Tip: For more flavor, you can glaze the chilled balls with melted dark chocolate (60% cocoa or higher) and sprinkle with mashed nuts.

Per Serving (1 ball)
calories: 146 | fat: 8.1g | protein: 4.2g
carbs: 16.9g | fiber: 1.0g | sodium: 70mg

Strawberries with Balsamic Vinegar

Prep time: 5 minutes | Cook time: 0 minutes | Serves 2

2 cups strawberries, hulled and sliced
2 tablespoons sugar

2 tablespoons balsamic vinegar

1. Place the sliced strawberries in a bowl, sprinkle with the sugar, and drizzle lightly with the balsamic vinegar.
2. Toss to combine well and allow to sit for about 10 minutes before serving.

Per Serving
calories: 92 | fat: 0.4g | protein: 1.0g
carbs: 21.7g | fiber: 2.9g | sodium: 5mg

Simple Spiced Sweet Pecans

Prep time: 4 minutes | Cook time: 17 minutes | Serves 4

1 cup pecan halves
3 tablespoons almond butter
1 teaspoon ground cinnamon

½ teaspoon ground nutmeg
¼ cup raw honey
¼ teaspoon sea salt

1. Preheat the oven to 350ºF (180ºC). Line a baking sheet with parchment paper.
2. Combine all the ingredients in a bowl. Stir to mix well, then spread the mixture in the single layer on the baking sheet with a spatula.
3. Bake in the preheated oven for 16 minutes or until the pecan halves are well browned.
4. Serve immediately.

Tip: Instead of almond butter, you can also use peanut butter.

Per Serving
calories: 324 | fat: 29.8g | protein: 3.2g
carbs: 13.9g | fiber: 4.0g | sodium: 180mg

Greek Yogurt Affogato with Pistachios

Prep time: 5 minutes | Cook time: 0 minutes | Serves 4

24 ounces (680 g) vanilla Greek yogurt
2 teaspoons sugar
4 shots hot espresso
4 tablespoons

chopped unsalted pistachios
4 tablespoons dark chocolate chips

1. Spoon the yogurt into four bowls or tall glasses.
2. Mix ½ teaspoon of sugar into each of the espresso shots.
3. Pour one shot of the hot espresso over each bowl of yogurt.
4. Top each bowl with 1 tablespoon of the pistachios and 1 tablespoon of the chocolate chips and serve.

Per Serving
calories: 190 | fat: 6.0g | protein: 20.0g
carbs: 14.0g | fiber: 1.0g | sodium: 99mg

Grilled Peaches with Whipped Ricotta

Prep time: 5 minutes | Cook time: 14 to 22 minutes | Serves 4

4 peaches, halved and pitted
2 teaspoons extra-virgin olive oil
¾ cup whole-milk Ricotta cheese
1 tablespoon honey
¼ teaspoon freshly grated nutmeg
4 sprigs mint
Cooking spray

1. Spritz a grill pan with cooking spray. Heat the grill pan to medium heat.
2. Place a large, empty bowl in the refrigerator to chill.
3. Brush the peaches all over with the oil. Place half of the peaches, cut-side down, on the grill pan and cook for 3 to 5 minutes, or until grill marks appear.
4. Using tongs, turn the peaches over. Cover the grill pan with aluminum foil and cook for 4 to 6 minutes, or until the peaches are easily pierced with a sharp knife. Set aside to cool. Repeat with the remaining peaches.
5. Remove the bowl from the refrigerator and add the Ricotta. Using an electric beater, beat the Ricotta on high for 2 minutes. Add the honey and nutmeg and beat for 1 more minute.
6. Divide the cooled peaches among 4 serving bowls. Top with the Ricotta mixture and a sprig of mint and serve.

Per Serving
calories: 176 | fat: 8.0g | protein: 8.0g
carbs: 20.0g | fiber: 3.0g | sodium: 63mg

Cherry Walnut Brownies

Prep time: 10 minutes | Cook time: 20 minutes | Serves 9

2 large eggs
½ cup 2% plain Greek yogurt
½ cup sugar
1/3 cup honey
¼ cup extra-virgin olive oil
1 teaspoon vanilla extract
½ cup whole-wheat pastry flour
1/3 cup unsweetened dark chocolate cocoa powder
¼ teaspoon baking powder
¼ teaspoon salt
1/3 cup chopped
walnuts
9 fresh cherries,
stemmed and pitted
Cooking spray

1. Preheat the oven to 375ºF (190ºC) and set the rack in the middle of the oven. Spritz a square baking pan with cooking spray.
2. In a large bowl, whisk together the eggs, yogurt, sugar, honey, oil and vanilla.
3. In a medium bowl, stir together the flour, cocoa powder, baking powder and salt. Add the flour mixture to the egg mixture and whisk until all the dry ingredients are incorporated. Fold in the walnuts.
4. Pour the batter into the prepared pan. Push the cherries into the batter, three to a row in three rows, so one will be at the center of each brownie once you cut them into squares.
5. Bake the brownies for 20 minutes, or until just set. Remove from the oven and place on a rack to cool for 5 minutes. Cut into nine squares and serve.

Per Serving
calories: 154 | fat: 6.0g | protein: 3.0g
carbs: 24.0g | fiber: 2.0g | sodium: 125mg

Grilled Stone Fruit with Honey

Prep time: 8 minutes | Cook time: 6 minutes | Serves 2

3 apricots, halved and pitted
2 plums, halved and pitted
2 peaches, halved
and pitted
½ cup low-fat ricotta cheese
2 tablespoons honey
Cooking spray

1. Preheat the grill to medium heat. Spray the grill grates with cooking spray.
2. Arrange the fruit, cut side down, on the grill, and cook for 2 to 3 minutes per side, or until lightly charred and softened.
3. Serve warm with a sprinkle of cheese and a drizzle of honey.

Per Serving
calories: 298 | fat: 7.8g | protein: 11.9g
carbs: 45.2g | fiber: 4.3g | sodium: 259mg

Watermelon and Blueberry Salad

Prep time: 5 minutes | Cook time: 0 minutes | Serves 6 to 8

1 medium watermelon	2 tablespoons lemon juice
1 cup fresh blueberries	2 tablespoons finely chopped fresh mint leaves
1/3 cup honey	

1. Cut the watermelon into 1-inch cubes. Put them in a bowl.
2. Evenly distribute the blueberries over the watermelon.
3. In a separate bowl, whisk together the honey, lemon juice and mint.
4. Drizzle the mint dressing over the watermelon and blueberries.
5. Serve cold.

Per Serving

calories: 238 | fat: 1.0g | protein: 4.0g carbs: 61.0g | fiber: 3.0g | sodium: 11mg

Rice Pudding with Roasted Orange

Prep time: 10 minutes | Cook time: 19 to 20 minutes | Serves 6

2 medium oranges	1 cup uncooked instant brown rice
2 teaspoons extra-virgin olive oil	1/4 cup honey
1/8 teaspoon kosher salt	1/2 teaspoon ground cinnamon
2 large eggs	1 teaspoon vanilla extract
2 cups unsweetened almond milk	Cooking spray
1 cup orange juice	

1. Preheat the oven to 450ºF (235ºC). Spritz a large, rimmed baking sheet with cooking spray. Set aside.
2. Slice the unpeeled oranges into 1/4-inch rounds. Brush with the oil and sprinkle with salt. Place the slices on the baking sheet and roast for 4 minutes. Flip the slices and roast for 4 more minutes, or until they begin to brown. Remove from the oven and set aside.
3. Crack the eggs into a medium bowl. In a medium saucepan, whisk together the milk, orange juice, rice, honey and cinnamon. Bring to a boil over medium-high heat, stirring constantly. Reduce the heat to medium-low and simmer for 10 minutes, stirring occasionally.
4. Using a measuring cup, scoop out 1/2 cup of the hot rice mixture and whisk it into the eggs. While constantly stirring the mixture in the pan, slowly pour the egg mixture back into the saucepan. Cook on low heat for 1 to 2 minutes, or until thickened, stirring constantly. Remove from the heat and stir in the vanilla.
5. Let the pudding stand for a few minutes for the rice to soften. The rice will be cooked but slightly chewy. For softer rice, let stand for another half hour.
6. Top with the roasted oranges. Serve warm or at room temperature.

Per Serving

calories: 204 | fat: 6.0g | protein: 5.0g carbs: 34.0g | fiber: 1.0g | sodium: 148mg

Crispy Sesame Cookies

Prep time: 5 minutes | Cook time: 8 to 10 minutes | Serves 14 to 16

1 cup hulled sesame seeds	butter
	2 large eggs
1 cup sugar	1¼ cups flour
8 tablespoons almond	

1. Preheat the oven to 350ºF (180ºC).
2. Toast the sesame seeds on a baking sheet for 3 minutes. Set aside and let cool.
3. Using a mixer, whisk together the sugar and butter. Add the eggs one at a time until well blended. Add the flour and toasted sesame seeds and mix until well blended.
4. Drop spoonfuls of cookie dough onto a baking sheet and form them into round balls, about 1-inch in diameter, similar to a walnut.
5. Put in the oven and bake for 5 to 7 minutes, or until golden brown.
6. Let the cookies cool for 5 minutes before serving.

Per Serving

calories: 218 | fat: 12.0g | protein: 4.0g carbs: 25.0g | fiber: 2.0g | sodium: 58mg

Crunchy Almond Cookies

Prep time: 5 minutes | Cook time: 5 to 7 minutes | Serves 4 to 6

½ cup sugar
8 tablespoons almond butter
1 large egg
1½ cups all-purpose flour
1 cup ground almonds

1. Preheat the oven to 375ºF (190ºC). Line a baking sheet with parchment paper.
2. Using a mixer, whisk together the sugar and butter. Add the egg and mix until combined. Alternately add the flour and ground almonds, ½ cup at a time, while the mixer is on slow.
3. Drop 1 tablespoon of the dough on the prepared baking sheet, keeping the cookies at least 2 inches apart.
4. Put the baking sheet in the oven and bake for about 5 to 7 minutes, or until the cookies start to turn brown around the edges.
5. Let cool for 5 minutes before serving.

Per Serving
calories: 604 | fat: 36.0g | protein: 11.0g
carbs: 63.0g | fiber: 4.0g | sodium: 181mg

Walnut and Date Balls

Prep time: 5 minutes | Cook time: 8 to 10 minutes | Serves 6 to 8

1 cup walnuts
1 cup unsweetened shredded coconut
14 medjool dates,
pitted
8 tablespoons almond butter

1. Preheat the oven to 350ºF (180ºC).
2. Put the walnuts on a baking sheet and toast in the oven for 5 minutes.
3. Put the shredded coconut on a clean baking sheet. Toast for about 3 to 5 minutes, or until it turns golden brown. Once done, remove it from the oven and put it in a shallow bowl.
4. In a food processor, process the toasted walnuts until they have a medium chop. Transfer the chopped walnuts into a medium bowl.
5. Add the dates and butter to the food processor and blend until the dates become a thick paste. Pour the chopped walnuts into the food processor with the dates and pulse just until the mixture is combined, about 5 to 7 pulses.
6. Remove the mixture from the food processor and scrape it into a large bowl.
7. To make the balls, spoon 1 to 2 tablespoons of the date mixture into the palm of your hand and roll around between your hands until you form a ball. Put the ball on a clean, lined baking sheet. Repeat until all the mixture is formed into balls.
8. Roll each ball in the toasted coconut until the outside of the ball is coated. Put the ball back on the baking sheet and repeat.
9. Put all the balls into the refrigerator for 20 minutes before serving. Store any leftovers in the refrigerator in an airtight container.

Per Serving
calories: 489 | fat: 35.0g | protein: 5.0g
carbs: 48.0g | fiber: 7.0g | sodium: 114mg

Frozen Mango Raspberry Delight

Prep time: 5 minutes | Cook time: 0 minutes | Serves 2

3 cups frozen raspberries
1 mango, peeled and pitted
1 peach, peeled and pitted
1 teaspoon honey

1. Place all the ingredients into a blender and purée, adding some water as needed.
2. Put in the freezer for 10 minutes to firm up if desired. Serve chilled or at room temperature.

Per Serving
calories: 276 | fat: 2.1g | protein: 4.5g
carbs: 60.3g | fiber: 17.5g | sodium: 4mg

Honey Baked Cinnamon Apples

Prep time: 5 minutes | Cook time: 20 minutes | Serves 2

1 teaspoon extra-virgin olive oil
4 firm apples, peeled, cored, and sliced
½ teaspoon salt
1½ teaspoons ground

cinnamon, divided
2 tablespoons unsweetened almond milk
2 tablespoons honey

1. Preheat the oven to 375ºF (190ºC). Coat a small casserole dish with the olive oil.
2. Toss the apple slices with the salt and ½ teaspoon of the cinnamon in a medium bowl. Spread the apples in the prepared casserole dish and bake in the preheated oven for 20 minutes.
3. Meanwhile, in a small saucepan, heat the milk, honey, and remaining 1 teaspoon of cinnamon over medium heat, stirring frequently.
4. When it reaches a simmer, remove the pan from the heat and cover to keep warm.
5. Divide the apple slices between 2 plates and pour the sauce over the apples. Serve warm.

Per Serving
calories: 310 | fat: 3.4g | protein: 1.7g
carbs: 68.5g | fiber: 12.6g | sodium: 593mg

Mascarpone Baked Pears

Prep time: 10 minutes | Cook time: 20 minutes | Serves 2

2 ripe pears, peeled
1 tablespoon plus 2 teaspoons honey, divided
1 teaspoon vanilla, divided
¼ teaspoon ground coriander

¼ teaspoon ginger
¼ cup minced walnuts
¼ cup mascarpone cheese
Pinch salt
Cooking spray

1. Preheat the oven to 350ºF (180ºC). Spray a small baking dish with cooking spray.
2. Slice the pears in half lengthwise. Using a spoon, scoop out the core from each piece. Put the pears, cut side up, in the baking dish.
3. Whisk together 1 tablespoon of honey, ½ teaspoon of vanilla, ginger, and coriander in a small bowl. Pour this mixture evenly over the pear halves.
4. Scatter the walnuts over the pear halves.
5. Bake in the preheated oven for 20 minutes, or until the pears are golden and you're able to pierce them easily with a knife.
6. Meanwhile, combine the mascarpone cheese with the remaining 2 teaspoons of honey, ½ teaspoon of vanilla, and a pinch of salt. Stir to combine well.
7. Divide the mascarpone among the warm pear halves and serve.

Per Serving
calories: 308 | fat: 16.0g | protein: 4.1g
carbs: 42.7g | fiber: 6.0g | sodium: 88mg

Easy Mixed Berry Crisp

Prep time: 15 minutes | Cook time: 30 minutes | Serves 2

1½ cups frozen mixed berries, thawed
1 tablespoon coconut sugar

1 tablespoon almond butter
¼ cup oats
¼ cup pecans

1. Preheat the oven to 350ºF (180ºC).
2. Divide the mixed berries between 2 ramekins
3. Place the coconut sugar, almond butter, oats, and pecans in a food processor, and pulse a few times, until the mixture resembles damp sand.
4. Divide the crumble topping over the mixed berries.
5. Put the ramekins on a sheet pan and bake for 30 minutes, or until the top is golden and the berries are bubbling.
6. Serve warm.

Per Serving
calories: 268 | fat: 17.0g | protein: 4.1g
carbs: 26.8g | fiber: 6.0g | sodium: 44mg

Orange Mug Cakes

Prep time: 10 minutes | Cook time: 3 minutes | Serves 2

6 tablespoons flour
2 tablespoons sugar
1 teaspoon orange zest
½ teaspoon baking powder
Pinch salt
1 egg
2 tablespoons olive oil
2 tablespoons unsweetened almond milk
2 tablespoons freshly squeezed orange juice
½ teaspoon orange extract
½ teaspoon vanilla extract

1. Combine the flour, sugar, orange zest, baking powder, and salt in a small bowl.
2. In another bowl, whisk together the egg, olive oil, milk, orange juice, orange extract, and vanilla extract.
3. Add the dry ingredients to the wet ingredients and stir to incorporate. The batter will be thick.
4. Divide the mixture into two small mugs. Microwave each mug separately. The small ones should take about 60 seconds, and one large mug should take about 90 seconds, but microwaves can vary.
5. Cool for 5 minutes before serving.

Per Serving
calories: 303 | fat: 16.9g | protein: 6.0g
carbs: 32.5g | fiber: 1.0g | sodium: 118mg

Fruit and Nut Chocolate Bark

Prep time: 15 minutes | Cook time: 2 minutes | Serves 2

2 tablespoons chopped nuts
3 ounces (85 g) dark chocolate chips
¼ cup chopped dried fruit (blueberries, apricots, figs, prunes, or any combination of those)

1. Line a sheet pan with parchment paper and set aside.
2. Add the nuts to a skillet over medium-high heat and toast for 60 seconds, or just fragrant. Set aside to cool.
3. Put the chocolate chips in a microwave-safe glass bowl and microwave on High for 1 minute.
4. Stir the chocolate and allow any unmelted chips to warm and melt. If desired, heat for an additional 20 to 30 seconds.
5. Transfer the chocolate to the prepared sheet pan. Scatter the dried fruit and toasted nuts over the chocolate evenly and gently pat in so they stick.
6. Place the sheet pan in the refrigerator for at least 1 hour to let the chocolate harden.
7. When ready, break into pieces and serve.

Per Serving
calories: 285 | fat: 16.1g | protein: 4.0g
carbs: 38.7g | fiber: 2.0g | sodium: 2mg

Cozy Superfood Hot Chocolate

Prep time: 5 minutes | Cook time: 8 minutes | Serves 2

2 cups unsweetened almond milk
1 tablespoon avocado oil
1 tablespoon collagen protein powder
2 teaspoons coconut sugar
2 tablespoons cocoa powder
1 teaspoon ground cinnamon
1 teaspoon ground ginger
1 teaspoon vanilla extract
½ teaspoon ground turmeric
Dash salt
Dash cayenne pepper (optional)

1. In a small saucepan over medium heat, warm the almond milk and avocado oil for about 7 minutes, stirring frequently.
2. Fold in the protein powder, which will only properly dissolve in a heated liquid.
3. Stir in the coconut sugar and cocoa powder until melted and dissolved. Carefully transfer the warm liquid into a blender, along with the cinnamon, ginger, vanilla, turmeric, salt, and cayenne pepper (if desired). Blend for 15 seconds until frothy.
4. Serve immediately.

Per Serving
calories: 217 | fat: 11.0g | protein: 11.2g
carbs: 14.8g | fiber: 6.0g | sodium: 202mg

Chapter 10 Sauces, Dips, and Dressings

Peanut Sauce with Honey

Prep time: 5 minutes | Cook time: 0 minutes | Serves 4

¼ cup peanut butter
1 tablespoon peeled and grated fresh ginger
1 tablespoon honey
1 tablespoon low-
sodium soy sauce
1 garlic clove, minced
Juice of 1 lime
Pinch red pepper flakes

1. Whisk together all the ingredients in a small bowl until well incorporated.
2. Transfer to an airtight container and refrigerate for up to 5 days.

Tip: The peanut butter can be substituted with the cashew butter or almond butter. This sauce works great with stir-fries, and it also can be used as a dip for the chicken fingers or topping for beef or seafood.

Per Serving
calories: 117 | fat: 7.6g | protein: 4.1g
carbs: 8.8g | fiber: 1.0g | sodium: 136mg

Cilantro-Tomato Salsa

Prep time: 10 minutes | Cook time: 0 minutes | Serves 6

2 or 3 medium, ripe tomatoes, diced
1 serrano pepper, seeded and minced
½ red onion, minced
¼ cup minced fresh cilantro
Juice of 1 lime
¼ teaspoon salt, plus more as needed

1. Place the tomatoes, serrano pepper, onion, cilantro, lime juice, and salt in a small bowl and mix well.
2. Taste and add additional salt, if needed.
3. Store in an airtight container in the refrigerator for up to 3 days.

Tip: This salsa can be used as a dip with chips, a topping on tacos or baked potatoes, or a sauce for grilled fish and meats.

Per Serving (¼ cup)
calories: 17 | fat: 0g | protein: 1.0g
carbs: 3.9g | fiber: 1.0g | sodium: 83mg

Simple Italian Dressing

Prep time: 5 minutes | Cook time: 0 minutes | Serves 12

½ cup extra-virgin olive oil
¼ cup red wine vinegar
1 teaspoon dried Italian seasoning
1 teaspoon Dijon mustard
¼ teaspoon salt
¼ teaspoon freshly ground black pepper
1 garlic clove, minced

1. Place all the ingredients in a mason jar and cover. Shake vigorously for 1 minute until completely mixed.
2. Store in the refrigerator for up to 1 week.

Tips: For a spicy kick, add a pinch of red pepper flakes to this dressing and mix well. If you want to enhance the flavor, you can add some shredded Parmesan cheese.

Per Serving (1 tablespoon)
calories: 80 | fat: 8.6g | protein: 0g
carbs: 0g | fiber: 0g | sodium: 51mg

Pineapple Salsa

Prep time: 10 minutes | Cook time: 0 minutes | Serves 6 to 8

1 pound (454 g) fresh or thawed frozen pineapple, finely diced, juices reserved
1 white or red onion, finely diced
1 bunch cilantro or mint, leaves only, chopped
1 jalapeño, minced (optional)
Salt, to taste

1. Stir together the pineapple with its juice, onion, cilantro, and jalapeño (if desired) in a medium bowl. Season with salt to taste and serve.
2. The salsa can be refrigerated in an airtight container for up to 2 days.

Per Serving
calories: 55 | fat: 0.1g | protein: 0.9g
carbs: 12.7g | fiber: 1.8g | sodium: 20mg

Cheesy Pea Pesto

Prep time: 5 minutes | Cook time: 0 minutes | Serves 4

½ cup fresh green peas
½ cup grated Parmesan cheese
¼ cup extra-virgin olive oil
¼ cup pine nuts
¼ cup fresh basil leaves
2 garlic cloves, minced
¼ teaspoon sea salt

1. Add all the ingredients to a food processor or blender and pulse until the nuts are chopped finely.
2. Transfer to an airtight container and refrigerate for up to 2 days. You can also store it in ice cube trays in the freezer for up to 6 months.

Tips: The green peas can be replaced with the edamame, if desired. This pea pesto pairs with the whole-grain pasta and risotto, and you can also serve it over the chicken, fish or shrimp.

Per Serving
calories: 247 | fat: 22.8g | protein: 7.1g
carbs: 4.8g | fiber: 1.0g | sodium: 337mg

Parsley Vinaigrette

Prep time: 5 minutes | Cook time: 0 minutes | Makes about ½ cup

½ cup lightly packed fresh parsley, finely chopped
⅓ cup extra-virgin olive oil
3 tablespoons red wine vinegar
1 garlic clove, minced
¼ teaspoon salt, plus additional as needed

1. Place all the ingredients in a mason jar and cover. Shake vigorously for 1 minute until completely mixed.
2. Taste and add additional salt as needed.
3. Serve immediately or serve chilled.

Tip: If the red wine vinegar isn't available, you can use the apple cider vinegar or rice wine vinegar.

Per Serving (1 tablespoon)
calories: 92 | fat: 10.9g | protein: 0g
carbs: 0g | fiber: 0g | sodium: 75mg

Hot Pepper Sauce

Prep time: 10 minutes | Cook time: 20 minutes | Makes 4 cups

2 red hot fresh chiles, deseeded
2 dried chiles
2 garlic cloves, peeled
½ small yellow onion, roughly chopped
2 cups water
2 cups white vinegar

1. Place all the ingredients except the vinegar in a medium saucepan over medium heat. Allow to simmer for 20 minutes until softened.
2. Transfer the mixture to a food processor or blender. Stir in the vinegar and pulse until very smooth.
3. Serve immediately or transfer to a sealed container and refrigerate for up to 3 months.

Tip: If you prefer a milder hot sauce, you can use a seeded jalapeño pepper or serrano pepper instead of the red chiles.

Per Serving (2 tablespoons)
calories: 20 | fat: 1.2g | protein: 0.6g
carbs: 4.4g | fiber: 0.6g | sodium: 12mg

Garlic Lemon-Tahini Dressing

Prep time: 5 minutes | Cook time: 0 minutes | Serves 8 to 10

½ cup tahini
¼ cup extra-virgin olive oil
¼ cup freshly
squeezed lemon juice
1 garlic clove, finely minced
2 teaspoons salt

1. In a glass mason jar with a lid, combine the tahini, olive oil, lemon juice, garlic, and salt. Cover and shake well until combined and creamy.
2. Store in the refrigerator for up to 2 weeks.

Per Serving
calories: 121 | fat: 12.0g | protein: 2.0g
carbs: 3.0g | fiber: 1.0g | sodium: 479mg

Lemon-Tahini Sauce

Prep time: 10 minutes | Cook time: 0 minutes | Makes 1 cup

½ cup tahini
1 garlic clove, minced
Juice and zest of 1 lemon
½ teaspoon salt, plus more as needed
½ cup warm water, plus more as needed

1. Combine the tahini and garlic in a small bowl.
2. Add the lemon juice and zest and salt to the bowl and stir to mix well.
3. Fold in the warm water and whisk until well combined and creamy. Feel free to add more warm water if you like a thinner consistency.
4. Taste and add additional salt as needed.
5. Store the sauce in a sealed container in the refrigerator for up to 5 days.

Tip: You can make this sauce ahead of time and keep it in the refrigerator. Remember to add a few tablespoons of hot water and stir well before using.

Per Serving (¼ cup)
calories: 179 | fat: 15.5g | protein: 5.1g
carbs: 6.8g | fiber: 3.0g | sodium: 324mg

Easy Aioli

Prep time: 5 minutes | Cook time: 0 minutes | Makes ½ cup

½ cup plain Greek yogurt
2 teaspoons Dijon mustard
½ teaspoon hot sauce
¼ teaspoon raw honey
Pinch salt

1. In a small bowl, whisk together the yogurt, mustard, hot sauce, honey, and salt.
2. Serve immediately or refrigerate in an airtight container for up to 3 days.

Per Serving
calories: 47 | fat: 2.5g | protein: 2.1g
carbs: 3.5g | fiber: 0g | sodium: 231mg

Vinaigrette

Prep time: 5 minutes | Cook time: 0 minutes | Makes 1 cup

½ cup extra-virgin olive oil
¼ cup red wine vinegar
1 tablespoon Dijon mustard
1 teaspoon dried rosemary
½ teaspoon salt
½ teaspoon freshly ground black pepper

1. In a cup or a mansion jar with a lid, combine the olive oil, vinegar, mustard, rosemary, salt, and pepper and shake until well combined.
2. Serve chilled or at room temperature.

Per Serving
calories: 124 | fat: 14.0g | protein: 0g
carbs: 1.0g | fiber: 0g | sodium: 170mg

Lentil-Tahini Dip

Prep time: 10 minutes | Cook time: 15 minutes | Makes 3 cups

1 cup dried green or brown lentils, rinsed
2½ cups water, divided
⅓ cup tahini
1 garlic clove
½ teaspoon salt, plus more as needed

1. Add the lentils and 2 cups of water to a medium saucepan and bring to a boil over high heat.
2. Once it starts to boil, reduce the heat to low, and then cook for 14 minutes, stirring occasionally, or the lentils become tender but still hold their shape. You can drain any excess liquid.
3. Transfer the lentils to a food processor, along with the remaining water, tahini, garlic, and salt and process until smooth and creamy.
4. Taste and adjust the seasoning if needed. Serve immediately.

Tip: To add more flavors to this dip, garnish it with finely chopped parsley, basil, dill, or rosemary.

Per Serving (¼ cup)
calories: 100 | fat: 3.9g | protein: 5.1g
carbs: 10.7g | fiber: 6.0g | sodium: 106mg

Ginger Teriyaki Sauce

Prep time: 5 minutes | Cook time: 0 minutes | Serves 2

¼ cup pineapple juice
¼ cup low-sodium soy sauce
2 tablespoons packed coconut sugar
1 tablespoon grated

fresh ginger
1 tablespoon arrowroot powder or cornstarch
1 teaspoon garlic powder

1. Whisk the pineapple juice, soy sauce, coconut sugar, ginger, arrowroot powder, and garlic powder together in a small bowl.
2. Store in an airtight container in the fridge for up to 5 days.

Per Serving
calories: 37 | fat: 0.1g | protein: 1.1g
carbs: 12.0g | fiber: 0g | sodium: 881mg

Asian-Inspired Vinaigrette

Prep time: 5 minutes | Cook time: 0 minutes | Serves 2

¼ cup extra-virgin olive oil
3 tablespoons apple cider vinegar
1 garlic clove, minced
1 tablespoon peeled and grated fresh

ginger
1 tablespoon chopped fresh cilantro
1 tablespoon freshly squeezed lime juice
½ teaspoon sriracha

1. Add all the ingredients in a small bowl and stir to mix well.
2. Serve immediately, or store covered in the refrigerator and shake before using.

Tips: You can adjust the spiciness by adjusting the sriracha quantity. If you'd like to raise the heat levels, you can add ½ teaspoon of Chinese hot mustard to the vinaigrette. It can be used as a marinade for poultry, meats, fish or seafood.

Per Serving
calories: 251 | fat: 26.8g | protein: 0g
carbs: 1.8g | fiber: 0.7g | sodium: 3mg

Creamy Grapefruit and Tarragon Dressing

Prep time: 5 minutes | Cook time: 0 minutes | Serves 4 to 6

½ cup avocado oil mayonnaise
2 tablespoons Dijon mustard
1 teaspoon dried tarragon or 1 tablespoon chopped fresh tarragon

½ teaspoon salt
Zest and juice of ½ grapefruit
¼ teaspoon freshly ground black pepper
1 to 2 tablespoons water (optional)

1. In a large mason jar with a lid, combine the mayonnaise, Dijon, tarragon, grapefruit zest and juice, salt, and pepper and whisk well with a fork until smooth and creamy. If a thinner dressing is preferred, thin out with water.
2. Serve immediately or refrigerate until ready to serve.

Per Serving
calories: 86 | fat: 7.0g | protein: 1.0g
carbs: 6.0g | fiber: 0g | sodium: 390mg

Basil Pesto

Prep time: 5 minutes | Cook time: 0 minutes | Makes 1 cup

2 cups packed fresh basil leaves
3 garlic cloves, peeled
½ cup freshly grated Parmesan cheese

½ cup extra-virgin olive oil
1/3 cup pine nuts
Kosher salt and freshly ground black pepper, to taste

1. Place all the ingredients, except for the salt and pepper, in a food processor. Pulse a few times until smoothly puréed. Season with salt and pepper to taste.
2. Store in an airtight container in the fridge for up to 2 weeks.

Per Serving
calories: 100 | fat: 10.2g | protein: 2.2g
carbs: 1.2g | fiber: 0g | sodium: 72mg

Peri-Peri Sauce

Prep time: 10 minutes | Cook time: 5 minutes | Serves 4

1 tomato, chopped
1 red onion, chopped
1 red bell pepper, deseeded and chopped
1 red chile, deseeded and chopped
4 garlic cloves, minced
2 tablespoons extra-virgin olive oil
Juice of 1 lemon
1 tablespoon dried oregano
1 tablespoon smoked paprika
1 teaspoon sea salt

1. Process all the ingredients in a food processor or a blender until smooth.
2. Transfer the mixture to a small saucepan over medium-high heat and bring to a boil, stirring often.
3. Reduce the heat to medium and allow to simmer for 5 minutes until heated through.
4. You can store the sauce in an airtight container in the refrigerator for up to 5 days.

Tips: If you prefer a milder sauce, you can omit the fresh chile. This sauce pairs perfectly with grilled chicken of any kind. It also tastes great with shrimp or white fish.

Per Serving
calories: 98 | fat: 6.5g | protein: 1.0g
carbs: 7.8g | fiber: 3.0g | sodium: 295mg

Not Old Bay Seasoning

Prep time: 10 minutes | Cook time: 0 minutes | Makes about ½ cup

3 tablespoons sweet paprika
1 tablespoon mustard seeds
2 tablespoons celery seeds
2 teaspoons freshly ground black pepper
1½ teaspoons cayenne pepper
1 teaspoon red pepper flakes
½ teaspoon ground ginger
½ teaspoon ground nutmeg
½ teaspoon ground cinnamon
¼ teaspoon ground cloves

1. Mix together all the ingredients in an airtight container until well combined.
2. You can store it in a cool, dry, and dark place for up to 3 months.

Tip: This seasoning can be used for grilled shrimp, clams, or crab.

Per Serving (1 tablespoon)
calories: 26 | fat: 1.9g | protein: 1.1g
carbs: 3.6g | fiber: 2.1g | sodium: 3mg

Ranch-Style Cauliflower Dressing

Prep time: 10 minutes | Cook time: 0 minutes | Serves 8

2 cups frozen cauliflower, thawed
½ cup unsweetened plain almond milk
2 tablespoons apple cider vinegar
2 tablespoons extra-virgin olive oil
1 garlic clove, peeled
2 teaspoons finely chopped fresh parsley
2 teaspoons finely chopped scallions (both white and green parts)
1 teaspoon finely chopped fresh dill
½ teaspoon onion powder
½ teaspoon Dijon mustard
½ teaspoon salt
¼ teaspoon freshly ground black pepper

1. Place all the ingredients in a blender and pulse until creamy and smooth.
2. Serve immediately, or transfer to an airtight container to refrigerate for up to 3 days.

Tips: To add more flavors to this dressing, you can add the thyme, oregano, and shallots. This dressing perfectly goes with the green salads and grain bowls.

Per Serving (2 tablespoons)
calories: 41 | fat: 3.6g | protein: 1.0g
carbs: 1.9g | fiber: 1.1g | sodium: 148mg

Homemade Blackened Seasoning

Prep time: 10 minutes | Cook time: 0 minutes | Makes about ½ cup

2 tablespoons smoked paprika
2 tablespoons garlic powder
2 tablespoons onion powder
1 tablespoon sweet paprika

1 teaspoon dried dill
1 teaspoon freshly ground black pepper
½ teaspoon ground mustard
¼ teaspoon celery seeds

1. Add all the ingredients to a small bowl and mix well.
2. Serve immediately, or transfer to an airtight container and store in a cool, dry and dark place for up to 3 months.

Tips: You can sprinkle the blackened seasoning on roasted potatoes or broccoli. It also pairs perfectly with blackened codfish or chicken.

Per Serving (1 tablespoon)
calories: 22 | fat: 0.9g | protein: 1.0g
carbs: 4.7g | fiber: 1.0g | sodium: 2mg

Guacamole

Prep time: 10 minutes | Cook time: 0 minutes | Serves 6

2 large avocados
¼ white onion, finely diced
1 small, firm tomato, finely diced
¼ cup finely chopped

fresh cilantro
2 tablespoons freshly squeezed lime juice
¼ teaspoon salt
Freshly ground black pepper, to taste

1. Slice the avocados in half and remove the pits. Using a large spoon to scoop out the flesh and add to a medium bowl.
2. Mash the avocado flesh with the back of a fork, or until a uniform consistency is achieved. Add the onion, tomato, cilantro, lime juice, salt, and pepper to the bowl and stir to combine.
3. Serve immediately, or transfer to an airtight container and refrigerate until chilled.

Tips: If you prefer a chunkier guacamole, leave some larger pieces of avocados when you are mashing it. If you prefer a smooth guacamole, you can purée the avocados in a blender. This guacamole can be used as a dip for veggies and a spread on sandwiches.

Per Serving (¼ cup)
calories: 81 | fat: 6.8g | protein: 1.1g
carbs: 5.7g | fiber: 3.0g | sodium: 83mg

Creamy Cucumber Dip

Prep time: 10 minutes | Cook time: 0 minutes | Serves 6

1 medium cucumber, peeled and grated
¼ teaspoon salt
1 cup plain Greek yogurt
2 garlic cloves, minced

1 tablespoon extra-virgin olive oil
1 tablespoon freshly squeezed lemon juice
¼ teaspoon freshly ground black pepper

1. Place the grated cucumber in a colander set over a bowl and season with salt. Allow the cucumber to stand for 10 minutes. Using your hands, squeeze out as much liquid from the cucumber as possible. Transfer the grated cucumber to a medium bowl.
2. Add the yogurt, garlic, olive oil, lemon juice, and pepper to the bowl and stir until well blended.
3. Cover the bowl with plastic wrap and refrigerate for at least 2 hours to blend the flavors.
4. Serve chilled.

Tips: For a unique flavor, you can add ½ teaspoon ground cumin to this cucumber dip. This dip perfectly pairs with the veggies, whole-grain pita, and falafel.

Per Serving (¼ cup)
calories: 47 | fat: 2.8g | protein: 4.2g
carbs: 2.7g | fiber: 0g | sodium: 103mg

Lemon-Dill Cashew Dip

Prep time: 10 minutes | Cook time: 0 minutes | Makes 1 cup

¾ cup cashews, soaked in water for at least 4 hours and drained well
¼ cup water
Juice and zest of 1

lemon
2 tablespoons chopped fresh dill
¼ teaspoon salt, plus more as needed

1. Put the cashews, water, lemon juice and zest in a blender and blend until smooth.
2. Add the dill and salt to the blender and blend again.
3. Taste and adjust the seasoning, if needed.
4. Transfer to an airtight container and refrigerate for at least 1 hour to blend the flavors.
5. Serve chilled.

Tips: If you want to make it a nut-free dish, you can substitute the soaked sunflower seeds for the cashews. This dip pairs perfectly with the chili or tacos. It also can be served as a sauce for steamed vegetables or gluten-free toast.

Per Serving (1 tablespoon)
calories: 37 | fat: 2.9g | protein: 1.1g
carbs: 1.9g | fiber: 0g | sodium: 36mg

Tzatziki

Prep time: 15 minutes | Cook time: 0 minutes | Serves 4 to 6

½ English cucumber, finely chopped
1 teaspoon salt, divided
1 cup plain Greek yogurt
8 tablespoons olive oil, divided

1 garlic clove, finely minced
1 to 2 tablespoons chopped fresh dill
1 teaspoon red wine vinegar
½ teaspoon freshly ground black pepper

1. In a food processor, pulse the cucumber until puréed. Place the cucumber on several layers of paper towels lining the bottom of a colander and sprinkle with ½ teaspoon of salt. Allow to drain for 10 to 15 minutes. Using your hands, squeeze out any remaining liquid.
2. In a medium bowl, whisk together the cucumber, yogurt, 6 tablespoons of olive oil, garlic, dill, vinegar, remaining ½ teaspoon of salt, and pepper until very smooth.
3. Drizzle with the remaining 2 tablespoons of olive oil. Serve immediately or refrigerate until ready to serve.

Per Serving
calories: 286 | fat: 29.0g | protein: 3.0g
carbs: 5.0g | fiber: 0g | sodium: 615mg

Harissa Sauce

Prep time: 10 minutes | Cook time: 20 minutes | Makes 3 to 4 cups

1 large red bell pepper, deseeded, cored, and cut into chunks
1 yellow onion, cut into thick rings
4 garlic cloves, peeled
1 cup vegetable

broth
2 tablespoons tomato paste
1 tablespoon tamari
1 teaspoon ground cumin
1 tablespoon Hungarian paprika

1. Preheat the oven to 450ºF (235ºC). Line a baking sheet with parchment paper.
2. Place the bell pepper on the prepared baking sheet, flesh-side up, and space out the onion and garlic around the pepper.
3. Roast in the preheated oven for 20 minutes. Transfer to a blender.
4. Add the vegetable broth, tomato paste, tamari, cumin, and paprika. Purée until smooth. Served chilled or warm.

Per Serving (¼ cup)
calories: 15 | fat: 1.0g | protein: 1.0g
carbs: 3.0g | fiber: 1.0g | sodium: 201mg

Orange-Garlic Dressing

Prep time: 5 minutes | Cook time: 0 minutes | Serves 2

¼ cup extra-virgin olive oil
1 orange, zested
2 tablespoons freshly squeezed orange juice
¾ teaspoon za'atar seasoning
1 teaspoon garlic powder
½ teaspoon salt
¼ teaspoon Dijon mustard
Freshly ground black pepper, to taste

1. Whisk together all ingredients in a bowl until well combined.
2. Serve immediately or refrigerate until ready to serve.

Per Serving
calories: 287 | fat: 26.7g | protein: 1.2g carbs: 12.0g | fiber: 2.1g | sodium: 592mg

Creamy Cider Yogurt Dressing

Prep time: 5 minutes | Cook time: 0 minutes | Serves 2

1 cup plain, unsweetened, full-fat Greek yogurt
½ cup extra-virgin olive oil
½ lemon, juiced
1 tablespoon chopped fresh oregano
1 tablespoon apple
cider vinegar
½ teaspoon dried parsley
½ teaspoon kosher salt
¼ teaspoon garlic powder
¼ teaspoon freshly ground black pepper

1. In a large bowl, whisk all ingredients to combine.
2. Serve chilled or at room temperature.

Per Serving
calories: 407 | fat: 40.7g | protein: 8.3g carbs: 3.8g | fiber: 0.5g | sodium: 382mg

Basic French Vinaigrette

Prep time: 5 minutes | Cook time: 0 minutes | Serves 2

3 tablespoons apple cider vinegar
2 tablespoons minced shallot (or 1 tablespoon minced red onion)
1 tablespoon balsamic vinegar
½ teaspoon dried thyme
1 teaspoon Dijon mustard
¼ cup olive oil
Salt and black pepper, to taste

1. Stir together the apple cider vinegar, shallot, and balsamic vinegar in a medium jar with a tight-fitting lid. Allow to sit for 5 minutes.
2. Stir in the mustard and thyme. Whisk in the olive oil in a slow, steady stream and season to taste with salt and pepper.
3. Store in an airtight container in the fridge for up to 5 days.

Per Serving
calories: 256 | fat: 27.1g | protein: 0.3g carbs: 3.4g | fiber: 0.4g | sodium: 207mg

Appendix 1: Measurement Conversion Chart

VOLUME EQUIVALENTS(DRY)

US STANDARD	METRIC (APPROXIMATE)
1/8 teaspoon	0.5 mL
1/4 teaspoon	1 mL
1/2 teaspoon	2 mL
3/4 teaspoon	4 mL
1 teaspoon	5 mL
1 tablespoon	15 mL
1/4 cup	59 mL
1/2 cup	118 mL
3/4 cup	177 mL
1 cup	235 mL
2 cups	475 mL
3 cups	700 mL
4 cups	1 L

WEIGHT EQUIVALENTS

US STANDARD	METRIC (APPROXIMATE)
1 ounce	28 g
2 ounces	57 g
5 ounces	142 g
10 ounces	284 g
15 ounces	425 g
16 ounces (1 pound)	455 g
1.5 pounds	680 g
2 pounds	907 g

VOLUME EQUIVALENTS(LIQUID)

US STANDARD	US STANDARD (OUNCES)	METRIC (APPROXIMATE)
2 tablespoons	1 fl.oz.	30 mL
1/4 cup	2 fl.oz.	60 mL
1/2 cup	4 fl.oz.	120 mL
1 cup	8 fl.oz.	240 mL
1 1/2 cup	12 fl.oz.	355 mL
2 cups or 1 pint	16 fl.oz.	475 mL
4 cups or 1 quart	32 fl.oz.	1 L
1 gallon	128 fl.oz.	4 L

TEMPERATURES EQUIVALENTS

FAHRENHEIT(F)	CELSIUS(C) (APPROXIMATE)
225 °F	107 °C
250 °F	120 °C
275 °F	135 °C
300 °F	150 °C
325 °F	160 °C
350 °F	180 °C
375 °F	190 °C
400 °F	205 °C
425 °F	220 °C
450 °F	235 °C
475 °F	245 °C
500 °F	260 °C

Appendix 2: Recipes Index

A

Air-Fried Flounder Fillets - 124

Almond-Crusted Chicken Tenders with Honey - 119

Apple and Berries Ambrosia - 145

Apple-Tahini Toast - 13

Artichoke and Arugula Salad - 28

Artichoke and Cucumber Hoagies - 57

Arugula and Fig Salad - 30

Arugula, Watermelon, and Feta Salad - 34

Asian-Inspired Tuna Lettuce Wraps - 128

Asian-Inspired Vinaigrette - 160

Avgolemono (Lemon Chicken Soup) - 43

Avocado and Egg Toast - 23

Avocado Shrimp Ceviche - 134

Avocado Smoothie - 25

Avocado Toast with Goat Cheese - 18

B

Baby Kale and Cabbage Salad - 103

Baby Potato and Olive Salad - 28

Baked Cod with Vegetables - 143

Baked Eggs in Avocado - 16

Baked Fish with Pistachio Crust - 136

Baked Halibut Steaks with Vegetables - 132

Baked Lemon Salmon - 127

Baked Oysters with Vegetables - 143

Baked Parmesan Chicken Wraps - 62

Baked Ricotta with Honey Pears - 25

Baked Rolled Oat with Pears and Pecans - 67

Baked Salmon with Basil and Tomato - 125

Baked Salmon with Tarragon Mustard Sauce - 126

Baked Teriyaki Turkey Meatballs - 117

Baked Tomatoes and chickpeas - 98

Balsamic Brussels Sprouts and Delicata Squash - 41

Balsamic-Honey Glazed Salmon - 135

Banana Corn Fritters - 22

Banana-Blueberry Breakfast Cookies - 18

Banana, Cranberry, and Oat Bars - 145

Barley, Parsley, and Pea Salad - 29

Basic French Vinaigrette - 164

Basil Pesto - 160

Basil Scrambled Eggs - 26

Bean and Veggie Pasta - 83

Beef Kebabs with Onion and Pepper - 120

Beef Stew with Beans and Zucchini - 116

Beef, Tomato, and Lentils Stew - 117

Beet and Watercress Salad - 87

Berry and Nut Parfait - 26

Berry and Rhubarb Cobbler - 146

Black Bean Chili with Mangoes - 68

Black-Eyed Pea and Vegetable Stew - 83

Black-Eyed Peas Salad with Walnuts - 70

Blackberry-Yogurt Green Smoothie - 15

Blueberry Smoothie - 15

Braised Branzino with Wine Sauce - 131

Braised Cauliflower with White Wine - 102

Breakfast Pancakes with Berry Sauce - 21

Breakfast Yogurt Sundae - 20

Broccoli and Carrot Pasta Salad - 84

Brown Rice and Black Bean Burgers - 50

Brown Rice Pilaf with Pistachios and Raisins - 74

Brussels Sprout and Apple Slaw - 32

Brussels Sprouts Linguine - 100

Bulgur Pilaf with Garbanzo - 81

Bulgur Pilaf with Kale and Tomatoes - 85

Butternut Noodles with Mushrooms - 104

Butternut Squash and Cauliflower Curry Soup - 31

C

Canned Sardine Donburi (Rice Bowl) - 128

Caprese Pasta with Roasted Asparagus - 69

Cauliflower Breakfast Porridge - 16

Cauliflower Hash with Carrots - 89

Cauliflower Rice Risotto with Mushrooms - 95

Cauliflower Steaks with Arugula - 102

Celery and Mustard Greens - 93

Cheesy Broccoli and Mushroom Egg Casserole - 24

Cheesy Fig Pizzas with Garlic Oil - 46

Cheesy Pea Pesto - 158

Cheesy Peach and Walnut Salad - 29

Cheesy Roasted Broccolini - 34

Cheesy Sweet Potato Burgers - 92

Chermoula Roasted Pork Tenderloin - 122

Cherry Walnut Brownies - 152

Cherry, Apricot, and Pecan Brown Rice Bowl - 76

Cherry, Plum, Artichoke, and Cheese Board - 33

Chicken and Pastina Soup - 37

Chicken Bruschetta Burgers - 120

Chicken Cacciatore - 115

Chicken Gyros with Tzatziki Sauce - 121

Chickpea Lettuce Wraps - 50

Chickpea Lettuce Wraps with Celery - 96

Chickpea Salad with Tomatoes and Basil - 83

Chocolate and Avocado Mousse - 148

Chocolate, Almond, and Cherry Clusters - 147

Cilantro-Tomato Salsa - 157

Cinnamon Oatmeal with Dried Cranberries - 14

Cinnamon Pistachio Smoothie - 21

Cioppino (Seafood Tomato Stew) - 131

Citrus Cranberry and Quinoa Energy Bites - 147

Citrus Salad with Kale and Fennel - 41

Classic Shakshuka - 27

Classic Socca - 49

Coconut Blueberries with Brown Rice - 147

Coconut Chicken Tenders - 112

Cozy Superfood Hot Chocolate - 156

Cranberry and Almond Quinoa - 76

Creamy Breakfast Bulgur with Berries - 20

Creamy Cauliflower Chickpea Curry - 96

Creamy Cider Yogurt Dressing - 164

Creamy Cucumber Dip - 162

Creamy Garlic Parmesan Chicken Pasta - 81

Creamy Grapefruit and Tarragon Dressing - 160

Creamy Peach Smoothie - 15

Creamy Polenta with Mushrooms - 99

Creamy Sweet Potatoes and Collards - 107

Creamy Vanilla Oatmeal - 17

Crispy Herb Crusted Halibut - 139

Crispy Pesto Chicken - 121

Crispy Sesame Cookies - 153

Crispy Tilapia with Mango Salsa - 130

Crunchy Almond Cookies - 154

Crustless Tiropita (Greek Cheese Pie) - 22

Cucumber Gazpacho - 35

Cumin Quinoa Pilaf - 86

Curry Apple Couscous with Leeks and Pecans - 76

D

Dill Baked Sea Bass - 138

Dill Chutney Salmon - 144

Dulse, Avocado, and Tomato Pitas - 56

E

Easy Aioli - 159

Easy Alfalfa Sprout and Nut Rolls - 47

Easy Blueberry and Oat Crisp - 145

Easy Breaded Shrimp - 140

Easy Buckwheat Porridge - 19

Easy Grilled Pork Chops - 112

Easy Mixed Berry Crisp - 155

Easy Pizza Pockets - 55

Easy Roasted Cauliflower - 36

Easy Simple Pesto Pasta - 81

Easy Tomato Tuna Melts - 141

Easy Walnut and Ricotta Spaghetti - 79

Easy Zucchini Patties - 106

Egg Bake - 14

Eggplant and Zucchini Gratin - 88

Eggplant, Spinach, and Feta Sandwiches - 47

F

Falafel Balls with Tahini Sauce - 54

Fava and Garbanzo Bean Ful - 80

Fennel Poached Cod with Tomatoes - 137

Feta and Olive Scrambled Eggs - 21

Feta and Spinach Frittata - 25

Fluffy Almond Flour Pancakes with Strawberries - 17

Freekeh Pilaf with Dates and Pistachios - 82

Fried Eggplant Rolls - 86

Frozen Mango Raspberry Delight - 154

Fruit and Nut Chocolate Bark - 156

G

Garlic and Parsley Chickpeas - 75

Garlic Lemon-Tahini Dressing - 158

Garlic Shrimp Fettuccine - 80

Garlic Shrimp with Arugula Pesto - 142

Garlic Shrimp with Mushrooms - 133

Garlic Skillet Salmon - 135

Garlic Wilted Greens - 28

Garlic-Butter Asparagus with Parmesan - 106

Garlic-Butter Parmesan Salmon and Asparagus - 140

Garlicky Broccoli Rabe - 101

Garlicky Zucchini Cubes with Mint - 89

Ginger Teriyaki Sauce - 160

Glazed Broiled Salmon - 124

Glazed Mushroom and Vegetable Fajitas - 57

Glazed Pears with Hazelnuts - 148

Greek Beef Kebabs - 122

Greek Chicken, Tomato, and Olive Salad - 27

Greek Salad with Dressing - 39

Greek Vegetable Salad Pita - 47

Greek Yogurt Affogato with Pistachios - 151

Greek-Style Lamb Burgers - 120

Green Bean and Halloumi Salad - 45

Green Beans with Tahini-Lemon Sauce - 41

Green Veggie Sandwiches - 61

Greens, Fennel, and Pear Soup with Cashews - 35

Grilled Bell Pepper and Anchovy Antipasto - 31

Grilled Caesar Salad Sandwiches - 51

Grilled Chicken and Zucchini Kebabs - 111

Grilled Lemon Chicken - 109

Grilled Lemon Pesto Salmon - 144

Grilled Peaches with Whipped Ricotta - 152

Grilled Romaine Lettuce - 103

Grilled Stone Fruit with Honey - 152

Grilled Vegetable Skewers - 96

Ground Beef, Tomato, and Kidney Bean Chili - 118

Guacamole - 162

Gyro Burgers with Tahini Sauce - 113

H

Haddock with Cucumber Sauce - 139

Harissa Sauce - 163

Hazelnut Crusted Sea Bass - 142

Healthy Chia Pudding - 15

Hearty Butternut Spinach, and Cheeses Lasagna - 68

Hearty Veggie Slaw - 32

Herbed-Mustard-Coated Pork Tenderloin - 118

Homemade Blackened Seasoning - 162

Honey Baked Cinnamon Apples - 155

Honey-Mustard Roasted Salmon - 127

Hot Pepper Sauce - 158

I

5-Ingredient Quinoa Breakfast Bowls - 19

5-Ingredient Zucchini Fritters - 90

Instant Pot Poached Salmon - 129

Israeli Couscous with Asparagus - 82

Israeli Style Eggplant and Chickpea Salad - 69

Italian Sautéd Cannellini Beans - 66

K

Kale and Apple Smoothie - 23

L

Lamb Kofta (Spiced Meatballs) - 123

Lamb Tagine with Couscous and Almonds - 111

Lebanese Flavor Broken Thin Noodles - 78

Lemon and Spinach Orzo - 31

Lemon Grilled Shrimp - 132

Lemon Rosemary Roasted Branzino - 130

Lemon-Dill Cashew Dip - 163

Lemon-Parsley Swordfish - 126

Lemon-Tahini Hummus - 37

Lemon-Tahini Sauce - 159

Lemony Blackberry Granita - 148

Lemony Farro and Avocado Bowl - 78

Lemony Shrimp with Orzo Salad - 134

Lemony Tea and Chia Pudding - 146

Lemony Trout with Caramelized Shallots - 142

Lentil and Mushroom Pasta - 84

Lentil and Tomato Collard Wraps - 93

Lentil and Vegetable Curry Stew - 63

Lentil-Tahini Dip - 159

Lush Moroccan Chickpea, Vegetable, and Fruit Stew - 64

M

10-Minute Cod with Parsley Pistou - 125

Macadamia Pork - 119

Mackerel and Green Bean Salad - 137

Mango and Coconut Frozen Pie - 149

Marinara Poached Eggs - 22

Marinated Mushrooms and Olives - 32

Mascarpone Baked Pears - 155

Mashed Beans with Cumin - 77

Mashed Grape Tomato Pizzas - 48

Mediterranean Braised Cod with Vegetables - 125

Mediterranean Cod Stew - 138

Mediterranean Eggs (Shakshuka) - 13

Mediterranean Greek Salad Wraps - 58

Mediterranean Grilled Sea Bass - 123

Mediterranean Lentils - 73

Mediterranean Omelet - 26

Mediterranean Tomato Hummus Soup - 40

Mediterranean-Style Beans and Greens - 84

Minestrone Chickpeas and Macaroni Casserole - 71

Mini Crustless Spinach Quiches - 103

Mini Nuts and Fruits Crumble - 149

Mini Pork and Cucumber Lettuce Wraps - 48

Mint Banana Chocolate Sorbet - 149

Mint Brown Rice - 77

Mixed Salad With Balsamic Honey Dressing - 40

Morning Overnight Oats with Raspberries - 16

Moroccan Lentil, Tomato, and Cauliflower Soup - 38

Moroccan Spiced Couscous - 38

Moroccan Tagine with Vegetables - 91

Mushroom and Caramelized Onion Musakhan - 51

Mushroom and Soba Noodle Soup - 33

Mushroom-Pesto Baked Pizza - 54

N

Not Old Bay Seasoning - 161

O

Open-Faced Margherita Sandwiches - 55

Orange Flavored Scallops - 129

Orange Mug Cakes - 156

Orange-Garlic Dressing - 164

Orange-Honey Glazed Carrots - 36

P

Paella Soup - 43

Panko Grilled Chicken Patties - 112

Papaya, Jicama, and Peas Rice Bowl - 70

Paprika Cauliflower Steaks with Walnut Sauce - 108

Parmesan Oatmeal with Greens - 23

Parmesan Roasted Red Potatoes - 44

Parmesan Stuffed Zucchini Boats - 97

Parsley Vinaigrette - 158

Parsley-Dijon Chicken and Potatoes - 115

Peanut Sauce with Honey - 157

Pearl Barley Risotto with Parmesan Cheese - 65

Pecan and Carrot Cake - 150

Peppercorn-Seared Tuna Steaks - 126

Peri-Peri Sauce - 161

Pesto Shrimp over Zoodles - 140

Pineapple Salsa - 157

Potato Lamb and Olive Stew - 114

Potato Tortilla with Leeks and Mushrooms - 92

Pumpkin Pie Parfait - 17

Pumpkin Soup with Crispy Sage Leaves - 39

Q

Quick Chicken Salad Wraps - 109

Quick Steamed Broccoli - 101

Quinoa and Chickpea Vegetable Bowls - 63

Quinoa with Baby Potatoes and Broccoli - 82

R

Ranch-Style Cauliflower Dressing - 161

Raspberry Yogurt Basted Cantaloupe - 150

Ratatouille - 100

Red Pepper Coques with Pine Nuts - 53

Rice and Blueberry Stuffed Sweet Potatoes - 77

Rice Pudding with Roasted Orange - 153

Rich Cauliflower Alfredo - 67

Rich Chicken and Small Pasta Broth - 36

Ricotta Toast with Strawberries - 13

Ritzy Garden Burgers - 56

Ritzy Summer Fruit Salad - 30

Ritzy Veggie Chili - 72

Roasted Broccoli and Tomato Panzanella - 30

Roasted Butternut Squash and Zucchini with Penne - 74

Roasted Chicken Thighs With Basmati Rice - 110

Roasted Ratatouille Pasta - 73

Roasted Root Vegetable Soup - 42

Roasted Tomato Panini - 59

Roasted Trout Stuffed with Veggies - 139

Roasted Vegetable Panini - 60

Roasted Vegetables - 90

Roasted Vegetables and Chickpeas - 105

Roasted Veggies and Brown Rice Bowl - 87

Root Vegetable Roast - 33

S

Salmon and Mushroom Hash with Pesto - 127

Salmon Baked in Foil - 135

Salmon Salad Wraps - 48

Salt and Pepper Calamari and Scallops - 141

Samosas in Potatoes - 49

Sardines with Lemony Tomato Sauce - 34

Sautéed Cabbage with Parsley - 101

Sautéed Green Beans with Tomatoes - 95

Sautéed Ground Turkey with Brown Rice - 116

Sautéed Kale with Olives - 44

Sautéed Spinach and Leeks - 98

Sautéed White Beans with Rosemary - 35

Savory Breakfast Oatmeal - 24

Seared Salmon with Lemon Cream Sauce - 136

Shrimp and Pea Paella - 144

Simple Apple Compote - 150

Simple Fried Cod Fillets - 124

Simple Honey-Glazed Baby Carrots - 106

Simple Italian Dressing - 157

Simple Lentil Risotto - 85

Simple Mushroom Barley Soup - 37

Simple Peanut Butter and Chocolate Balls - 151

Simple Spiced Sweet Pecans - 151

Simple Zoodles - 94

Slow Cook Lamb Shanks with Cannellini Beans Stew - 110

Slow Cooked Turkey and Brown Rice - 65

Slow Cooker Salmon in Foil - 136

Small Pasta and Beans Pot - 79

Sole Piccata with Capers - 137

Spaghetti with Pine Nuts and Cheese - 70

Spiced Citrus Sole - 128

Spiced Roast Chicken - 114

Spicy Black Bean and Poblano Dippers - 52

Spicy Grilled Shrimp with Lemon Wedges - 129

Spicy Haddock Stew - 133

Spicy Italian Bean Balls with Marinara - 66

Spicy Tofu Tacos with Cherry Tomato Salsa - 58

Spinach and Egg Breakfast Wraps - 19

Spinach Cheese Pie - 20

Steamed Trout with Lemon Herb Crust - 141

Stir-Fried Eggplant - 108

Stir-Fry Baby Bok Choy - 97

Strawberries with Balsamic Vinegar - 151

Stuffed Portobello Mushroom with Tomatoes - 97

Stuffed Portobello Mushrooms with Spinach - 99

Sumptuous Greek Vegetable Salad - 29

Sumptuous Vegetable and Cheese Lavash Pizza - 45

Super Cheeses and Mushroom Tart - 59

Super Mushroom and Red Wine Soup - 42

Sweet Pepper Stew - 98

Sweet Potato Chickpea Buddha Bowl - 105

Sweet Spiced Pumpkin Pudding - 146

Swoodles with Almond Butter Sauce - 72

T

Tomato and Egg Breakfast Pizza - 24

Tomato and Egg Scramble - 14

Tomato Basil Pasta - 85

Tomato Sauce and Basil Pesto Fettuccine - 75

Tricolor Summer Salad - 39

Triple-Green Pasta with Cheese - 80

Tuna and Hummus Wraps - 55

Tuna and Olive Salad Sandwiches - 46

Tuna and Zucchini Patties - 138

Turkish Canned Pinto Bean Salad - 71

Turkish Eggplant and Tomatoes Pide with Mint - 61

Tzatziki - 163

V

Veg Mix and Blackeye Pea Burritos - 52

Vegan Lentil Bolognese - 94

Vegetable and Red Lentil Stew - 95

Vegetable and Tofu Scramble - 94

Vegetable Fagioli Soup - 40

Veggie Rice Bowls with Pesto Sauce - 104

Veggie-Stuffed Portabello Mushrooms - 88

Vinaigrette - 159

W

Walnut and Date Balls - 154

Warm Bulgur Breakfast Bowls with Fruits - 18

Watermelon and Blueberry Salad - 153

White Pizzas with Arugula and Spinach - 60

Wild Rice, Celery, and Cauliflower Pilaf - 64

Wilted Dandelion Greens with Sweet Onion - 93

Y

Yogurt Chicken Breasts - 113

Z

Za'atar Pizza - 49

Zesty Spanish Potato Salad - 38

Zoodles with Beet Pesto - 104

Zoodles with Walnut Pesto - 91

Zucchini and Artichokes Bowl with Farro - 89

Zucchini Crisp - 107

Zucchini Hummus Wraps - 53

Made in the USA
Monee, IL
28 December 2020